RICHARD STERBA
THE COLLECTED PAPERS

RICHARD STERBA
THE COLLECTED PAPERS

Edited and Arranged by Herman Daldin, Ph.D.
Foreword by Alexander Grinstein, M.D.
Translations from the German by Richard Sterba, M.D.

North River Press, Inc.
CROTON-ON-HUDSON
NEW YORK

Copyright © 1987 Richard Sterba and Herman Daldin

All rights reserved. Except for the usual review purposes, no part of this work may be reproduced or transmitted in any form or by any means, electronic or mechanical, including photocopy, recording, or any information retrieval system, without the written permission of the publisher.

Manufactured in the United States of America

Library of Congress Cataloging-in-Publication Data

Sterba, Richard F.
   Richard Sterba, the collected papers.

   1. Psychoanalysis. 2. Sterba, Richard F.
I. Daldin, Herman, 1951-   . II. Title. [DNLM:
1. Psychoanalysis—collected works. WM 460 S838r]
RC509.S74 1987   616.89'17   87-11129
ISBN 0-88427-071-8

Table of Contents

Foreword/vii
Editor's Preface/xiii
On Latent Negative Transference/1

A Compulsive Action from The Latency Period/9

An Examination Dream/11

On the Oral Origin of Envy/13

Jealous of . . . ?/16

A Contribution to the Theory of Sublimation/20

Equation of Mother and Prostitute/29

The Resistance to Symbol Interpretation/31

On The Oedipus Complex in Girls/35

The Theory of Anxiety/50

The Fate of the Ego in Analytic Therapy/62

Psychoanalytic Therapy/71

On Criteria of The Libido/87

Critique of the Theory of Transference/95

Two Cases of Fetishism/108

The Psychic Trauma and
the Handling of the Transference.
(The Last Contributions of Sandor Ferenczi
to Psychoanalytic Technique)/114

Aggression in the Rescue Fantasy/121

The Dynamics of the Dissolution of
the Transference Resistance/124

The Relaxation of the Analyst/137

The Abuse of Interpretation/143

The Significance of a Missed Diagnosis/149

The Formative Activity of the Analyst/154

Dreams and Acting Out/161

On Spiders, Hanging and Oral Sadism/165

A Case of Brief Psychotherapy by Sigmund Freud/171

Character and Resistance/177

Clinical and Therapeutic Aspects
of Character Resistance/181

Oral Invasion and Self-defence/197

Foreword

Richard Sterba was born in Vienna, over three quarters of a century ago, on May 6, 1898, into a middle class Viennese family. His father, Joseph, of Czech ancestry, was a college professor of mathematics and physics. His mother, Mathilda, née Fischer, was Viennese. Both were liberal, non-practicing Catholics.

Young Richard began his education at the age of six at the Volkschule on Copernicus Gasse. Four years later he transferred to the then new Staatsgymnasium (in VII Wiener gemeindebezirk). At that time there were only two classes and a small number of students so that each student received a great deal of personal attention. The faculty, men of high academic stature, experts in their particular fields, were inspiring teachers and exerted their influence throughout his life. During these years, history, geography, Latin, oratory and religion were among the required subjects he studied.

During Richard's adolescence he developed interests in music and literature that have continued to the present day and which, in addition to enriching his life, became a valuable background for his chosen profession. He had started to play the violin at the age of seven. He studied the instrument seriously and at fourteen became a member of a musical group. His enthusiasm for the world of culture and his curiosity were both stimulated and sustained by the people with whom he associated, people who provided the impetus for his avid and extensive reading. Among the writers who most influenced him were E. T. A. Hoffmann, Rainer Maria Rilke and Schopenhauer.

Richard entered military service at eighteen and served for three and a half years, seeing action on the Italian front where he was wounded. During his years of service his intellectual development was greatly influenced by Arthur Ruessler, an Austrian writer. An account of his experiences of his formative years may be found in his paper entitled, "Multiple determinants of a minor accident" (1970).

After his military service, Sterba began his medical education in Vienna. Toward the end of his studies, he became familiar with some of Freud's writings which impressed him so much that during his medical residency he decided to enter psychoanalytic training, contravening the prevailing opinion of his colleagues who vigorously opposed this discipline. He undertook his personal analysis with Dr. Edward Hitschmann.

Early in his training, he was influenced by the lectures of Paul Schilder and Julius Wagner-Jauregg. In 1927, after a period of supervision, he was certified as a psychoanalyst by Freud and Helene Deutsch. There was only one other such certification, that of Grete Bibring, before this practice was discontinued. For several years, Richard Sterba presented clinical material in technical seminars of Wilhelm Reich, Helene Deutsch, and Hermann Nunberg. During these years he was librarian of the Psychoanalytic Institute and Society. He became a training analyst in the Vienna Institute, and, in 1931, conducted his first course on the Libido Theory. He attended Freud's Wednesday evening seminars and at one of these meetings presented a paper on Sublimation which is included in this collection. Many of his experiences and impressions are detailed in his book, *Reminiscences of a Viennese Psychoanalyst* (1982).

While he was with the Vienna Institute, Richard Sterba met his future wife, Editha. They were married in 1926, and have two daughters, Monica and Verena, both now married with children of their own.

As for so many people, Hitler's rise to power and with it the political and social events in Austria brought many threats and conflicts into the lives of the Sterbas. Richard described this period in these words:

> I once had the opportunity to express my solidarity with my Jewish colleagues in the presence of Freud. In the fall of 1936 Dr. Felix Boehm came from Berlin to Vienna to report on the status of Psychoanalysis in Nazi-Germany. A meeting of the Board of the Vienna Psychoanalytic Society was called at Freud's home on a Sunday afternoon. Dr. Boehm, who was a gentile, had stayed in Berlin under Nazi domination, and tried to point out how much he had done for the survival of psychoanalysis in Hitler's Reich by achieving through his efforts that psychoanalysis was taught at par with Jung's and Adler's systems at the Berlin Institute of Psychotherapy, which was headed by Professor Goering, a relative of the fieldmarshall Hermann Goering. And in order to demonstrate the Berlin Institute's permissive attitude toward psychoanalysis, Dr. Boehm said that he would gladly invite one of the Viennese psychoanalysts to present a paper there. Freud said, looking at him questioningly over the rim of his glasses: "Whom would you invite?" Dr. Boehm's quick answer was: "Dr. Sterba for

example." When Freud looked at me, obviously curious what my answer would be, I said: "I will be willing to present a paper at the Berlin Institute after one of the Jewish members of the Vienna society has been invited to speak there," to which Dr. Boehm had no reply and the matter was dropped.

The real test, however, came when Hitler and his German army invaded Austria and occupied Vienna on Saturday, March 12, 1938. The following day, on Sunday afternoon, the board of the Vienna Psychoanalytic Society met at Freud's home in order to decide what had to be done. Anna Freud, then president of the Society, chaired the meeting. She asked each member what he intended to do. When it was my turn to answer this question I declared that I would emigrate at the earliest possibility. The group received this declaration with obvious relief and Anna Freud said: "We expected that you would not like to play the role here which Felix Boehm plays in Berlin." The rest of the meeting is faithfully reported by Ernest Jones in the third volume of his Freud biography where he writes:

"A meeting of the Board of the Vienna Society had, however, been held on March 13 at which it was decided that everyone should flee the country if possible, and that the seat of the Society should be wherever Freud would settle. Freud commented: 'After the destruction of the Temple in Jerusalem by Titus, Rabbi Jochanan ben Sakkai asked for permission to open a school at Jabneh for the study of the Torah. We are going to do the same. We are, after all, used to persecution by our history, tradition, and some of us by our personal experience,' adding laughingly and pointing at Richard Sterba, 'with one exception.' Sterba, however, decided to share the fate of his Jewish colleagues and left for Switzerland two days later: he sternly refused the blandishments of the German analysts to return and become Director of the Vienna Institute and Clinic." [p.221]

Sterba continues his account of those troubled times:

Shortly after the Anschluss, Dr. Mueller-Braunschweig, another gentile Berlin psychoanalyst, had come to Vienna from Berlin in order to arrange the psychoanalytic situation. He wrote me a special delivery letter in which he urged me to come back to Vienna and to take charge of the Psychoanalytic

Institute as a branch of the German Psychotherapeutic Institute. He stated at the same time that the Vienna Psychoanalytic Society, after exclusion of the Jewish members, had been fused with the German Psychotherapeutic Association. The letter was signed with "Heil Hitler." . . .

I declined the offer and wrote to Jones asking whether he would make it possible for me and my family to settle in England. His answer was an unexpected blow. He wrote that he had no intention to do anything for me: "You will be the last one who will obtain any assistance from the International Psychoanalytic Association since you (being gentile) should have stayed in Vienna as a memory of Psychoanalysis for a happier future."

(1970, pp. 115–116)

In 1939, after considerable difficulties the Sterbas were finally able to emigrate from Switzerland to the United States and settled in Detroit. The story of their troubles with emigration is the basis of a somewhat fictionalized account by Laura Z. Hobson, entitled *The Trespassers*. Strangers in a strange land, disciples of what appeared to outsiders as an unholy cult, they were regarded by some as trespassers in their new community.

With the United States' entry into World War II, special problems arose for them. Because they were aliens who spoke German fluently, the Sterbas were looked upon with hostile suspicion. And yet, despite these problems, their deep commitment and dedicated work inspired the establishment of the true spirit of psychoanalysis in the Detroit area.

The ensuing years were marked by further writing and a continuation of publication of many scientific papers that attest to the breadth and diversity of Richard Sterba's interests. Many, but by no means all of those dealing with the clinical or theoretical aspects of psychoanalysis, have been included in this volume. His papers on applied psychoanalysis have been omitted. Among these are publications dealing with holidays, "A Dutch celebration of a festival" (1941), "On Christmas" (1944), and "On Hallowe'en" (1948). In 1948 a delightful paper on a then popular expression, "Kilroy was here," appeared. During this period he wrote on the "Metapsychology of morale" (1943). Three years later, he began an exploration of the problem of the musical process (1946) which was continued in a subsequent publication. Some years later he wrote a paper, "On some psychological factors in pictorial advertisement" (1950), which was received with a good deal of interest. During the 50's, Richard Sterba became interested in studying Michelangelo's personality from a psychoanalytic standpoint, a study that clearly provided him as well as the reader, the lover of art and the art historian an opportunity to see how psychoanalysis can provide an added dimension of appreciation and knowledge of that Titan of the Renaissance. A complete bibliography of Richard Sterba's publications is included in this book.

In the analytic community at large, nationally and internationally, Richard Sterba has unceasingly exemplified the highest standards of scientific integrity. In his teaching and in his clinical practice he provided an unique model of keen scientific observation, critical acumen and a depth of compassion and empathy. In addition his background in the humanistic tradition, with its cultural and intellectual derivatives, has served distinctively to enrich the teaching and scientific discipline of psychoanalysis to a depth and perspective rarely seen in the world today.

Alexander Grinstein, M.D.
Birmingham, Michigan

BIBLIOGRAPHY

Hobson, Laura Z. (1943), *The Trespassers*. New York: Simon and Schuster.

Jones, Ernest (1957), *The Life and Work of Sigmund Freud*. New York: Basic Books, Vol. 3, p. 221.

Sterba, Richard (1970), "The multiple determinants of a minor accident. *Israel Annals of Psychiatry and Related Dis.*, 8(2): 111–122.

——— (1982). *Reminiscences of a Viennese Psychoanalyst*. Detroit: Wayne State University Press.

Editor's Preface

For over sixty years, Richard Sterba has been an important figure in the creation and development of psychoanalysis as both a science and a clinical profession. He continues to be involved in teaching, clinical supervision, publishing and treatment of patients. The field of psychoanalysis has benefitted from his contributions which are widely recognized by his peers. His works reflect the shift from the ego as a helpless victim to the concept that the ego is the controller of the id. The foundation which Dr. Sterba helped lay, set the stage for the present day theories of psychoanalytic therapy.

Dr. Sterba had the unequaled privilege to be a student, an active member and board member of the Vienna Psychoanalytic Institute and Society (1924–1938). Besides having direct contact with Sigmund Freud, Dr. Sterba worked with such distinguished colleagues as August Aichhorn, Edward and Greta Bibring, Marie Bonaparte, Felix and Helene Deutsch, and Wilhelm and Annie Reich, to name just a few. However, his contacts with Sigmund Freud influenced Dr. Sterba throughout his career in which his devotion to the psychoanalytic movement never waned.

Besides over sixty papers, Dr. Sterba authored "Psychoanalytic Theory of the Libido" (1942), "Beethoven and His Nephew" (1954) (written with his wife Editha Sterba) and most recently, "Reminiscenses of a Viennese Psychoanalyst" (1982).

In this book, I present a collection of Dr. Sterba's papers, which influenced both the theories and practice of psychoanalysis. These papers are rich with clinical material, which Dr. Sterba believes is crucial in presenting theories and technical concepts. Many of the papers are familiar to the practicing psychoanalytic therapists, while some may be new, primarily due to the fact that several of these papers have never been published in the English language. I am certain the reader will be able to share in the excitement which surrounded and inspired Dr. Sterba when he wrote each paper.

Herman J. Daldin, Ph.D.
Birmingham, Michigan

On Latent Negative Transference

Discussion in our seminar reveals that the manipulation of the transference presents the most difficult technical task. These difficulties are greater than Freud has indicated in his technical papers since the transference has assumed an increasingly greater role in analytic therapy. Accordingly, the significance of transference for the therapeutic result is increased and the dissolution of the resistances which proceed from the transference become the central problem of analytic therapy.

Freud has called attention in his work to the positive transference and to the resistance which proceeds from the unconscious part of it. Negative transference, which upon more exact observation constitutes the chief resistance in many analyses, particularly those which are endangered and have to be broken off, has had less emphasis in Freud's technical works which, however, was published more than a decade ago. Nevertheless, the dissolution of this negative transference, by retracing it to its infantile origin as a reaction to traumata and frustrations, constitutes a powerful therapeutic agent. It derives its power from the fact that it takes hold very often on the deepest aetiological layer of the symptom, on its characterological basis.

From this deep root of negative transference, proceeds, of course, the intensity of the resistance based upon it. But from the fact that it is a resistance proceeds the frequent difficulty in discovering and undoing it, which is so necessary for therapeutic purposes. It often happens that long before its infantile motives are made conscious, the negative transference itself must be liberated from its latency, by forcing the patient to acknowledge it as a resistance. This has to be achieved through consistent disregard for all the material that is advanced by the patient as a front and by continuous interpretation of this particular resistance.

From the Seminar on "Psychoanalytic Therapy" in Vienna
Uber latente negative Ubertragung. *Internationale Zeitschrift fur Psychoanalyse*, 1927, *13*, 160–165.

In "Future Chances of Analytic Therapy", Freud has called attention to the fact that progress in therapy lies in recognition of the connections between typical cases of illness, and that a similar need for classification exists in the case of the resistances.[1]

I believe that the chief task of a therapeutic technical seminar consists in classifying the various forms of resistances according to types, and I shall consider the task set before me accomplished if I am successful in presenting types of resistance from my clinical material and in clearly formulating it.

It has been pointed out repeatedly in our seminar that the resistance character of the negative transference is responsible for the fact that it is difficult to discover. It is typical that the negative transference is hidden behind the appearance of a positive one.

A twenty-five year old patient sought the help of analysis because of erective impotence which had been troubling him for four years. The patient, an intelligent Jew, of Russian descendence, was a skilled laborer. Quite in contrast with his background, he had developed a considerable degree of education. His appearance was that of a strong person and thoroughly masculine. He was employed and managing his father's business, quite in opposition to the extremely conservative and often impractical, narrow-minded intentions of his father, whose orientation was strictly orthodox. The patient received hardly any compensation for his work, even though he was fed and clothed at home. The rest of the family consisted of his mother and a sister about five years younger. The stinginess, obstinacy, and orthodox piety of the father, to which the liberal minded son stood quite in opposition, constituted the basis for frequent conflicts, in which the father continually remained the victor, because the son always gave in.

The impotence first appeared four years before the beginning of the analysis; previously he had had intercourse normally from the age of sixteen on. However, he had to have intercourse very frequently as a compensation for his apprehension that he might be impotent and had considerable anxiety over evil consequences of his masturbation, which he continued practicing. After he had given up the masturbation, he actually became impotent. He made repeated attempts at intercourse, which resulted in him being incapable of an erection. When he left the woman, after an unsuccessful attempt, he felt a momentary relief, but this was quickly followed by a deep depression. The patient had to think continually about his lack of sexual success, and was in despair over his misfortune. Everything reminded him of his

---

[1] S. Freud Collected Papers, Vol. 2, pg. 288.

impotence. This would last for a few days, after which he became calm again. Then, after a short while, when he again attempted to have intercourse, he would fail again and become depressed, and so on. On rare occasions, he proved to be potent, but then later he would doubt whether he had been efficiently potent. A new attempt at intercourse would then convince him of his impotence. In addition to his genital disturbance, he developed anxiety about women and a more generalized anxiety in public places, such as restaurants, etc. Concomitantly, he had the feeling that his nose and lips were too large, that his hair was standing on end, so that he had to go to the washroom several times in order to brush it down. The patient became self-conscious in many situations and felt inferior and inhibited.

After working through the superficial resistances, the analyst approached the castration complex, which forms the core of the analysis; a transference relationship developed in which the patient got stuck for a considerable time, and which seriously endangered the progress of the analysis. This came about in the following manner: after a few superficial interpretations which touched upon the castration complex, and to which the patient reacted with understanding, he suddenly began to show a positive attitude towards the analysis. Up until this time he had extreme ambivalent feelings about the therapy. Simultaneously, an intense positive transference with strong passive castration wishes developed. In numerous dreams, the analyst appeared as a castrating person. He would, for example, reach for the patient's penis and find it shriveled up. The patient sometimes woke from the dreams with a seminal emission. The primary attitude of the patient towards the analyst at this time was completely passive-feminine. He wanted to have a thorough physical examination by the analyst. He was of the opinion that the treatment should be directed towards his genitals, and that medical procedures should focus on the location of the problem. He came to the analysis gladly and found his hours pleasant. He was looking forward to his appointments and was unhappy over any interruption. He willingly accepted any interpretations which had to do with his passive feminine wishes. He even wished to be a girl. He dreamed that he had female genitals, and came to his hours perfumed like a girl for a *rendezvous*.

In this phase of apparently completely positive transference, the analysis came to a halt. In spite of all my efforts, the analytic situation remained static for weeks. The material presented by the patient consisted of variations of one theme: a passive feminine attitude with the wish to be castrated. During this period, the patient was completely free of anxiety. He had abandoned all attempts at intercourse with women.

At this point the case was presented in the technical seminar. The discussion drew attention to the fact that the latent negative transference had not been recognized and analyzed. This was pointed out to the patient during the analytic situation resulting in a change almost immediately. It was revealed that the patient had for a long time begun and ended each analytic hour with a secret inner smile. Though numerous other actions which remained unnoticed he had undermined the apparently positive relationship to the analyst. Hidden behind this existed an intense hate-readiness, which was inhibited by anxiety only, and which now trickled through in the form of small hints, which, when attention was called to them, led finally to a vehement outbreak. Suddenly the anticipated negative transference became manifest. It had been there all along, but now it emerged from behind the apparent positive transference. Before long, it became the focal point of the analysis. Tardiness, insults, a tendency towards flight and the deepest doubts about the therapy became the order of the day. This negative attitude was transferred from the father onto the analyst. Tracing it back to its original object gave the clearest insight into the source of this negative attitude.

The patient had not always been employed in his father's business. He had originally taken up the profession of being a merchant, had served his apprenticeship, and worked his way up to an advanced position in a company. One day he suddenly left the company, without being able to give any account of his motives in this action. He entered the business of his father, as an apprentice, and with little interruption, remained there under unfavorable conditions. Simultaneously, with his return into his parents' house, he gave up masturbation and became impotent. The explanation of this unintelligible return to the father was the following: the patient had had intercourse with a young woman who was staying at his parents' apartment on a trip through the city and he had caught scabies from her. He went to the clinic for treatment. As he was waiting there in the dermatological department, he saw a patient urinating in the lavatory with an amputated penis; he had only a small stump remaining. The sight of this terrified the patient. During the dermatological treatment, some of the Wilkinson ointment got on his foreskin, where it caused an excoriation that became infected and confined the patient to bed for weeks. Through these various reactivations of his castration complex, his castration anxiety was considerably intensified. The neurosis which had up until this time been latent now became manifest.[2] His return to his father was caused

---

[2] Just before he acquired scabies he had a talk with his father in which the latter warned him about the consequences of extramarital intercourse. "He would no longer be able to do it." This took direct effect in the disturbance of his potency.

chiefly by guilt feeling, but in the deeper layers was also a homosexual passive tie to the father, which found expression in the subordinate position which he took in his father's business. The basic reason, at least for the change in occupation was an identification with the father on an anal basis.[3]

The anal cathexis of the genitals was particularly marked in this patient. Money meant to him anality, and, on a higher level, genital potency. He gave up this potency when he worked for his father for little money. Just before his entrance into his father's business, the patient went through a phase when he compulsively gambled away his earnings. In the analysis too, the patient remained dependent upon his father up until the time when the latent negative transference broke through. Then the return of the hate impulses which he directed against the analyst were also operative on the father: the patient went on strike, demanded twenty-five percent of the profits from the business and got it. However, the money which he thus obtained, he gambled away compulsively, a repetition of an early passion for gambling which occurred before the beginning of his impotency. This passion for gambling could easily be interpreted to him as self-castration, and disappeared completely after the interpretation had been given him. A second consequence of alteration in this patient's attitude in the transference was of wide-reaching significance for the progress of the analysis. The patient developed anxiety. This anxiety could be mobilized from its numerous deposits where it had been displaced. It was recognized more and more clearly as anxiety aroused by his father and about his genitals. Ultimately, both anxiety experiences could be traced to their common infantile source, that of childhood masturbation.

The phenomenon of latent negative transference was particularly clear in this case. The positive and accepting attitude towards the analyst screened powerful latent hate impulses, the manifestations of which did not appear because of castration anxiety (anxiety-protection, *Angstschutz*). The chief element of the apparently positive relationship, for the sake of which the negative relationship remained hidden, namely castration, was preserved but out of fear was converted into a wish.

There were numerous other analyses reported in this seminar where the transference relationship in question played a more or less important role. Two of these analyses had to be terminated unsuccessfully. The following dream, which derives from one of these two analyses, can serve as the classical manifestations of latent negative transference.

---

[3] There was, of course, in this passivity and patience shown toward his father ample room for indications of his hate impulses. For example, he could not look at the Kaddish prayer, which is said by the son after the father's death. Even the sight of the prayer book terrified him. He could not lay any dark object on his father's bed and became terrified when he saw a hearse.

A woman patient dreams that the analyst is sitting in the first row at the movies. It was emphasized in the associations to this dream that the much respected analyst could be thought of as sitting in no other place but the first row. When it was pointed out to the patient that the first row in a moving picture theatre was also the worst, the patient excused this by saying that the analyst might not go to the movies often, and probably did not know this. The associations, therefore, made a visible effort to hide and belie the negative relationship which had broken through in the dream, and to emphasize the positive aspects of the dream.

We shall now discuss several theoretical questions in connection with our presentation of the latent negative transference. First, as to the motives for concealment of the negative transference: in the case of impotence presented, the chief motive is clear throughout, perhaps so clear that other motives can be easily overlooked. The castration anxiety, or better perhaps, the avoiding of the discomfort of the anxiety related to punishment for the aggressive tendencies directed against the father caused these aggressive tendencies to remain hidden.

In the search for further motives it is necessary to discuss the resistance character of the negative transference more thoroughly. A hostile attitude is particularly well-adapted to resistance.

According to Freud's presentation in the "Introductory Lectures on Psychoanalysis", analytic therapy consists of the elimination of repression through reactivation of the conflicts in the transference. This elimination is made possible through an alteration in the Ego due to the suggestive influence of the analyst.

A hostile attitude on the part of the Ego, through which the analyst's influence is counteracted from the very beginning, is a means of resistance; it is a means, to be sure, which can be dealt with relatively easily, using technical training and skill.

It is different, however, when interpretations, or even everything the analyst presents, is immediately accepted by the patient but afterwards or even simultaneously but in a deeper layer, negated. In this double attitude of this topical difference between these two antagonistic reactions lies the difficulty in recognition and combating the depreciation.

We know that where difficulties develop during the therapy, resistances are at work. From the size of the difficulty it is certainly admissible to draw conclusions as to the quantitative factor of the resistance concerned. During the phase of latent negative transference one has to do, therefore, with particularly intense resistances against the therapy. The next point we may take up for discussion is the origin of the resistances, by examining under what conditions these resistances create and preserve the specific transference relationship which is the subject of our discussion.

The essential point is that the latent negative transference is a *transference*; that is the repetition of an attitude towards a person of significance in the infantile phases of the patient. Without such an infantile model of covering up hostile feelings by an apparently positive attitude can the transference phenomena in question not be established. In general this emotional constellation originates in the Oedipus complex.

The origin of the resistances, which participate in the formation of the latent negative transference is manifold. In the case discussed, castration anxiety was the main factor in the formation of the transference relationship. Resistances which proceed from the Super-Ego, for example guilt-feeling, can be active in the relationship. *Repression* resistance also has its part in the resistance expressed in the form of the latent negative transference.

We should not forget that resistances which stem from different sources can be joined together, and that they even have a tendency to coalesce. If a resistance, for example, a transference resistance out of castration anxiety, has led to the establishment of a latent negative transference, this relationship is not only preserved by the resistance due to castration anxiety, but other resistances against the analysis also contribute to and support this form of transference relationship, because it effectively counteracts the analytic process.

Freud seems to have had this support of a transference situation through resistances other than the transference resistance in mind when he says in the "Introductory Lectures on Psychoanalysis",

"That which probably prevents single effects of suggestion from arising during the treatment is the struggle that is incessantly being waged against the resistances, which know how to transform themselves into a negative (hostile) transference." (Introductory Lectures, p. 394.)

The negative, particularly the latent negative transference, becomes thereby the chief resistance to the cure.

How does it come about, then, that particularly with beginners the hidden negative transference is so difficult to recognize, and often eludes them entirely? It is very easy for us to recognize a positive relationship, even from the slightest indications. But we can also recognize and interpret manifestations of hostile impulses, correctly and easily, when they are not directed towards ourselves. The overlooking of hidden hate impulses which are directed against ourselves occurs because we want to avoid the narcissistic injury which every hate impulse implies for the person against whom it is directed. It is by no means easy for the beginner to recognize himself the target of the hidden anger, which is usually well-aimed and hits directly at the most sensitive areas of the analyst and of his environment. After the negative transference has become manifest, one is much better equipped to deal with the crude approaches than one with the refined and cleverly chosen insinuations about the weaknesses of the analyst. Beginners frequently scotomize themselves against these and thus avoid the unpleasure of injury to their narcissism.

The latent negative transference, with its consistent appearance of an apparently positive relationship, is often elaborated characterologically. I am familiar with this character type from an analysis. Friendly and devoted to everyone, these people at the same time, or perhaps later, often have fantasies about the unpleasant things that they should have said or will say to them. Nevertheless, in their behavior, they are markedly cowardly and upon meeting the persons the next time they react with the same obsequious submission.

The task then arises in treatment, of making the hate manifest, and of tracing the anxiety to its source, which is usually possible only after the overcoming of further resistances which proceed from the anxiety experience that has become manifest. The result of such analyses is then a basic characterological change, which is usually externally recognizable as a change in attitude, greater security and more self-assertive behavior.

A Compulsive Action From the Latency Period

An internal conflict is the basis of every psychoneurotic symptom. The hysterical symptom is a compromise between an instinctual wish and a corresponding repressive tendency. In the obsessional symptom, one can observe that the symptom is the expression of the antagonistic forces of love and hate, as well as that of acceptance and rejection. The conflict characteristic of the compulsion neurosis occurs between two contrary emotional attitudes toward one and the same object, which we call the *conflict of ambivalence*. Often this ambivalence, this simultaneous occurrence of emotions of opposite tendency toward a definite object, leads to two compulsion actions, wherein the second action is intended to cancel out the first, and with it the result of the emotional attitude which is the basis of it, and to convert it into its opposite. Freud describes a typical example of such a compulsive action in his "Notes upon a Case of Obsessional Neurosis"[1]: "On the day of her departure (the lady whom that patient loved) he knocked his foot against a stone lying in the road, and was *compelled* to put it out of the way by the side of the road, and because the idea struck him that her carriage would be driving along the same road in a few hours' time and might come to grief against the stone. But a few minutes later it occurred to him that this was absurd, and he was *obliged* to go back and replace the stone in its original position in the middle of the road.'' The patient's conflicting emotions toward the woman are clear in this example of a compulsive action.

My patient related that from his seventh to his eighth year—at a time, therefore, when the infantile compulsive neurosis usually becomes manifest, he had to perform the following compulsive action: if he was given the task of carrying an object, particularly if it was breakable, he was compelled to say according to his religious attitude at the time, "with the

[1] Collected Papers, III, 327f.Eine Zwangshandlung aus der Latenzzeit. *Zeitschrift fur Psychoanalytische Padagogik*, 1927–1928, 2, 322–323.

help of God," so that nothing would happen to the object. But at the same time, and this was the compulsive action disasterous for the object, he had to fold his hands as in praying. The result was that frequently enough the object fell to the floor and broke. This compulsive action, which was intended to protect the object, and for this purpose called upon God's help, had the result, and therefore also the purpose of destroying the object or at least of damaging it. This reveals the ambivalent attitude toward the object, and behind this the ambivalence against its owner and against the person who imposed the task, which in both cases was usually one of the parents. But at the same time God's help was called upon in such a fashion and under such conditions that his inability to help was questioned. Thus, the deepest layer of ambivalance was expressed in the doubt of God's existence.

The negative side of this ambivalence was completely unconscious to the patient. He blamed his hands for the misfortune that befell him when he was given the task to carry something precious and breakable. The complicated task of carrying and protecting, by the praying position, was just too much for such little hands. His mishap was therefore attributed to external circumstances, and was not recognized as the consequence of an unconscious emotional attitude directly opposed to his conscious purpose.

An Examination Dream

One of my patients had fairly regularly, at intervals of two or three months, a dream about his matriculation examination. In the dream he was always doing a paper in Latin or mathematics. Invariably the dreamer lived through the last few minutes before the time was up. He had not yet begun to translate or to work out the problems, and the examiner announced that there would be five minutes more. His comrades held out their papers for him to copy and tried to prompt him, but he was incapable of even guiding his pen; the figures or letters became a blur, and he experienced the whole torment of the situation of not being able to perform or complete a task—only to awake with a sense of great relief and satisfaction at the thought that his school-days were long since over. So far, these dreams are typical and do not require any special mention; but the subject's previous history is worth noting from a theoretical point of view. In the *Traumdeutung* we read that a colleague had remarked to Freud that, so far as he knew, the matriculation dream only occurred in people who had passed the examination, and never in those who had failed in it.

Now the dreams in question are peculiar owing to the fact that the dreamer had never taken the matriculation examination.

Let me first give some analytical data in connection with the dream. The fact that the examination was always in mathematics or Latin is easily explained. The patient's father was a professor of mathematics; the Latin Professor at the time when the patient was a schoolboy was clearly a father-substitute.[1] The father and the Professor had certain qualities in common: both were one-sided and immersed in their own narrow scientific work, both were unsociable and delighted in books and astronomy, and both smoked pipes. The boy, who was otherwise very alert and of good intelligence, could make no progress in Latin, thus giving vent to his negative

---

An Examination Dream. *International Journal of Psychoanalysis*, 1928, 9, 353–354. From: Ein Prufungstraum, *Internationale Zeitschrift fur Psychoanalyse*, 1927, *13*, 456–457.

[1] When he dreamt of an examination in mathematics the patient never saw the examiner, but if it was a Latin paper the examiner was always there.

feelings towards his father. It was in accordance with the somewhat protracted duration of puberty that he retained his dislike of Latin right up to the highest form in school. The Latin Professor liked him. Every badly performed task was regarded by him as a personal slight from the patient, and thus he added to the negative transference. He saw to it that, in spite of the boy's defective knowledge, he was moved up every year to a higher form. With horror the patient saw his matriculation examination becoming more and more imminent. When he thought of this public examination, in which the gaps in his knowledge would inevitably be revealed, he was seized with violent anxiety. He was anticipating punishment for the many occasions on which he had neglected his tasks: that is to say, for the unconscious hate towards his father which had caused this neglect. The examination was anticipated as a punishment, so to speak, for his guilt in relation to his father.

Then came the War and with it the 'War-matriculation' [i.e. reaching the status of manhood without the test of a school-examination], and the boy eluded the anticipated punishment. Shortly afterwards the examination-dream occurred for the first time, and from then on it recurred regularly. The patient could not recollect that there was any connection between the dream and some responsible task which he was required to perform on the following day.

The analytical material associated with this dream shews that, although it was about an examination, it has not the characteristics which Freud ascribes to examination-dreams in general but must be placed in another category, amongst those which he calls 'punishment-dreams'. According to him 'punishment-dreams' fulfil the wishes of the critical institution in the ego (ego-ideal, censorship, conscience). The fact that in the dreams under consideration the father appeared as the examiner would accord with this view.[2] Only it is rather remarkable that this punishment-dream took the form of an examination-dream and had in it much of the mechanism which Freud discovered in the latter type of dream.

Thus we have here a mixture of two types: the examination and the punishment-dream. This is the explanation of the remarkable fact that anyone who had never stood for this examination should nevertheless dream of it in this typical way.

Richard Sterba, Vienna.

---

[2] Cf. Reik, *Geständniszwang und Strafbedürfnis*, p. 65.

On the Oral Origin of Envy

It was inevitable that psychoanalysis, in the course of its investigations, should consider basic behavior and attitudes which are not differentiated from the rest of mental life, such as we observe in the case of slip-actions, dreams, and symptoms, as well as those which are built into the conscious mental life and serve to give direction to the latter. We designate such behavior and attitudes as character traits. Psychoanalysis succeeded in establishing the fact that their particular and sometimes pathological determination was to be ascribed to a fixation of the libido to a certain erotogenic zone. With those character traits, which are pathological, there is regularly some connection with an erotogenic zone which the libido of the adult has normally given up, to a considerable extent, in order to subject it in its ultimate disposition to the primacy of the genital zone. The retention of an organizational level of libidinal development, which normally would have been abandoned in favor of progress to a higher level, is fixated at this level. All organizational levels of the libido contribute to normal character formation. The character of the normal individual remains in the oral, anal-sadistic, and urethral phases of the libido. The features of this pathology and character trait are disturbing to the individual or to the community. In correspondence with such a character trait of a pathology, there is a particularly strong fixation at the erotogenic zone from which the character trait is derived. This fixation at a particular zone finds expression through early childhood behavior.

Freud, who was a pioneer in discovering the basis of character traits from manifestations of pleasure in specific erotogenic zones, was particularly interested in obstinacy, parsimoniousness and orderliness. He found that these characteristics derived from the anal zone, that is, individuals in whom these character traits were particularly marked. During childhood, all those forms of "naughtiness" were for the purpose of obtaining anal

Zum oralen Ursprung des Neides. *Zeitschrift fur Psychoanalytische Padagogik*, 1928–1929, *3*, 472–473.

pleasure. Here belong primarily the retention of the stool, the stubborn refusal of the infant and also of older children to empty their bowels at the time the person caring for them wishes it to occur. Performing this function, at the time when the accumulation of the stool provides them with a particularly intense experience of pleasure in passing this through the anus, is of great importance.

Abraham, in his "Supplement to the Theory of Anal Character" extended Freud's concepts. In a later work, "Contributions of Oral Eroticism to Character Formation," he has indicated that manifestations of pleasure in the oral zone, as they correspond to the act of sucking of the infant and later the "naughtiness" of sucking in the child, can be reckoned among the contributions to character formation. One character trait which is derived from the oral zone is *envy*. Envy is likely to develop if the child is already beyond the suckling stage, but has experienced weaning as a severe disappointment, and has then had the opportunity to observe how a sibling who has arrived in the meantime enjoys the happiness at the mother's breast which is denied to him forevermore.

I had the opportunity to observe a patient in whom envy was a predominant character trait. Jealousy and envy had completely overwhelmed him in both his professional and private life. They did not leave him a moment's peace. He was completely incapable of pleasure, because on every opportunity he had for pleasure, he was disturbed by the fact that others had more. He was literally *eaten up* by his envy. Because the analysis had to be broken off due to external reasons, it was not possible to discover the ultimate determinants of this patient's envy. But a series of memories were uncovered providing sufficient proof for the origin of the envy in the oral zone. The patient was the oldest of four brothers, and therefore had a threefold opportunity to observe how younger siblings enjoyed the pleasure of mother's breast, which was denied to him at the end of a normal nursing period. He developed into a child who was a literal "sucker." From five to seven years it would happen that if hard candies were distributed among the children, the patient broke out into a furious rage when he saw his brothers sucking on the candies, although he himself had received an equal share. He threw himself upon them and, since he was much stronger, forced them to open their mouths, snatched out the candies, and with the greatest satisfaction put them into his own mouth. We may assume that these attacks upon the younger brothers represent an attempt to assuage a feeling of envy which had already developed earlier. It becomes clear that the hard candy is a substitute for the mother's breast with reference to the nipple. The derivation of envy from the oral zone and its development out of the attitude of competition with a younger sibling was particularly clear in this case. The attack upon the brothers was an expression of his attempt to win back the mother's breast by way of a substitute object, namely the hard candy. He would then force the brothers from the position of oral happiness, which he longed for so much and to which he could never again attain. The intense envy which this patient manifested as an adult showed that these attempts at an oral robbery could not completely fulfill their purpose psychically. The remainder of the rivalry relationship to the brothers had been characterologically modified and found its ultimate and continual expression in the envy of the patient.

Jealous of . . . ?

An Equivocal Expression of Our Everyday Language

In the course of its development and during the rapid extension of its area of validity psychoanalysis has had at its disposal an extraordinarily easily accessible and constant source of pointers for the trend of its research, and for confirmation of the results of its findings. This source must be doubly welcome, because its living force is active in every individual; not only does every individual develop through it, but at the same time has a living participation in its development as well; and the influx to scientific research of the human mind created by it is convincingly effective with an intense directness and active liveliness. This source is our language.

We are not concerned here with the fact that the use of spoken language plays a predominant role for the understanding of dreams and in slip-actions, and that the recognition of the usage of words in their infantile, primitive sense, according to the 'primary process' with its employment of displacement and condensation, is the key to psychopathological mechanisms which enable us to understand the meaning of dreams and the symptom formations of the neuroses and psychoses. The current and correct expression of our daily speech itself can surprise us when we recognize the depth of psychological insight which it betrays, if we are only able to grasp its significance. One could be so bold as to say that the ignorance about our mental life is so vast, that we do not know what we are saying, even when we speak with complete conscious clarity and full deliberation. It is Freud who we again owe the first insight into the hidden meaning of many expressions of daily speech, an insight which proved so very useful. The examination of many dreams in Freud's 'Interpretation of Dreams' already gives ample opportunity for the examination of expressions and

Elfersuchtig auf . . . ? Ein doppelsinniger Ausdruck unserer Umgangssprache. *Psychoanalytische Bewegung*, 1930, 2, 167–170.

sayings in our daily speech which are astonishing in their symbolic value and their imminent psychological knowledge. As often happens, a word was inserted where a concept was lacking, and helped to reveal the psychological secret if one only hit upon the hidden meaning of the word. And contrariwise, one learned to understand the hidden meaning of certain common phrases used in everyday language. Many speech usages and many daily expressions have a deep meaning due to the fact that the deeper layers of our mental apparatus, which are not accessible to our consciousness, send derivatives up into consciousness, which are difficult to decipher. These derivatives remain unrecognized through their participation in consciousness, bring relief and lessen to a certain degree the tension under which the repressed material is maintained. Part of the power which proceeds from words, not only when the poet shapes them, but also in the simple speech from man to man, is due to those derivatives from the deeper and powerfully repressed areas of our mind. For also in speech all strong effects proceed from such repressed instinctual dynamics.

The expression which we wish to examine here is a simple everyday usage: '*to be jealous of someone*'. It can readily be observed that when someone speaks about jealous impulses, either his own or those of another, a difficulty in expression for the understanding of these feelings arises, which frequently makes further explanation necessary. This necessity grows out of the double meaning of our expression 'to be jealous of someone'. For in daily speech, we are accustomed to use this expression, not only for our feeling concerning the *beloved object*, but also for that toward the *rival*. If someone wishes to say that he has a feeling of jealousy toward the rival A because of his love for B, then the common usage permits him to say that he is jealous of A, as well as that he is jealous of B. This is intelligible without further clarification, if it is known which is the love object and which the rival.

But if the relationships are not clear, then the inexactness of our expression, requires further exploration as to which is the love object and which is the rival. For if I merely say that I am jealous of someone, it still remains unclear whether he is the object of my love impulses or of my jealous hate and feelings of rivalry; and within the framework of this common expression, love object and rival are interchangeable.

It is my opinion that we will not go wrong if we assume that such a striking lack of precision in our daily speech is the reflection of a double meaning in the psychological situation which is so expressed.

Pathology is acquainted with a strange delusional mental illness that is termed *delusion of jealousy*. This delusion consists in the fact that the sick person, completely without justification, accuses his marriage or sexual partner of sexual relationships with one or more other persons, although the conduct of the accused person does not give the slightest occasion for or justification of the suspicion of such accusation. It is very striking that the aggression which arises out of this jealousy is directed, not against the rival but regularly against the individual's own love partner, usually in a brutal, often dangerous form. Depth psychological investigation of the delusional formation permits us to recognize that it *represents the defense against a strong homosexual instinctual impulse*, the object of which is the supposed rival. This defense follows the formula: It is not I who loves him, *she* is the one that loves him. This jealousy, therefore, does not arise out of love for the person who is apparently the love object, but out of an unconscious homosexual love for the person, who in the conscious psychotic formation appears as the *rival*. In this case, homosexual wishes are the deep unconscious motivation for the jealous impulse.

Not seldom one finds that such a positive relationship to the rival also appears in normal jealousy. Freud, in his paper, 'Certain Neurotic Mechanisms in Jealousy, Paranoia and Homosexuality' (Coll. Papers, II, 232f) says about jealousy, 'Moreover, it is noteworthy that in many persons it is experienced bisexually; that is to say, in a man besides the suffering in regard to the loved woman and the hatred against the male rival, grief in regard to the unconsciously loved man and hatred of the woman as a rival will add to its intensity.' The bisexual experience of jealousy is here made as generally applicable as bisexuality itself, which is present in all of us at the beginning of the libidinal development. Mastery of the homosexual components of this bisexuality is in the normal outcome of psycho-sexual development in our culture. A homosexual intensification of jealousy, which becomes so clear in pathological cases, is then generally operative only in a small degree. But, as so often, there is nevertheless, a remainder of this already mastered early developmental phase, which is usually overlooked by us, because of its insignificant influence. I consider the ambiguity of our expression 'to be jealous of someone', the residue of bisexuality in the experience of normal jealousy with its interchangeability of love object and rival. It is a matter of great wonder that our speech, which is otherwise so concerned with precise formulation of affective states is here so lacking in precision that it makes more exact inquiry necessary whether, when I say 'I am jealous of someone', he is my love object or my rival. The possibility of reversal in a jealous relationship, from love object to rival and vice versa, which is a regular occurrence in pathological cases, and often noticeable in normal ones, is derived from a common point of origin, namely, the original bisexual disposition, to us a striking ambiguity of a verbal expression which is so commonly used, finds this genetic explanation.

It is interesting that in the German language the expression '*auf jemanden eifersuchtig sein*' is just as ambiguous as the English 'to be jealous of someone'. If I say 'Ich bin eifersuchtig auf ihn', or 'auf sie', it remains unclear whether the person of whom I speak is the love object or the rival, since the same interchangeability of love object and rival is present in this verbal expression. The same holds true for the French expression '*etre jaloux de quelqu'un.*'

A Contribution To The Theory Of Sublimation

Sublimation is one of the vicissitudes which an instinct can undergo after it is denied satisfaction for internal or external reasons. The vicissitudes 'turning around upon the subject' and 'reversal into its opposite' have been thoroughly discussed by Freud in the paper, 'Instincts and Their Vicissitudes'; to the vicissitude 'repression', Freud devoted a whole paper. In contrast, the vicissitude sublimation was given no unified presentation by Freud. Bernfeld, in his study "Observations on Sublimation", (Imago, VIII, 1924) attempted to resolve several of the inconsistencies which became noticeable if one compiles the scattered remarks on sublimation found in Freud's writings. The following paper concerns itself with a consideration of the two most important points in Bernfeld's critique, and with proving these invalid on the basis of Freud's more recent formulations.

The first point to which Bernfeld objects is the definition of sublimation as it is formulated by Freud. Bernfeld considered it inappropriate that a cultural or social value factor is operative in the definition of sublimation. If we consider one of Freud's earliest definitions, the one in the lectures 'On Psychoanalysis,' which Freud gave in 1909 at Clark University, Worcester, Massachusetts, there can be no doubt that a cultural value factor plays a decisive role in it: "We know a far more purposive process of development, the so-called sublimation, by which the energy of infantile wish-excitations is not secluded, but remains capable of application, while for the particular excitation, instead of becoming useless, a higher, eventually a non-sexual goal is set up." (The Origin and Development of Psychoanalysis, The American Journal of Psychology, XXI, 2, 1910). There the designation "Higher" goal serves to a certain extent as a criterion as to whether a sublimation has taken place. But from Freud's later definitions, one gains the impression that the evaluation "Higher" new goal

Zur Problematik der Sublimierungslehre. *Internationale Zeitschrift fur Psychoanalyse*, 1930, *16*, 370–377.

is not the essential criterion of the sublimatory process, but rather a by-product of the sublimation. Thus, for example, we find this in considering the most recent definition from the *Marcuse's Handbook of Sexual Sciences*, which reads:

> "The most important vicissitude which an instinct can undergo seems to be sublimation. Here both object and aim have changed so that what was originally a sexual instinct, finds satisfaction in some achievement which is no longer sexual but has a higher social or ethical evaluation."[1]

The diction here gives the impression that if the diverted goal is evaluated more highly socially or ethically, this is only a by-product of the sublimation process, not the essence of it. The definition in "Narcissism, An Introduction", runs:

> "Sublimation is a process that concerns object libido and consists of the instinct's directing itself towards an aim other than and remote from that of sexual satisfaction. In the process the accent falls upon deflection from sexuality."[2]

Here the emphasis rests upon the deviation from the sexual and the higher evaluation of the new goal is definitely placed in the background. It seems to us a clear conclusion from the quotation that Freud himself was attempting to exclude the cultural evaluative factor in his judgment as to what psychic process should be called sublimation. The suggestion of Bernfeld that any deviation of an object libidinal striving from its original goal, insofar as it takes place without repression and is ego-syntonic be primarily and explicitly termed a sublimation seems to me completely in accord with Freud's definition of the term, and even to be implied in that definition. I shall return to the cultural evaluation factor and its possibilities of application later in my discussion, for the purpose of resolving certain theoretical difficulties in the problem of sublimation.

Now as to the presentation of the *mechanism* of sublimation as it is found in Freud's writings. The first and most important place where Freud makes a statement about the mechanism of sublimation is in the "Three Contributions to the Theory of Sex," and runs as follows:

> "*Reaction Formation and Sublimation.* What are the means

---

[1] *The Complete Psychological Works of Sigmund Freud*, Vol. 18, pg. 258.
[2] S. *Freud*, Standard Edition, 14, 94)

that accomplish these important constructions so important for the later personal culture and normality? They are brought about at the cost of the infant sexuality itself. The influx of this sexuality does not stop even in this latency period, but its energy is deflected either wholly or partially from sexual utilization and conducted to other aims. The historians of civilization seem to be unanimous in the opinion that such deflection of sexual motive powers from sexual aims to new aims, a process which merits the name of *sublimation*, has furnished powerful components for all cultural accomplishments. We will, therefore, add that the same process acts in the development of every individual, and that it begins to act in the sexual latency period.

We can also venture an opinion about the mechanisms of such sublimation. The sexual feelings of these infantile years would on the one hand be unusable, since the procreating functions are postponed—this is the chief character of the latency period; on the other hand, they would as such be perverse, as they would emanate from erogenous zones and from impulses which in the individual's course of development could only evoke a feeling of unpleasure. They, therefore, awaken psychic counterforces, which build up the already mentioned *psychical dams* of disgust, shame and morality.''
(Standard Edition, 7, 178)

Our great reaction formations are here termed sublimations; for the mechanism described in the text is the one of reaction formation. A footnote is supplied by Freud at this point to clarify this:

"In the case here discussed, sublimation of the sexual motive powers proceeds on the path of reaction formations. But in general it is necessary to separate sublimation from reaction formation. They are two diverse processes. Sublimation may also result through other and simpler mechanisms.''
(Standard Edition 7, 178)

Bernfeld takes exception to the lack of distinction between sublimation and reaction formation, and would like to have sublimation clearly differentiated from reaction formation. He holds valid only the mechanism of sublimation indicated in the footnote, and refuses to designate reaction formation as sublimation.

Through the presentation in the "Three Contributions", which fuses sublimation and reaction formation, we actually meet with a considerable dilemma. We are generally accustomed to distinguish between sublimation and reaction formation, but here we find them identified. It is my belief that Bernfeld's suggestion to make both concepts distinct one from the other, and to call only that sublimation which can be regarded as a simple deviation from the original aim does not necessarily have to be accepted, and I can think of two possibilities for the solution of this theoretical difficulty. The first attempt at a solution consists in a re-introduction of the value factor into the definition. It would have to then run as follows: if from an instinctual vicissitude an action results which is culturally, socially and ethically more valuable than the instinctual gratification originally striven for, this vicissitude is to be called sublimation. Against this solution, one object that the value factor, the deletion of which from the definition was to be commended, has been reinstated. In addition to this, the definition is contradicted by many passages in Freud, where it is emphasized that repression excludes sublimation, and that only after the lifting of repression is the way to sublimation free. For repression and sublimation are repeatedly presented by Freud as in opposition, while on the other hand, the presentation of the mechanism of sublimation in the 'Three Contributions' makes repression a pre-requisite for it. In order to solve this difficulty one must assume that there are two paths of sublimation: first, a direct deviation from the goal, which is only possible without repression. (This would be sublimation in the sense of the simple mechanism in the footnote quoted above), and secondly, a sublimation after previous repression. The difficulty consists in the fact that sublimation is defined as an instinctual vicissitude, while in the reaction formation the vicissitude of the instinct is repression.

There is a solution to all this, if one consults Freud's later metapsychological writings. In speaking of *identification* in "The Ego and the Id," he says that this process implies a sublimation of the libido. The giving up of the object, which is a necessary experience in childhood, is accomplished by a process of alteration in the Ego, in that the Ego makes itself like the object. The libido is then diverted from the object back to the Ego and is thus transformed from object libido into narcissistic libido. "The transformation of object-libido into narcissistic libido which thus takes place obviously implies an abandonment of sexual aims, a process of desexualization; it is consequently a kind of sublimation." (*The Ego and the Id*, 37f)

The recognition of the fact that sublimation plays a part in the process of identification increases the significance of the sublimation process for the individual to a great degree. For through the individual's capacity to promote his libido to such sublimation, it is possible for the Ego to make the Id serviceable to it; sublimation makes the Ego master of the Id. Freud also tells us something about the fate of the sublimated libido. It is turned into indifferent, displaceable cathexis energy of the mental apparatus. The assumption of such an indifferent cathexis energy is necessary, because without it various phenomena of transformation within the mental apparatus could not be explained. Thus, for example, one must assume the existence of such indifferent energy to explain the so frequently observed transformation of love into hate, to explain the paranoid transformation of an erotic impulse into a hostile one, the hostile rivalry into homosexual tendencies, and so on. "Without assuming the existence of a displaceable energy of this kind we can make no headway."[3] This energy, however, consists of desexualized, therefore sublimated Eros.

The assumption of such a displaceable, indifferent cathexis energy, which originally was goal-directed energy, offers solution for the contradiction of our concepts 'sublimation' and 'reaction formation.' We may say, that is, that the reaction formation is in fact the result of the process of sublimation. If a drive cannot be satisfied, because of its forbidden aim, it is a possibility that *its energy becomes desexualized and is discharged in the form of a reaction formation, in the opposite direction to the original drive goal.*

The reaction formation is then certainly a result of sublimation, but the application and discharge of the indifferent cathexis energy, which derives from the originally sexually directed drive energy lies beyond the actual process of sublimation or takes place only afterwards in the direction of the reaction formation. However, in order to allow for the possibility of such discharge in the direction of the reaction formation, a sublimation of the original drive energy to indifferent cathexis energy is a necessary prerequisite. In order to understand the so frequent application of the desexualized and therefore sublimated drive energy in the direction of a reaction formation, opposite to the original drive goal, it is well to contemplate the dynamic-economic meaning of sublimation.

In 'Civilization and Its Discontents,' Freud described sublimation as a technique of defense against suffering pain which is 'unpleasure.' Unpleasure is an increase in tension or the lack of decrease in it. Therefore, in a psycho-dynamic sense defense against pain means the avoidance or lessening of tension. Sublimation is, therefore, *a technique of lessening tension*. The drive provides the tension (energy), the discharge of tension

---

[3] *The Ego and the Id*, Standard Edition, 19, 44.

is accomplished through action with the help of the motoric system. The deviation from its original aim through the process of sublimation makes the discharge of the drive energy possible.

If we ask ourselves whence the inhibiting forces proceed that compel a deviation from the original aim, the answer is not difficult to find: it is civilization with all its ethical, social and other standards, which in form of external or incorporated demands forces the instinctual vicissitude of sublimation. It is self-explanatory that the result of an instinctual vicissitude compelled by civilization will correspond more to the values of civilization than the original aim of the drive. Thus, the cultural value factor in the concept of sublimation is reinstated. For if civilization compels the deviation from the original goal, this deviation can occur only in a direction which is in conformity with the values of civilization.

We shall now consider the different possibilities for direction of the deviation from the goal. This can be illustrated by means of a comparison. Let us suppose that I am given the task of taking the energy of a waterfall, which in its place and position cannot be used, and of making it usable in another place. It is then possible for me to conduct the water into canals, and to make the potential energy inherent in it usable in another place, by watermills, of course only downstream, that is, in the direction that it is falling. This is the case in sublimation, according to the *simple* mechanism of deviation from the goal. It can happen, however, that the application in the direction of the fall through cultural limitation, is impossible. There then remains a second possibility for the use of this energy, for its discharge, with the water in the same place and position. I can *transform* its energy into another form; namely, into electric energy. This electric energy, in our comparison, corresponds to the indifferent, displaceable cathexis energy. It is then possible to dispatch this movable energy in any direction, because it has been completely divested of the original character of directedness toward its drive aim. I can also use (i.e., discharge) it upstream, and will do this particularly if I find the best ego-syntonic possibilities for discharge in the direction of inhibition of the drive. *The result of this discharge of energy in the direction of an inhibition of a drive is made possible through the transformation into indifferent displaceable cathexis energy we call reaction formation.*

It is perhaps well to distinguish between two types of reaction formation. The intensity of the repressed drive residue may serve as a mark of distinction between them. In the case of a relatively high drive residue what we designate as a reaction formation is identical with what is otherwise called counter-cathexis. The high consumption of energy, which must be withdrawn from other functions, brings about the compulsive and exaggerated character of this type of reaction formations identical with counter-cathexis. Wilhelm Reich has given a phenomonological demonstration of this type of reaction formation, and has contrasted it with genuine sublimation (Der genitale und neurotische Charakter, Int. Zeitschr. f. PsA Bd. SIV, 1928). In this case, the second type of reaction formation, which is what I would like to call reaction formation proper, nothing or very little is left repressed of the original instinct.

I consider the normal superego a type of reaction formation according to Freud's presentation, "The Passing of the Oedipus Complex", (Standard Edition), it rises out of the oedipus complex after complete transformation of the oedipal drive energies. In the transformation of the superego, one can observe most clearly the change of the original drive energies through desexualization and their discharges in the direction opposite to the original drive aim.

To demonstrate the distinction between the reaction formation identical with counter-cathexis and the reaction formation proper, we may consider the two types of pity. In exaggerated forms of pity, such for example as that for animals, associated with a phobic avoidance of butcher shops, etc., even superficial analysis meets with great drive residues of a sadistic kind. In the efficacious rendering of help in active (masculine) pity (Jekels) there is nothing in the nature of a counter-cathexis indicated; rather this pity represents *a discharge of psychic energy* of a sadistic origin in the form of a reaction formation which has to be considered a sublimation.

It seems justifiable to deduce from the material heretofore presented a scale of the results of sublimation, wherein the degree of deviation from the original aim serves as the basis for the scale. This scheme naturally makes no claims to completeness and attempts merely to designate the most striking points within the range of possible deviations from the goal. As such we may mention the following:

I) The simplest form of deviation from the aim is the inhibition of the sensual drive to a tender one. Its cultural value is clear, and lies in the durability of such strivings with an inhibited aim (object constancy). The object and the direction of the drive remain the same; it is only that the drive stops its demand, short of its original aim. One could speak of this process as a moderation of the aim rather than a deviation from it.

II) As the next point along the line of deviations from the aim, we may consider the simple displacement, somewhat in the manner of primitive symbolism. An example of this would be the preparation of fire among primitives, in which it is difficult to distinguish whether a sexualized Ego process or a desexualized Id drive is represented.

III) Artistic sublimation. Its essence lies in its presentation of the fantasied drive satisfaction in such a way that it can be shared by others. The creation of the artist is thereby still clearly derived from erotic wishes. The desexualization consists of the transformation of the original instinctual gratification into the narcissistic cathexis of the work.

IV) The rendering of social aid, which contains on the one hand considerable amounts of homosexuality, modified in the form of "pauline love," on the other reaction formations against aggressive tendencies.

V) The performance and activity of the scientific research worker. For this form of sublimation, we have Leonardo da Vinci as an example which has been brilliantly investigated by Freud. Regarding points one to five on our scale, what Freud says about sublimation in the 'Introductory Lectures' is valid; namely, that the new goal has a genetic connection with that which has been given up. In the activity of the scientific investigator, to be sure, this genetic connection has already been extended a considerable distance toward the periphery.

As point VI, we find the sublimation to indifferent displaceable cathexis energy, in which we can no longer recognize the connection with the original instinctual goal. A few words about its possible applications: the indifferent cathexis energy is at the disposal of the Ego. It is employed in the formation and structure of the Ego and the Ego-ideal, increases the cathexis of ego-syntonic, libidinal or destructive tendencies, it supplies the counter-cathexis, and finds discharge in reaction formations. Finally, its most desexualized application is found in the form of small quantities, the displacement of which within the mental apparatus results in the activity which we call thinking. The process of thought can be called the purest manifestation of the usage of indifferent instinctual energy resulting from sublimation.

Freud warns against an over-evaluation of the therapeutic possibilities through sublimation. "In my opinion, therefore, efforts invariably to make use of the analytic treatment to bring about sublimation of instinct are far from being in every case advisable." (Recommendations on Treatment, Standard Editions, 12, 119)

This applies to points one through five on our scale, like so many other generalities about sublimation. However, insofar as our therapeutic goal is a strong Ego, sublimation cannot be excluded from the therapeutic process. For a strong Ego is one which has a rich supply of indifferent cathexis energy at its disposal. This, however, stems from the drive, and is therefore sublimated instinctual energy. Insofar as we set for our therapeutic goal a strong Ego, and thereby a combination store of sublimated energy, our therapy rests upon the capacity of the Ego for such extreme sublimation. The specific conditions of such a conversion to a cathexis energy, without specific quality among which secondary narcissism plays the essential role, do not yet seem accessible to a more exact examination.

Equation of Mother and Prostitute

"It is not an infrequent observation that certain men can only fall in love or have sexual relations with women who either are prostitutes or behave in a manner which is close to that category". The paradox that mother and prostitute are identified Freud tries to explain by events which take place in prepuberty. The realisation that sexual intercourse takes place also between the parents and the awareness that women use the sex act for monetary gain as prostitutes are connected to the formula: "My mother is no better than these women". The pubertal boy then starts to desire his mother from this new-won aspect, and renews his hate for his father. Thus the boy is again psychologically dominated by the Oedipus complex. That much by Freud.

A clinical experience made me aware that the equation mother-prostitute can be understood in a deeper sense. A patient who from his puberty on frequented bordellos developed during and after his visits intense anxiety caused by the following idea: "If during my visits with the prostitutes a murder should be comitted in the 'stetl', and I would be suspected and would have to prove my innocence by an alibi, I could not possibly admit that I was in a house of ill repute". Here the two evil deeds of the oedipal crime are obviously united. While he makes love to the mother-prostitute a murder occurs and he cannot prove his innocence. Dreams and other analytical material proved without any doubt that the murdered person was the patient's father. Here the visit with the prostitute implied the father-murder. This case evoked in me the idea that a visit to the prostitute regularly implies the murder of the father. One might venture the following contemplation:

The frequent fantasy the mother might be unfaithful to the father provides the possibility that the son might be among those with whom the mother is unfaithful to the father. This can be enlarged to the equation of mother

Zur Gleichstellung von Mutter und Dirne. *Internationale Zeitschrift fur Psychoanalyse*, 1931, *17*, 386.

and prostitute. If the mother is equated to a prostitute this makes mother available to all men. But this is the hoped for situation after the killing of the primal father. But the murder of the primal father is committed with the expectation that the primal mother will be accessible to all sons. If the woman who is available to all men is endowed with the significance of the mother, this means that the murder of the father is implicitly committed. More experiences will demonstrate whether this hypothesis can be upheld.

The Resistance To Symbol Interpretation

The symbol serves the purpose of indirect representation. According to Rank and Sachs, it is a vicarious and manifest substitute expression of something hidden, with which it has obvious characteristics in common, or with which it is bound up associatively through inner connections (Otto Rank and Hans Sachs, *Die Bedeutung der Psycho-analyse fur die Geisteswissenschaften*, Wiesbaden, 1913, p. 11). The dynamic meaning of the use of the symbol is easily ascertained. We find it universally used to avoid the direct representation of *forbidden* and therefore frequently *sexual* material that presses for expression due to the power of the motivating drive. Symbolism has to a certain degree the character of a compromise formation; it heeds the domain of the instinctual wish as well as that of the repressing agent. The result of the compromise is therefore a substitute for the original and direct representation similar to the neurotic symptom. The possibility of the efficacy of the symbol as a substitute, which rests upon the original identity of the symbol and that which should be represented, will not be treated further here.

There are two areas for which sexual symbolism has a predilection: dreams and folklore. If one examines the resistance which opposes itself to symbol interpretation, one will be soon aware that the intensity of the refusal to recognize the translation of the symbol is incomparably greater in the area of the dream than it is in the area of folklore. The translation of the *dream symbolism* meets a powerful resistance in persons who still have resistances against the analysis. In folklore material, on the other hand, in wit, or in obscene jokes these symbols are recognized without further ado, their meaning is understood and their translation accepted. One can confirm this experience everywhere and at any time. How are we

Der Widerstand gegen die Symbolumbersetzung. *Psychoanalytische Bewegung*, 1932, *3*, 246–249.

to explain and make intelligible this difference in the understanding of the symbol in one and the same individual? We must here go into the forces as the resultant of which the symbol appears, namely into the tendency which seeks expression for the forbidden content and that which inhibits the wish of the former and forces it to take on the symbol as a mask.

All of us, insofar as we respect certain barriers erected by culture, avoid the direct discussion and representation of the sexual in the presence of others as something indecent. Now there can be no doubt that there are powerful drive forces active within us which want to precipitate this direct manifestation that is involved by direct naming and representation. Here we rely upon the expedient of the sexual symbol. We represent the acts and organs of sexual intercourse and of excretion, therefore, the *sexual* acts in the analytic sense symbolically in wit, in the obscene joke, etc. In those who are willing to accept our symbolic representation there is the tendency to understand the symbol for the purpose of pleasure which is otherwise inhibited. They translate it themselves in order to procure the same gain in pleasure which the originator has clothed with the symbolic representation. The translation of the symbol follows automatically and without difficulty. The distortion, as which the symbolization comes about under the pressure of an inhibiting institution, takes place as a conscious process which is enacted between those portions of the Ego which affirm the instincts and those which inhibit them. The act of censoring, which in the representation of sexual material forces a detour through symbolism, was, therefore, an act of the conscious personality. The rapid understanding of the symbol results from the *inclination* to understand it, and thereby to enjoy the easily forbidden pleasure which is woven into the form of folk-lore disguise.

It is otherwise in the dream. For the most part the dreamer is completely lacking in the understanding of the symbolism in his dreams. And his lack of understanding derives from his *disinclination* to understand his dream, because the content of the dream was unpleasureful for him. For just as in the symbolic material of folklore, the dream has contents which are not permitted open representation. But the reason for which it is disguised is not that the material is merely obscene, therefore, that it offends the refined ear and would be obnoxious in a social gathering, but it must be clouded in such a lack of understanding because its existence rises up against and offends the whole conscious personality. Also, the translation brings with it so much unpleasure, the dreamer does not understand it. He dares not understand symbols which are self-explanatory and self-evident to him in the folklore material, because that which they represent has some connection with his dearest relatives for whom he has esteem, and honor which he cannot connect with anything sexual. The entire conscious and normative personality devotes itself to this disinclination; the Ego as well as the Super-Ego bar the direct representation which urges toward expression from the unconscious instinctual wishes, and compels a detour through the symbolic disguise. This latter is permitted only because the state of sleep eases conscience with the assurance that what is forbidden can only be dreamed of and not acted upon. If the dreamer wakens, the dream dissolves, or remains in the mind like a strange picture to the secret content of which the dreamer has no access without analysis. But he *dare* not understand the symbol, because there is a vigorous disinclination and shying away from such understanding.

And because the understanding of the symbolism of others' dreams must lead to an understanding of one's own, the resistance also is extended to the translation of the dreams of others.

We now use the fact that the resistance to the interpretation of folklore symbolism is so much less intense to make the dreamer who refuses to accept our symbol interpretation more receptive to our interpretation by intellectual detours. An example from analytic practice will serve to demonstrate this.

A patient dreamed that *he watched with anxiety while his father pounded vigorously in a mortar with a pestle.* The interpretation that the activity of the father in the dream was a symbol for coitus was rejected by this dreamer, as by anyone who still has resistance against the analysis. The dreamer, a Viennese, was then reminded that in Viennese land an overnight hotel was called a *Stosspudel* (stossen: pound), sexual intercourse *Stösserl*, and understood this folklore symbolism without going any further. He had further to recognize that also in a dream *stossen* could have a sexual-symbolical meaning, and quickly found the current and infantile sources of the dream.

The efficacy of reference to the parallel of folklore symbolism in dream analysis we must construe as follows: the convincing insight into folklore symbolism which is so easily gained because the affective resistance of the total personality is not marshalled against it, leads to an alteration in the Ego in the sense of a decrease of the resistance to the dream symbolic in a purely intellectual way. A reasoning intellect grasps such parallels and is ready to admit that what has served as a symbol in one case might also serve in the other. For the time being, it accepts the suggested interpretation and thrusts back its resistance against recognition of the symbol, whereby free access to wider, deeper and more convincing associations is given.

Therefore, a consideration of the dynamic conditions of the resistances to the various uses of symbols furnishes the basis for application of a technical device which the analyst will often have occasion to use.

On The Oedipus Complex In Girls

The presentation of such a complicated phase of development as the Oedipus situation involves considerable difficulties. These difficulties lie primarily in the general deficiency of our technique in presentation, which is inadequately equipped to describe the psychological material of a period in development so rich in relationships. This is because our technique, with its linear construction can never attain through mere words the richly intricate psychic formations and processes with sufficient precision. Among the exigencies imposed upon this presentation the result will be simplification of the topic. If I permit such simplification in the material of this article, it is not without warning to the reader and for didactic reasons. Whoever deliberately holds to a simplified scheme for the exact representation of the complicated and intricate structures of one of the most important developmental periods in childhood, will be in error. But the drawing-up of such a scheme remains nevertheless the best guide for an initial orientation into the abundance of manifestations. The enlargement and subdivision of this scheme, to the extent that it can embrace the abundance of relevant material not mentioned here, must be left to those who apply it themselves to their observations of children's behavior.

We define as Oedipus Complex the psychological situation at a certain phase in the child's development in which the child's love is directed toward the parent of the opposite sex. The parent of the same sex is experienced as a disturbing rival whom the child wishes to push out of the way and to replace. In the developmental series of libidinal phases, the establishment of the Oedipus Complex corresponds to the *genital* organization, or, more exactly, to the *phallic* stage in the boy, the *post-phallic* stage in the little girl. The psychological situation of the Oedipus Complex comes at a later point in libidinal development for the girl than for the boy which is an important discovery first revealed to us by Freud in 1925.[1]

Uber den Oedipuskomplex beim Madchen. *Zeitschrift fur Psychoanalytische Padagogik*, 1933, 7, 334–348.

[1] S. Freud, Some Psychic Consequences of the anatomical Distinction between the Sexes, Coll Pap . . . .

The following material attempts to explain this difference in time on the basis of the development. It also elaborates the phases of development relating to the Oedipus Complex of the girl, which can then be easily derived from the presentation.

The developmental stages of the libido can be recognized as already prescribed. They are oral, anal, and finally the phallic stage. Even the phallic stage is common to both sexes. Its designation rests upon the fact that the phallic organ, that is, the penis of the little boy and the clitoris of the little girl corresponds to the development of the penis, as the prevailing erotogenic zone dominates over the other erotogenic zones (phallic primacy). The chief expression of the sexual drives, of this period, is phallic masturbation, that is, the rhythmical rubbing of the phallic organ (penis or clitoris respectively) for the purpose of deriving pleasure and for the discharge of sexual excitement. Masturbation, however, does not appear for the first time at this period. We know that even the suckling infant can discover the highly erotogenic genital zone and can employ it to derive pleasure. In the phases following the suckling period, the pleasure value of the genital region is by no means neglected. But in the phallic phase masturbation becomes particularly intense, whereby the child enters into bond with the love impulses of the Oedipus Complex. It becomes the open sexual expression of the Oedipal impulses, whereby sexual tension is discharged.

We are accustomed to unravel the course of psycho-sexual development in the little girl through comparison with the development of the boy, because the complicated path which the development of the female child follows can be most readily followed by this method. This clarifies the deviations from the relatively simple developmental scheme of the boy.

The greater simplicity of the developmental line in the male child lies in the fact that during all phases of the psychosexual development in childhood, the principal object of the sexual strivings remain the same. The *mother* is the object of the *oral* strivings. A part of her body constitutes the object during the act of sucking, while during the biting phase the breast and later the mother's entire body represents the object to be incorporated. During the *anal* phase, the fact that the regulation of the toilet training, the administration of enemas, the procedures of cleaning, are all done by the mother. This accounts for the taking over of the original object for the new sexual aims. And in the *genital* phase, which transpires from the fourth to the fifth year of life, the mother again serves as the object of the active love strivings which culminate in the grossly sensual desire to make a conquest of the mother with the phallic organ. The *father*, who up until the phallic phase has also been loved and respected, is at this stage experienced as a rival and is rejected with hatred.

Masturbation is widely practiced as the expression of the sensual impulses of the Oedipus Complex. Masturbation can be frequently observed in children, while the psychosexual strivings and impulses which go on under the psychic surface, seldom reveal themselves directly and clearly. They are instead disguised in manifestations which adults, without the analytic technique of interpretation, can hardly understand. If they express themselves openly, the child is usually rapidly suppressed, and the child naturally guards against repetition of such open revelation. It can therefore scarcely be a matter for astonishment if what the most careful analytic observation with a schooled sensitivity that is free from repression, has detected in the psyche of the child is not so readily visible to others who are not analytically aware.

During this excessive masturbation during the phallic phase the little boy is almost always discovered. It is prohibited him and he is threatened upon repetition of it with a typical punishment through physical injury, primarily a threat to the genitals. If the threat concerns the hand, such for example that one will cut off the evil hand that does this, it is transferred to the genitals.

Historical accounts of tribal events, which are preserved in weakened form in the circumcision of primitives and which must be interpreted as castration of the sons by the primal father, are regularly handed down as an hereditary possession and support the supposition that the threat made because of masturbation was originally uttered directly against the genitals.

If now the little boy discovers at the same time that there are creatures who have no penis, or if a previous observation which he has made of the female genitals is reactivated by this regularly made threat to him, there then results a very powerful and tormenting experience of anxiety about his genital which he so highly prizes as a pleasure organ. The working out of this anxiety, which must be reckoned among the most intense anxiety experiences of the child, can hardly be described in its full significance. The after-effects reach into maturity; its transformations, which are a direct result of the appearance of this anxiety in the infantile psyche are of incisive importance, and occasion such a radical alteration in the instinctual impulses of the child that no other influence can compare with it in intensity, so far as its influence upon the psychic systems is concerned.

The most direct result of the appearance of castration anxiety is that the strivings of the Oedipus Complex are given up, that is, the sensual wishes which are directed toward the mother and the hostility and desire to replace the father are all repressed, while the tender feelings for both parents are retained. This repression occurs because of anxiety about the genital, because these impulses are intimately bound up with masturbation and the threat against the genitals is made because of masturbation. The intensity of the anxiety is so great that in normal cases the repression of the prohibited impulses is very thorough, so thorough that even in the unconscious, relatively little of the original impulse is preserved. Freud uses the word "shattering" for the catastrophic passing of the Oedipus Complex. The Oedipus Complex is shattered by anxiety.

For the second part of this resume of developmental conditions during infantile periods which we have to treat, it is necessary to deal with the fate of the instinctual energy of those impulses which have been repressed because of castration anxiety in order to understand the formation of the Super Ego. The complete repression makes possible a relatively free disposition of the instinctual energies. For the most part, it achieves their detachment from the original instinctual representatives. The greater part of the object tendencies of the Oedipus Complex now undergoes a transformation into a narcissistic formation, that is, into a relationship to the individual's own Ego rather than to a parental object. This is the usual manner in which object relationships are given up. The love that was formerly devoted to the object the individual now turns to the task of his relationship with himself. He comforts himself about his loss with his own self-esteem and prizes himself in place of the object.

But the returned libido, which directs itself towards the Ego is designate as *secondary narcissism*. To distinguish it from the state prior to any object relationship, in which all libido from the beginning applies to the individual's own person, and which is called primary *narcissism*, this returned libido bears traces of the former object relationship with it. It has experienced the object and does not want to forego the features of the latter in the Ego. Therefore the Ego takes over features of the object, a process which we call identification.

Therefore, the giving up of the Oedipus Complex results in a narcissistic state. But that part of the Ego which has taken over the features of the object, does not remain at the level of the Ego. To a certain extent, it advances to a higher level and sets up an institution in the Ego which is in opposition to the rest of the latter, maintaining numerous relationships to the Ego and keeps the rest of the Ego dependent upon it, just as the parents did with the child. This new super-structure erected in the interior of the Ego and cathected with narcissistic libido developed out of idealized features derived from the pattern of the parents through assimilation of these features into the psyche we call the Super Ego. Its perceptible expression is moralistic conscience, which from within the psyche governs each of our actions and our processes of thought. The numerous hostile tendencies which the boy has turned toward his parents, toward his father as a rival and toward his mother because of his extreme disappointment in her, return in the strict and inflexible character of the moral demands of the Super Ego. The Ego's minute obedience to the Super Ego is at the same time a new form of the old self-overestimation in primary narcissism. The omnipotence of the Ego is transformed into omnipotence of the Super Ego. Overstepping the boundaries set up by the Super Ego is punished by guilt feeling, as well as by voluntary and unconscious acts of expiation which we find in particular abundance among neurotics (tendency towards self punishment).

The Super Ego is therefore, as Freud calls it, the inheritance of the Oedipus Complex as well as the inheritance of the primary narcissism.

We must make at least one correction in this simplified scheme of the development of the male child during the Oedipus period. We have spoken of the fact that from the very beginning the father appears next to the mother as love object, in that he is the recipient of numerous tender and admiring impulses in the child's psyche. There now appear in varying intensity and in accordance with the bi-sexual disposition of human beings, sensual impulses which are directed toward the father, which can attain to a particular intensity during the Oedipus phase and which culminate in the wish to bear the father a child, just as the mother had done. An intensification of passive anal eroticism whether it be on the basis of constitutional disposition or the result of experiences during the anal phase which causes this desire for the father to attain to considerable intensity. In this situation the mother is put in the role of a rival.

This situation, which we designate as *inverted* or *negative* Oedipus Complex, manifests itself merely in hints or else in open declaration *in addition to* the positive Oedipal development. The instinctual impulses directed towards the parents have friendly and hostile qualities towards the object, at any time. This phenomenon is called *ambivalence*. The formation of the Super Ego now makes possible a resolution of the ambivalence conflict. The positive impulses are converted into narcissistic libido, the negative into the aggressive activity of the Super Ego, which is turned against the individual's own Ego.

Let us make a brief summary. The little boy loves his mother through all the phases of libido development. During the phallic phase his masturbation is the expression of an intense sexual desire for his mother. The threat to his genitals, after his masturbation is discovered, and his observation of the female genitals, which, he presumes, sh s the possibility of the loss of the penis, results in an overpowering anxic about the danger of losing his genitals. We call this castration anxi ty. As a result of this anxiety, the parent-objects become introjected an cathected with narcissistic libido in order to form the Super Ego. The prohibitive and punitive function of the parents from within the psyche continues. This is the case with boys.

With this schematic presentation of the development of the boy during the Oedipal period we shall now undertake to study the development of the girl during the same period. The first and most significant difficulty for the understanding of the development of the girl during this period is the *change of object* which the little girl has to accomplish as she enters the Oedipal phase. It is characteristic of the Oedipus Complex of the girl, that the father is the object of her love impulses, while the mother assumes the role of rival. Just prior to this period of the Oedipus Complex, the mother was the love object of the girl during the oral and anal phases, just as with the little boy. This is also the case during the phallic phase, which requires some explanation. We have said that the clitoris is the conveyor of the genital tendencies and sensations during this phase. At this time, the clitoris has for the little girl the pleasure value and the meaning of an organ for the active acquisition of the love object (the mother) just as the penis has this value and meaning for the little boy. Masturbation of the clitoris is the process of discharge for the sexual impulses towards the mother. The development of the girl, therefore, runs parallel to that of the boy in so much that during the phallic phase, the significance of the erotogenic zones (penis and clitoris respectively), in the active relationship to the object (the mother) and in the kind of sexual activity (masturbation of the phallic organ) are certainly common to both. Therefore, as Helene Deutsch emphasizes, the clitoris is psycho-sexually equal to the penis, and is charged with the same high quantities of libido.

From this situation, the mother is desired with the phallic organ by the little girl. Regularly but in varying degree, cruel pleasure-laden sadistic wishes against the mother play a part in their fantasies. This situation results in a relatively abrupt transition to a new object with new instinctual tendencies. It is the transition to the father of which we speak. The relationship to the mother now takes on a clearly negative aspect. She becomes the hostilely rejected and hated rival. We shall now examine this reversal in the psyche of the little girl.

Freud supplies us with two groups of causes for this, which are complementary in their operation. Those of the first group have a common nature and are connected with the general reactions to the frustrations which infantile wishes must necessarily undergo.

The child reacts to the frustration of libidinous or aggressive impulses, which the mother has to establish, with hostility. If younger siblings appear during the course of the first years of life, often the result is *jealousy*. The child experiences a set-back and feels himself at a disadvantage because the younger sibling enjoys in the care, nourishment and necessary general protectiveness which is essential if it is going to thrive at all. Satisfactions and pleasures are being denied to him as an older child. The infantile instincts are so unbridled that the child reacts to this denial with intense hate towards the sibling and the mother. But the child also considers the relationship of his mother to the other adults in his environment, particularly that towards the father as a serious interruption of his own relationship with his mother. Of particular influence are the *prohibitions* which are actively given by the mother. It is usually the mother who prohibits the masturbation of the child, because she usually is the one who will discover it. Upon prohibition of the masturbation, the child rejects the mother. This rejection is accompanied by intense hate and an attitude of defiance. It is just the active impulses toward the mother which are necessarily frustrated. The child would also like to take the active role and involve himself with the mother in all those processes which were part of her care of him. This instinctual impulse is doomed to disappointment, and the child will find only partial gratification through its handling of its doll.

But all these things, which are applicable to both male and female children, would not be enough to undermine the positive relationship to the mother, if there were also not a circumstance of great consequence which first liberates the already formulated negative reactions and causes them to express great hatred against the mother. In order to develop a deeper understanding of this circumstance which is the basis for the second group of reasons that cause detachment from the mother, we must examine what we have said about the pre-Oedipal masturbation of the boy, which is equally applicable to the little girl. The pleasure value of the clitoris is discovered very early. This is because of the stimulation which is provided by the secretions, the urine, the mucous discharge of the genitals and their decomposition. In addition, the cleansing processes, such as washing and powdering which includes minor stimulation soon make the little girl aware of her clitoris. Masturbation in the earliest stages then occurs as an almost objectless bodily gratification, without any particular psychic content. During the phallic phase the masturbation enters into combination with the active and partially sadistic wishes of the little girl toward her mother. We emphasize again that in its psychosexual significance, its capacity for stimulation, and discharge of pleasure, the clitoris during this phase is fully comparable to the penis of the boy.

Now the little girl, who has developed sexual curiosity and who is attentive to the genitals of her playmates, makes a discovery of great consequence. She notices the much larger genital pleasure organ of the boy, the penis, and "is at once ready with her judgement and her determination." She has seen it, knows that she does not have it and subsequently wants it.[2] She blames her mother for the fact that she does not possess an organ like the boy's. She is very quick in making this judgement and re-forms her hate impulses confirmed by the opinion, "My mother has made me like this, and it is she whom I have to thank for not having a penis."

She quickly turns away from the mother, and in addition to the tender relationship develops an openly hostile and aggressive attitude. A second factor is added, which further damages the relationship to the mother. The little girl, who up to this time has often exceeded the little boy in the liveliness of her intelligence, in her self-confidence, rapid understanding and psychic activity, now begins to develop an intense feeling of inferiority, which is the result of the constitutional inferiority of her genitals. At the same time she begins to generalize her feeling of "inferiority" to all persons of the female sex. But the mother is also of the female sex, and with this fact comes a considerable devaluation and contempt from her little daughter. Thus the observation of her own lack of a penis has a double influence in undermining the good relationship to the mother.

Both reactions to her own lack of a penis can be observed in the daughter's relationship to the mother until maturity. One finds very often that a daughter blames her mother for everything which she considers as inferior in herself. She has failed to make progress and feels that her intellect lacks the capacity to compete with the male. There often results a very poor relationship with the mother, who tries in vain to do everything possible for the daughter in order to improve the relationship. But this is all without effect, because this hate feeds upon a level of the unconscious which is entirely inaccessible to the love of the mother. It comes from that period of childhood in which the little girl's discovery of her own lack of a penis has caused her to direct a strong reproach towards her mother. Again, in other cases, one can observe that daughters (up to the time when they develop an adult capacity for judgement), harbor a boundless contempt for the mother, merely because she is a woman.

Simultaneously with this goes a limitless admiration for the father which easily extends to all males. We can assume that the reaction is based on the recognition of the physical plus with which the male gender is equipped.

The five main reasons for the spoiling of the relationship to the mother are, 1) the disappointment of the infantile love tendencies, 2) the jealousy of other siblings, 3) the rejection of prohibitions, 4) the blame for the lack of a penis and 5) the contempt towards females.

---

[2] Freud

We shall now consider the further effects which are caused by the discovery of the loss of the penis. These effects are of incisive significance, not only for the detachment from the mother, but also for the establishment of the erotic relationship to the father, and therefore for the setting up of the Oedipus Complex.

At first the little girl, in her pride and self-love feels very bitter over the fact that she cannot keep up with the boy. Frequently during the ensuing period she gives up masturbation because the comparison with the male member and the feeling that she does not possess a pleasure organ which is comparable to the boy's, spoils masturbation for her. We shall speak later about the alteration of the fantasy content of the masturbation. In pathological cases, the repression of pleasure activity with the genital goes so far that the little girl retreats in her unconscious from everything that is sexual. The result is a serious sexual disturbance in the form of frigidity or sexual anaesthesia. In normal cases, the active genital-sadistic instinctual aims become useless through the lack of a penis. If an active instinctual aim is useless because it is unattainable, discharge for the instinct is turned into the opposite direction. Instead of an active instinctual aim, a passive one is chosen. Gratification is found through the attainment of this passive goal. Therefore, the sexual impulses of the little girl, which up to this time have been of an active sadistic nature, and similar to those of the male, are now converted into passivity and pleasure through suffering. The instinctual aim which was active and directed outwards is now turned around upon herself. As object of these passive masochistic instinctual tendencies, the father is chosen as the most active personality of the family group. Therefore, the father becomes the active sadistic partner of the passive and partially masochistic sexual impulses. The Oedipus Complex is introduced in this fashion.

The conversion of the actual sexual tendencies into the passive, which Helene Deutsch terms "thrust into passivity" and which is of enormous importance for the development of femininity, harbors certain dangers, just in respect to this development of femininity. If the active tendencies were, as a result of liberal admixture from the anal-sadistic organization, particularly cruel and combined with great quantities of destructive pleasure, then the conversion from activity into passivity becomes dangerous for the Ego. For with the conversion of the wishes into passivity, this pleasure in destruction retains its negative quality. It is turned around upon the individual's own person and the goal of the wishes is correspondingly masochistic. The content of these wishes then becomes: to be treated cruelly, to be cut, wounded, and to be bloodily maltreated. All of these contents enter into a relationship with genital wishes, because the genital, and at first the clitoris still functions as the chief locus of sexual excitement. Most of the genital processes of the woman retain in the unconscious, that bloody-masochistic character which so often remains with them, and which so often causes neurotic reactions in these processes. The first menstruation in particular, but also every following one, defloration, birth, entering menopause and even the sexual act itself, becomes a cruel and bloodily passive experience in the unconscious of the woman. Helene Deutsch stated that in being unconsciously prepared to experience cruelty and bloody passivity, lies an imminent danger for the development of femininity. On the other hand a moderately masochistic passive instinctual foundation is the prerequisite for a woman to function normally.

The conversion into the passive, belongs among the most important consequences of the girl's discovery that she has no penis. Through it the father becomes the active partner in the content of the sexual wishes, and in it the entire sexuality of the girl preserves its distinctive, specifically feminine, passive masochistic feature.

There is still another factor which, proceeding from the lack of a penis, directs the sexual wishes of the little girl specifically toward her own father. The renunciation of the penis is not completely accomplished through the conversion into passivity. The hope for it is not completely given up and continues to constitute a strong tendency in the female psyche. But the wish is displaced onto a new object which replaces the penis, namely *the child*. Instead of a penis, therefore, a child is desired, which is a shift from the series of reactions which we call masculinity complex into femininity. Herein lies the possibility for an extensive identification with the mother the opportunity for the turning of love impulses and sexual wishes to the father. At this time, the child has some idea of the role which the father plays in the birth of a child. It has overheard nightly scenes between the parents, which is certainly misinterpreted as bloody and cruel, and is connected to creating of children. The wish to produce a child, as a substitute for the coveted penis, gives the little girl another reason to direct her sexual wishes towards her father. The mother, who has already borne the father a child, and who can always bear him a new one, becomes a hostile rival.

Let us at this point summarize the consequences of the little girl's observation of a penis and her discovery that she lacks one:

1. The little girl makes the mother responsible for this lack and viciously takes revenge upon the mother.

2. Creatures without a penis are despised, the mother included. Both of the foregoing reasons spoil the relationship to the mother.

3. The girl avoids active phallic masturbation because it is a narcissistic

blow to her not to be able to compete with the boy because of her rudimentary organ.

4. The active impulses are converted into passive masochistic ones, wherein the father is desired as the active sexual partner.

5. The narcissistic cathexis is transferred from the penis to the desired and fantasied child. The wish to have a baby appears, and the father as the begetter of children is taken as a love object. Numbers four and five account for the fact that the father becomes the object for the sexual impulses.

We might say that the discovery of her own lack of a penis puts a pressure upon the libidinal attitudes and the whole libidinal economy of the little girl similar to that which the treat of castration puts upon the little boy. We shall now include penis envy and the feeling of genital injury in the castration complex. We define castration complex as the sum of those groups of ideas which are highly charged with affect and are concerned with the threatened, supposedly accomplished or wished for loss of the phallic organ.

Therefore Freud defines the relationship between castration complex and Oedipus Complex in comparing boys and girls as follows: "While the Oedipus Complex of the boy passes because of the Castration Complex, it is made possible for and introduced to the little girl through the castration complex." It is this alone which is responsible for the chronological difference in the establishment of the Oedipus Complex for girls and for boys. For the girl it is only the period following the phallic stage that is devoted to the Oedipus Complex, while the boy experiences the Oedipus Complex during the phallic phase, and represses it when he gives up phallic masturbation because of castration anxiety.

The girl continues to practice phallic masturbation for a while longer. This is not with the phallic tendencies of conquest and penetration, but rather with passive masochistic wishes which are directed towards the father. First, the clitoris remains the executive-organ for the passive wishes and also for the wishes for cruel suffering. They are first connected with the clitoris as a source of sexual excitement to the point where the supposed inferiority of the organ becomes the occasion for gradually giving up clitoral masturbation, which need not always be the case. The discovery of the *vagina* as a pleasure organ occurs, if no early seductions draw attention to this zone, usually after the first coitus, therefore in connection with defloration. And even then the clitoris retains the function of the kindling which has to fire the vaginal excitement.

Therefore while the castration complex causes the passing of the Oedipus Complex in the boy, it first introduces the Oedipus Complex of the girl in that it (1) activates the negative tendencies against the mother, and (2) inaugurates the conversion from activity to passivity.

The fact that the relationship to the love object in the Oedipus situation of the girl is a secondary one, and not, as with the boy, a primary one, can frequently be confirmed in the relationship of the girl to her father or to objects which are substituted for him. Frequently strong oral elements enter into this relationship, and these are to be evaluated as a transference of the oral relationship to the mother. The symbolic equation of penis = mother's breast is frequently used as the displacement of these wishes onto the father or another man. Thus, hysterical girls have the typical reaction to the sexual approach of a man. They become nauseated and vomit as an expression of the defense against oral wishes. These wishes have their deepest origin in connection with the mother's breast. The tormenting reproachful attitude which many wives have towards their husbands is also a transposition of the bad relationship to the mother over to the husband. Where there is an intense relationship with the father that is difficult to dissolve, an intensely negative relationship to the mother is a regular occurrence. Freud used the words "deeded over" to describe the transference of the relationship to the mother over to the father. It is derived from legal vocabulary and is used to denote the making over of property to a new possessor. The land remains the same; it is only the owner who is different, and the traces of the previous possessor are still clearly recognizable on the property. The relationship to the mother is deeded over to the father by the establishment of the Oedipus Complex. While the boy quickly breaks off the Oedipus Complex, because of castration anxiety, so that it leads rather precipitously to the establishment of the Super Ego. This becomes relatively consolidated in a short period of time. It is just the castration experience which introduces the girl into the Oedipus situation. Resolution of the Oedipus Complex in boys and castration anxiety is spared to the little girl. It is now our task to demonstrate from what motives and in what form the little girl abandons the Oedipus Complex.

What causes the little girl to abandon the Oedipus situation? Freud furnishes us with the insight that it is not easily given up. It dies out much more slowly, is often preserved into later times and can be pointed out much more frequently in girls who are approaching adulthood than in boys of the same age. Freud suggests that it is the *disappointments* which the little girl experiences in the Oedipus situation, as the motive for the ultimate abandoning of the Oedipus Complex. The sexual wishes are not fulfilled. The child which is so eagerly desired as a substitute for the penis does not come, and for this reason, the girl turns slowly and gradually away from her love object. Helene Deutsch suggests several other motives which seem to play an important role in the casual series which accounts for the giving up of the Oedipus Complex. There are *guilt feeling* and the phenomena consequent upon the transformation into the *masochistic*.

According to Helene Deutsch, the genesis of the guilt feeling can be attributed to two factors; first, the guilt feeling is bound up with phallic masturbation. The discovery of her lack of a penis causes the little girl to believe that her masturbation has resulted in such a serious punishment as the loss of her penis. She therefore thinks, that because of her masturbation, she has lost her penis. This associative connection between masturbation and guilt either results in an inhibition of the masturbation, or, if the masturbation is continued further, creates an intense feeling of guilt. On the other hand the renunciation of the masturbation strengthens the guilt feeling by means that the active-sadistic impulses which are bound up with the masturbation are converted into destructive instinctual manifestations against the individuals own person, to which the guilt feeling is joined. Secondly, this guilt feeling is concerned with the activation of the thrust into passivity, in that it encourages the masochistic behavior of the Ego.

The second factor which is the occasion for the development of guilt feeling is, according to Helene Deutsch, the hostility towards the mother. Up until the entrance into the Oedipus situation the mother was the girl's love object. Remains of this positive relationship are preserved during the Oedipus Complex. These positive feelings towards the mother are strong enough to enter into gradual opposition to the negative impulses towards the latter, and to restrain them. Now it is in the very nature of the Oedipus Complex that positive desires towards one parent and negative impulses towards the other parent are intimately bound up and cannot be separated. A love relationship with the father during the Oedipal period is impossible without a simultaneous hostility towards the mother, which constitutes the Oedipus Complex. If the remains of the good relationship to the mother gradually make it possible to hold the negative impulses towards her in check, while on the other hand every love impulse towards the father strengthens the child in her wish to put the mother aside, both impulses of the Oedipus Complex must be given up. This is because the negative impulses towards the mother are not tolerated by the psyche. Therefore, the guilt feeling which derives from that hatred of the mother leads gradually to abandonment of the love for the father.

We have already spoken of the dangers which the *conversion into masochism* involves for the development of femininity. The more active and the more sadistic the relationship to the mother was, the more masochistic will be the conversion into the opposite. But the Ego develops anxiety because of the masochistic wishes of the Id, since the content of these wishes has resulted in some disturbance of or damage to the individual's own person. The anxiety of the Ego, as well as the passive-masochistic behavior in the Oedipus complex, contribute to the repression of the Oedipus Complex. In pathological cases, a regression to the relationship to the mother results from the anxiety cause of the masochistic relationship to the father. This is one of the possible reasons for female homosexuality. In other cases this anxiety results in a mis-identification with the active father; the un-feminine attitude of the woman which we call the *Masculinity complex.*

We thus see that there is a variety of reasons which are responsible for the little girl's giving up of the Oedipus Complex. We must imagine that in each case, these causes operate with varying intensity, and operate in the same direction.

With the female child, as well as with the male, the Super Ego proceeds from the repressed Oedipus relationship. For the formation of the Super Ego, it is not just a matter of indifference in what form the Oedipus Complex was abandoned. We connect the severity and inflexibility of the male Super Ego with the rapid passing of the Oedipus Complex. Sachs speaks of the threatening character of the male Super Ego, which it obtains in connection with castration anxiety. In actuality, the Super Ego of the woman is of a different form from that of the man. Freud speaks of a difference in level of the moral customs of men and women. The Super Ego of the woman is not so inflexible and so personally independent of its affective origins as that of the man. From this proceeds a lesser need for law and a weaker inclination to submit to the necessities of life. Women are more emotional, less inclined to follow rigidly logical consequences and preserve stubbornly in their desires against the strong demands of the reality principle than men.

For the qualities and attitudes described, precision and rigid limits proceed from the solidity and fund of energy of the Super Ego. The slow abandonment of the Oedipus Complex also results in the fact that the formation which comes from renunciation of the Super Ego, is less stable and less endowed with energy. This, of course, cannot be taken as a broad generalization and there are numerous exceptions in each individual case.

The further development of the Super Ego of the girl is, like that of the boy, founded upon the given object relationships of the Oedipus Complex. According to Helene Deutsch, the active strivings in the phase of phallic masturbation, which are based upon similarly directed demands of the mother condition (an identification with the father) are not entirely converted into passivity. Instead a certain part of them is desexualized after the renunciation of active phallic masturbation and directed toward the higher level of Super Ego formation. The sublimated male demands of the father ideal are taken up by the Super Ego. This results from the male-active portion of the Super Ego which demands active performance upon intellectual, social and cultural levels. In women who from a strict and inflexible inner demand choose occupations suited to the male, and who fulfill the demands of these perfectly with an unswerving devotion to duty, this active male portion of the Super Ego is in predominance. But just as with the object choice, the Super Ego of the woman has a double disposition. The second part derives from the relationship to the mother in respect to the identification with her upon the higher level of the Super Ego after the giving up of the ambivalent attitude towards the mother. Its content is the demands of idealized motherhood. The ideal demands of pure, madonna-like motherhood and the sexual morality and sexual inhibition which are of particular concern to the women of our culture, derive from this introjection of the idealized mother into the Super Ego formation.

The more detailed opinions of various authors on the partial processes in the formation of the woman's Super Ego, which are not completely harmonious, and which in any case attest to the impenetrability and inaccessibility of these processes, fall outside of the limits of this presentation, having a more didactic purpose.

We hope to have succeeded in avoiding with this paper both the Scylla of over-simplification and the Charybdis of too great complexity which would have been inevitable in a more exact presentation. If the development of the female appears complicated enough in this presentation that one can see what difficulties lie in the path of normal development to full femininity, and how much more prone to neurosis the woman is, and if the development as such has become an intelligible process for the reader, we believe that the purpose of this presentation has been achieved.

The Theory of Anxiety

Anxiety is a basic experience in our mental life. We may attribute to it an influence upon our behavior as great as that of hunger and love. Every individual regulates his behavior, whenever he can, in such a way that he avoids anxiety, and the large communities which men form among themselves exercise their attraction upon the individual and their power over him chiefly through the fact that their religious or social institutions are so constituted that for one who participates the anxiety is either avoided or decreased. Our striving to avoid anxiety is so great because anxiety is an unbearably painful experience.

With this last statement, we have assigned to anxiety a place among the mental manifestations: we consider it primarily as an emotional experience. But it is characteristic of such experiences that they are mental processes which take place in our Ego, therefore in that which we perceive and know as our own self. Thus we have further assigned to anxiety a particular place in the totality of the mental structure. Anxiety is a conscious mental process in the Ego.

We include anxiety among the *affects*. Affects are emotional experiences of such intensity that next to them little else can find a place in consciousness. The angry man is only angry; there is room in his consciousness for nothing except the fullness of his anger. We know that those who are deeply grieved concentrate their entire interest upon their grief, and whoever experiences violent anxiety has no other desire than that of escaping from the situation in which the anxiety has made its appearance.

Affects such as rage, anxiety, sadness, and shame are of very complex formation. The psychic experience of these affects is accompanied by a series of physical reactions which the subject feels, and which one can observe in him, as for instance, blushing from a sense of shame, growing red or pale with anger, weeping out of sadness, besides which there are reactions which occur in the chemical processes of the body, such as

Theorie der Angst. *Zeitschrift fur Psychoanalytische Padagogik*, 1933, 7, 421–432.

discharge of secretions of the endocrine glands into the blood, disappearance of certain of these secretions from the blood, changes of the distribution of the blood throughout the body through contraction and dilation of the different blood vessels. In short, a violent affect brings about manifold changes in the realm of physical and mental functions.

This is applicable to anxiety as well as to the other affects. A man suffering from anxiety also feels this anxiety somatically. If his anxiety is extremely violent, one can observe it in him. He trembles, perspires and shivers. He becomes pale, or grows red in splotches; he is restless, moves about nervously or cowers in a shrinking attitude. His mouth gets dry, his heart pounds. He breathes laboriously and still feels out of breath. He has a sensation of choking, his urine production is increased, and sometimes he even feels a strong need for bowel movement and has diarrhea. In particularly intense anxiety, such as occurs almost only in psychotic states, the motor unrest can even amount to frenzy and rage. The anxiety affect is also accompanied by more refined chemical changes in the body. The inner secretions of the adrenal glands are increased, the blood pressure rises, the thyroid gland secretions are also increased.

We will now turn to the psychic experience of anxiety, which of course cannot be separated from the somatic experience, for anxiety is, as an affect, a somatic-psychic occurance.

Most prominent in the mental course of the anxiety affect is the great discomfort which accompanies it. This unpleasure is very difficult to describe. But it is not necessary to do so, as everybody knows the experience of anxiety and has felt its torture. In every experience of anxiety there is some anticipation. Anxiety is, so to speak, a prospective affect. As the most essential factor in the psychic experience of anxiety we have to consider the feeling of constriction which is felt, particularly in the chest, but sometimes also in the stomach. The other psychic characteristics are to a great extent nothing other than the disagreeable sensations which are bound up with the physical changes described above; thumping of the heart, shortness of breath, and muscular trembling.

The prospective character of the anxiety affect, the anticipatory expectation, leads us to the conclusion that there is an essential relationship between the anxiety affect and something which is anticipated. What is anticipated is an approaching injury or pain. We therefore can formulate: *Anxiety is the reaction to a danger.*

Such a formula must be tested with regard to the extent of its validity. Is every anxiety experience a reaction to a danger? There is no doubt about this in the case where a real peril is to be expected. The anxiety affect, however, in connection with a real danger is very slight with the normal adult individual; one could say that there is only an indication of it, and that when the danger arrives, the anxiety is dissolved and passes over into other reactions: flight or defense. But if such measures cannot be taken against the danger, then the anxiety affect can break out in its full strength. As long as anxiety appears in its initial state, it serves to heighten the attention, and is accompanied by an increased readiness for defense, and thus must be called appropriate; the full outbreak of anxiety is, on the contrary, inappropriate, since it paralyzes and hinders clear thinking and defense measures. The appropriateness, therefore, of the early stages of anxiety-development is converted into a severe handicap when anxiety fully breaks out.

The appropriateness of anxiety-readiness consists in an increased cathexis of all the perceptive parts of the psychic apparatus, and in increased readiness for flight or defense which accompanies the early stages of anxiety development. The purpose which anxiety readiness serves can be best understood by observing anxious animals at liberty. Anxious animals are those which have little or no means of defense, and whose only protection is the swiftest flight. The hare and the rabbit are both proverbially well-known as anxiety animals, as are so many herbivores.

Movies of animals in the African prairies, for example, give us the opportunity to observe big herds of wild animals in their natural environment. There is hardly anything more impressive than the anxious caution of these animals when they go to drink. They look carefully in every direction, listen attentively and probe the air cautiously for danger before daring to bend down to the water, which action will, as they know, severely handicap their powers of observation. But even then they are ready at an instant's notice to escape swiftly. The lives of these animals consist of lightning changes from anxiety-readiness to panic-stricken flight, with *but few moments left between* for nourishment, watering and propagation. However, anxiety is their life-saving principle, for to slacken their anxiety-readiness is to be overcome by the thousands of lurking perils with which the wilderness is full for these poor creatures. We civilized human beings have hardly any idea of the perils of wilderness except in war; we are comparatively secure owing to our victory over nature. That we must, of course, pay for this security by anxiety experiences of another kind is a considerable limitation of the security which humanization brings us.

We call the appropriate anxiety, which is only indicated and appears as a reaction to a danger which is actually expected *real anxiety*. We would prefer to give to this reaction to a real danger the name *fear*, if speech usage would permit a sufficient distinction to be made between fear and anxiety. But it is often very hard to distinguish between these two, because fear, which we would equate with real anxiety is always accompanied by traces of neurotic anxiety, or a high degree of it. *Neurotic anxiety* is the reaction to a danger which is primarily not an actual one, therefore anxiety appearing where the external circumstances do not warrant it. It is the reaction to a danger from another source than that of external reality. Neurotic anxiety is the reaction to an inner danger, and this danger is presented by the individual forces of his unconscious.

Neurotic anxiety is that considerable limitation of security in our human existence about which we spoke above. This arises out of the fact that what we consider human in ourselves has not penetrated to the lower depths of our psyche, but that it covers the surface like a thin film, while in the depths all is still in seething ferment, savage and unsubdued. And this thin film-like surface, which we call the Ego, is afraid of the depths, it pays heed to every movement down below with delicate organs, just as the anxiety animal constantly watches its surroundings.

We have represented figuratively here an essential factor in the production of neurotic anxiety. This is the fact that our psyche is not a unified structure, but that it is divided into an anxiety ready part and dangerous forces. The locus of instincts in the mental apparatus, the source from which they are generated and arise out of inner somatic stimuli we call the Id. The Ego is afraid of the Id, if neurotic anxiety makes its appearance. The Ego, however, is not only the frightened gazelle which our comparison has expressed in too one-sided a fashion, but at the same time that part of our psyche with which we live in reality, and which we mean when we speak of ourselves as "I". The Ego is, as it were, the bearer of consciousness, which links us to the real environment and to the community to which we belong. It is the Ego which sees to it that in general we do what we hold to be right, and we do this to avoid the tortures of a bad conscience, which the Ego would otherwise have to suffer. We have mentioned, therefore, two important functions of the Ego, two tasks with which it is faced. The first is the testing of the outside world by means of the sensory organs, which bring stimuli to us from the outside. We have to make this test continuously in order to know if the outside world is able to satisfy our needs, from the bodily need of hunger to our most sublime desires and in order to meet dangers coming from the outside world. The second important function of the Ego is to try to avoid doing what an inner voice tells us is wrong; it obeys an inner moral law. If the Ego neglects the outside world, it is threatened by unbearable tension from unsatisfied needs, or with other real dangers; if, on the other hand, it does not listen to the conscience, it is threatened with the torments of a 'bad conscience.' The Id, however, instinctually desirous, greedy, violent, amoral, continually demanding and refusing to be put off, pays no heed to reality and to conscience. But the Id is surrounded by the Ego, and has no access to the external world, except through the Ego, to which the power of decision over every action is given. But all energy which we direct toward the external world is ultimately instinctual energy and derives from the Id.

Thus, the Ego stands between two powers, the Id and reality; and still a third institution makes demands upon the Ego, conscience, which we regard as a function of our own psychic judge, the Super-Ego. The Ego must mediate among all three, for danger threatens from each side. If it does not heed outside reality, it is threatened by tensions from unsatisfied needs, i.e. unpleasure, by damage and injury, or even destruction, briefly, by whatever can happen to one from the side of the external world if one acts imprudently. If it does not pay attention to the commands of the Super Ego, the Ego is punished by remorse and guilt feelings, which can only be relieved by acts of atonement. Both dangers, those from the outside world, and those from the Super Ego, threaten the Ego if it gives in too much to the Id, if it is too permissive of the Id's impetuous, unreasonable and forbidden wishes. Thus, ultimately, all inner dangers come from the Id. But the most powerful weapon at the disposal of the Ego in its struggle against the Id is *anxiety*. The Ego can help itself against the threatening instinctual dangers by generating anxiety. It is this anxiety which plays a dominant part in neurosis.

To understand more fully this function of anxiety in neurosis, it is necessary to follow Sigmund Freud's thought processes about the first anxiety experience in life. Our first anxiety experience occurs at the very beginning of our extra-uterine existence. We enter the world experiencing anxiety. It is well known how Freud first came upon the connection between anxiety and birth. When he was still a young doctor in a hospital, a colleague of his told the other doctors at the dinner table a story of an incident which had occurred at the midwivery examination. One of the candidates was asked what it meant if at birth one finds meconium (that is, feces of the child) in the amniotic fluid. She answered that this was a sign that the child had been very frightened during the birth, and was flunked by the examiner. Freud, however, when listening to the story, divined that there was a connection between birth and anxiety, which the poor candidate so naively expressed because she probably was anxious herself and had felt the intestinal sensations of anxiety. Psychoanalysis actually considers the act of birth, this most traumatic experience at the youngest age, as a prototype of anxiety. In general, if we think of the suffering during birth, we incline to sympathize with the woman giving birth; her terrible cries of pain, her desperate struggle during the last part of the birth grips our hearts and we breathe freely when at last the child is safely in the world. But we don't see the child itself in the birth canal, nor how it is exposed to the heaviest of mechanical strains, how the enormous power of the contracting uterus muscles squeeze it as though it were a cork being pressed through the neck of a bottle, how the inner breathing of the baby stops, how the bones of the tiny cranium are pushed one above the other, how the softer parts of the infant's body are chafed against the walls of the birth canal. For hours the child has to suffer under the constricting pressure and the marks and bruises can be seen for many days afterwards. So, in birth, the most fragile organism that exists has to suffer the hardest trial. No wonder that a permanent impression is left on the young psyche, undeveloped as its functions may be. The numb sensations of an unheard of experience, of being helpless and forced to submit to the most brutal irruptions by stimuli from all sides is preserved by the young psychic organism for all time as the most distant memory, a memory which, as is characteristic of earliest experiences, cannot be revived in consciousness, but only in the form of repetitions of the sensations which were experienced at the time of the trauma.

But this repetition of the birth experience is the affect of anxiety. Even the *word* anxiety, derived from the Latin word *angustiae*, meaning narrowness, names one of the essential repetitions of the sensations of being born, namely, the compression, the tightness, the paralyzing oppression against which there is no defense in the state of intense anxiety. The lack of breath in the anxiety state corresponds to the restriction of oxygen of the infant in the birth canal during labor through pressure of the umbilical cord and similar mechanical hindrances. The heart acceleration belonging to the anxiety affect repeats the accelerations of the heart action of the child during birth in order to conpensate for the deficiency of oxygen. How the intestinal sensations at birth and the anxiety affect correspond, the midwife mentioned above has already taught us. Thus we can say with Sigmund Freud that anxiety is patterned after the birth experience, copied faithfully, even in the somatic details. This relation between anxiety and birth has already been established by the experiences of innumerable generations, so that it still appears, even if a child is spared the normal birth experiences by a Caesarian operation on the mother. We do not find that such children live without anxiety. The birth experiences as the prototype of the anxiety affect is inherited through countless generations, so that its pattern is innate.

This relation between anxiety and birth experience, recognized by the genius of Sigmund Freud, throws light upon the meaning of the anxiety experience and its application in the battle of the Ego against the instinctual forces. To understand this thoroughly, it is necessary to investigate more deeply the anxiety of the *child*. There is no child who does not experience anxiety; especially with the infant the readiness to produce anxiety is very marked, if not immediately after birth, then during the first phases of psychic development, when the first object relationships are developed and the child begins to recognize his mother. Among these otherwise vague anxiety experiences, *one* has an obvious relationship to the mother, namely, the anxiety in connection with the dark and with strange persons.

To understand this clearly, we have to examine the significance of the mother for the baby. The mother, or the nursing person, is the source of every satisfaction for the baby. The care which the mother devotes to him satisfies all his needs; we must take into consideration that gratifying these needs takes up most of the time of the person caring for the child, but also that this continual satisfaction of the baby's needs through the nursing is a psychic and somatic *necessity* for preservation of the tiny existence.

From the psychological standpoint however, the situation of the well-nursed infant is a continuation of the state of equilibrium, free from stimulus and need, which the unborn child enjoys before birth. One may say that to a great degree the situation of the suckling infant is psychologically equivalent to that of the situation in the womb, that insofar as the psychic economy is concerned, it is a continuation of the intrauterine existence. Through the mother's care, the state of peace in the mental economy, so violently disturbed by the act of birth, is reinstated. The presence of the mother is to a certain extent the guarantee that such a disturbance as the act of birth signified for the child will not be repeated. The state of psychic equilibrium depends upon her presence and upon her care. If the mother is absent, then the infant is exposed to the increasing need tensions, which he cannot satisfy himself, and he recognizes very early the connection between the mother and the gratification of all needs. Thus, the absence of the mother threatens the child with the danger of a disturbance of the mental equilibrium. If he misses the mother just at the moment of increasing need tension, he reproduces, as though from memory, the sensations of the first economic disturbance in his life. He experiences unpleasure, which can be intensified to anxiety. Actually, his cries of anxiety call the mother to him, she satisfies his needs and thus restores his psychic equilibrium. Thus, the production of anxiety gradually becomes a signal of appeal to the mother, a signal of the threatening dangers of unsatisfied need tensions.

We must now examine the process by which anxiety in its further development is employed as a *signal* of the danger of increasingly unpleasureful need tensions. We have spoken already about the psychological significance of the mother for the infant. The mother herself is aware of this significance and uses it for the education of the child. The first acts of education occur through indications to the child by which the mother shows him that she is displeased if he has done something to which she objects. We call this means of education the threat of *love privation*. Love privation means to the infant absence of the mother, means a threat of irruption of unpleasure through lack of the most necessary gratifications, means a reinstatement of the disturbed situation in the mental economy equal to the experience of birth. The child responds to this threat with anxiety, i.e., with a signal-like repetition of the sensations accompanying birth, and through his anxiety, he is forced into obedience to the educating person. For anxiety is such a painful experience that the Ego of the child retreats before the undesired instinctual impulse and refuses to give way to it. One might say that he flees from it, in that he withdraws perception from the undesired instinctual impulse as if it did not exist. What we have described here is the process of *repression*, and we see what an important and decisive part anxiety plays in this process. Anxiety becomes the motive for repression, because its extreme unpleasure forces the individual to do everything possible to get away from this unpleasure. This flight before the instinctual impulse in the form of repression is the most immediate and earliest reaction which the child can utilize against those instinctual impulses which are forbidden by the educating person and, thus, dangerous for the infant. If the child is first afraid of the mother's absence and reacts to it with anxiety, it soon grows afraid of the instinctual impulse, which brings with it the danger of the mother's absence, the danger of love-privation. The child, therefore, develops anxiety over the forbidden Id impulses, but this anxiety, when it is used as a signal, is at the same time the most powerful means the Ego can employ against forbidden instinctual impulses. And almost all neurotic anxiety is of this kind. It is *signal anxiety*, and shows that forbidden wishes are active in the unconscious, against the assault of which the Ego brings into operation the most powerful means at its disposal, namely, the development of anxiety.

Thus, neurotic anxiety is, with children as with grownups, an indication that forbidden wishes from the Id are assaulting the Ego. These wishes may be of a libidinal or of an aggressive character. Often, and this is typical of the anxiety of children, the anxiety is displaced from a person whom the child is afraid to love or to hate, onto an animal, an object, or a locality. The typical *phobias* of children consist of such anxiety displaced from the original objects, which are the goal of forbidden impulses. In the phobia of Little Hans (Analysis of a Phobia in a Five Year Old Boy, S. Freud, Collected Papers, Vol. III), whose analysis serves as the first example of a child analysis, the aggressive impulse against the father is feared, because as an instinctual impulse disapproved of by the parents, it involves the danger of love privation. Simultaneously, however, the anxiety is displaced from the object "father" onto the object "horse," from which the great advantage is derived that the horse can be avoided easily, whereupon, because of anxiety, little Hans refused to go out on the street, while his association with the father, who was really to be feared, was in this way preserved (displacement of anxiety object).

Since the bad wishes in the child's psyche are very violent, and since the possibilities of bringing them to mitigated discharge through displacement of the instinctual goal, which we call sublimation, are very limited, the child cannot defend itself against the instincts without the help of anxiety, and it thus comes about that no child escapes from anxiety experiences.

We have to emphasize a particular form of anxiety which plays an important role in connection with the genital excitations of early childhood, culminating in the fourth or fifth year. This is *castration anxiety*. It is destined to take over the role of anxiety over love privation. At a certain period in the psychic development—from the fourth to the fifth year—among the instinctual wishes forbidden by the adults are primarily those in the center of which are genital excitations. These are not only forbidden, because they manifest themselves in masturbation, but also because their goals are bound up with sensual wishes directed towards the parents as objects. At this time, the genital organs, that is, the penis of the boy and the clitoris of the girl, are the centers of pleasurable physical sensations of an erotic nature, and these phallic organs, the penis and the clitoris, are very highly valued as the bearers of such intense pleasure. If, as usually happens, the child is discovered masturbating and is threatened with losing his penis in one way or another, that it will be cut off, that it will rot away, or that something else will happen to it, then, especially in connection with observation of the female genitals, maybe of the sister or of little girl playmates, through which he becomes convinced that there are human beings possessing no penis, an intense anxiety develops over the threatened genital. The significance of this anxiety about the genital consists in the fact that it is of such a traumatic and intense nature that it gives occasion for the most incisive alteration in the child's mental constellation through the complete repression and relinquishment of the Oedipus Complex and the establishment of the Super Ego.

With the little girl, the anxiety experiences of this period of childhood are still primarily anxiety over love-privation, but there is also genital anxiety developed in the girl, because the clitoris is equivalent to the penis in regard to its pleasure value. Furthermore, anxiety over masochistic wishes appears, because these have as their content injuries of the genitals.

When, in our psyche, the moral institution is established which we call the Super Ego, which criticizes our behavior and punishes transgressions of its prescriptions with guilt feeling, our obedience to this institution is again enforced by anxiety. The Super Ego is an intrapsychic repetition of the first authority, the parents, who seemed omnipotent to us. And we continue our dependent relationship to the parents, their wishes concerning our behavior, their criticism, even their functions of punishment and reward through the establishment and activity of the Super Ego. Thus we preserve intrapsychically our childhood attitude towards our parents throughout our lives, although we have long been adult in our external circumstances. But this dependence in the normal individual is stripped of all that is personal; the parents become the moral law. This critical intrapsychic institution is another source of anxiety (conscience anxiety).

In our moral anxiety, the old anxiety of losing the protecting and loving parents is still active. Transgression of a command or prohibition that is internally maintained leads to qualms of conscience which are not appeased until a conscious or unconscious act of atonement, psychologically equivalent to punishment by the parents, conciliates conscience and obtains pardon from the Super Ego. The moral anxiety is, therefore, a continuation of the infantile anxiety over love privation. The severity of the Super Ego, and, therefore the anxiety which the Ego must have because of it varies considerably in cases of obsessional neurosis, the Super Ego is so strict and the moral anxiety so great that almost every action of the Ego must either be compulsively transformed so that it simultaneously has the character of atonement, or it must be followed by a compulsive act of atonement. If this gratification of the conscience is hindered by impeding the obsessive act, violent and tormenting anxiety appears. Thus, we see that anxiety forces the compulsive neurotic to his compulsive actions. The obsessive neurotic individual shows in extreme exaggeration the results of the Ego-Super Ego relationship which we find in milder form with smaller quantities of affect in the normal person. Our obedience to the moral law within ourselves is guaranteed by anxiety. And in this connection, we must speak about the anxiety-binding functions of religion and of the other great social institutions, of the state, the army, political parties, even common ideologies, etc., which we mentioned at the beginning of this paper. The binding of anxiety results from the transference of the Super Ego role to the leader or leading ideas of such organized groups. Obedience to the demands or prescriptions of this leader, made considerably easier through participation of all the other members, means a great relief for the individual conscience. If this schematization of the prescripts of conscience through membership in an organized group is brought to an end by decomposition of the group, we can clearly observe the appearance of anxiety or even panic in the former members of the group. This anxiety can frequently be mastered only through entrance into another group formation.

I should like to mention another form of anxiety which appears under very definite, almost experimentally set conditions. It is that anxiety which manifests itself as an anxious expectation or as an indefinite feeling of anxiety if the discharge of genital sexual excitement is hindered. This type of anxiety appears for instance in people who are engaged, when there is occasion for sexual excitement, but if strict maintenance of abstinence until the marriage furnishes no opportunity to discharge the excitement in the sexual act. Or the premature interruption of intercourse may, as a sexual disturbance, have such an anxiety arousing after-effect (practice of coitus interruptus). Women often develop such anxiety states if the man experiences his satisfaction earlier in the act than the woman, and in this way leaves her unsatisfied. Sexual abuses of different kinds beget this form of anxiety, which we call *anxiety neurosis*. Remedy of the sexual abuse and the attainment of full gratification removes this state of actual neurosis. The observation that interrupted sexual excitement causes anxiety first led Freud to the assumption that sexual excitement which cannot be discharged is converted into anxiety. Libido, he thought, is transformed into anxiety, like wine into vinegar. In accordance with this first theory of anxiety, Freud was of the opinion that the anxiety of all neuroses was of this type, and that it arose out of the transformation of libido which became pent up after the repression of the instinctual impulses (In Introductory Lectures). A careful consideration of the material which he had at hand in the case of Little Hans, as he tells us in "Inhibition, Symptom and Anxiety—1926" caused him, on the basis of material from his experience, which he had obtained from many neuroses in the meantime, to recognize that anxiety is the *cause* of repression, and not the opposite, that repression creates anxiety.

We think of the anxiety of the anxiety neuroses as the result of irruptions of great quantities of stimuli into the mental apparatus, the mastery of which through discharge is not possible because of inner or outside hindrances. This economic disturbance begets anxiety as a repetition of the effect of the first economic disturbance which birth represented. Irruptions of great quantities of stimuli, mastery of which in the mental apparatus does not succeed, we call *traumatic* irruptions. Traumatic irruptions beget anxiety to a certain extent as a re-creation of the experiences during the first traumatic situation, namely, birth. In the case of the anxiety neurosis, the undischarged sexual excitement represents the irrupting traumatic stimulus. In correspondence with this, the anxiety of the anxiety neurosis *has no mental content*; it is fed from the somatic source of the genital excitement. The anxiety of the phobia, or of anxiety hysteria in general, on the other hand, reveals under analytic investigation the forbidden rejected instinctual wish, against the impetus of which anxiety is engendered as a signal, warning of the danger of punishment attendant upon the fulfillment of the wish, as we have described above.

The early anxiety of children has frequently the character of traumatic anxiety. Situations of need with high tension occur all too easily with the infant, for which situations the weak young mental organ is not yet ready. But the small child soon learns to develop anxiety as a precautionary measure against the economic disturbance awaited from instinctual dangers, as a signal against this danger, as we have presented it here.

It can be seen from the above of what eminent importance the manifestations of the child's anxiety are for the educator. The anxiety of the child is the earliest indication of a neurotic disturbance. For the anxiety of the small child is to a certain extent a measurement of how weak the young Ego still is in relation to the instinctual forces which it has to master. It will certainly be the effort of every educator to preserve the child from anxiety to the greatest possible extent; for anxiety, mastery of which often succeeds only in a phobia, regularly implies a more or less extensive limitation of the child's mental freedom. On the other hand, the anxiety-signal in the Ego of the child is the most powerful weapon which the educator can use, in the battle against the instincts which must be suppressed, and he cannot dispense with this means, because he must provide for repressions in the child if he wishes to make a useful social being out of him. But repression, as we have shown above, is caused by anxiety. The educators' most powerful means in his battle against the instincts is the privation of love, or threat of the latter, and we have attempted to show how the child reacts to his danger with anxiety. In this antagonism of tasks, namely, the provocation of anxiety because instinctual mastery cannot succeed otherwise, and the avoidance of anxiety because the Ego of the child suffers so from it, the educator must always choose the correct moment for the one or the other. The empathetic judgment of the mental situation of the child is his best guide. Through his knowledge about the conditions of the anxiety and about its function in the mental apparatus, this judgment will considerably facilitate his weighty decisions.

The Fate Of The Ego In Analytic Therapy

That part of the psychic apparatus which is turned towards the outside world and whose business it is to receive stimuli and effect discharge-reactions we call the ego. Since analysis belongs to the external world, it is again the ego which is turned towards it. Such knowledge as we possess of the deeper strata of the psychic apparatus reaches us by way of the ego and depends upon the extent to which the ego admits it, in virtue of such derivatives of the Ucs as it still tolerates. If we wish to learn something of these deeper strata or to bring about a change in a neurotic constellation of instincts, it is to the ego and the ego alone that we can turn. Our analysis of resistances, the explanations and interpretations that we give to our patients, our attempts to alter their mental attitudes through our personal action upon them—all these must necessarily start with the ego. Now amongst all the experiences undergone by the ego during an analysis there is one which seems to me so specific and so characteristic of the analytic situation that I feel justified in isolating it and presenting it to you as the 'fate' of the ego in analytic therapy.

The contents of this paper will surprise you by their familiarity. How could it be otherwise, seeing that it is simply an account of what you do and observe every day in your analyses? If, nevertheless, I plead justification, it is because I believe that, in what follows, adequate recognition is given for the first time to a factor in our therapeutic work which has so far received too little attention in our literature. The nearest approach to my theme is to be found in a paper on character-analysis by Reich,[1] in which he talks of 'isolating' a given character-trait, 'objectifying' it and 'imparting psychic distance' to it, referring thereby no doubt to that therapeutic process which I shall now present in a much more general form.

The Fate of the Ego in Analytic Therapy. *International Journal of Psychoanalysis*, 1934, *15* (2 & 3), 117–126. Also in: Das Schicksal des Ichs im therapeutischen Verfahren. *Internationale Zeitschrift für Psychoanalyse*, 1934, *20*, 66–73.

[1] *Internationale Zeitschrift für Psychoanalyse*, Bd. XIV, 1928.

For the purposes of our incomplete description it will suffice if we regard the ego in analysis as having three functions. First, it is the executive organ of the id, which is the source of the object-cathexis of the analyst in the transference; secondly, it is the organization which aims at fulfilling the demands of the super-ego and, thirdly, it is the site of experience, i.e. the institution which either allows or prevents the discharge of the energy poured forth by the id in accordance with the subject's previous experiences.

In analysis the personality of the analysand passes first of all under the domination of the *transference*. The function of the transference is twofold. On the one hand, it serves to satisfy the object-hunger of the id. But, on the other, it meets with opposition from the repressive psychic institutions—the super-ego, which rejects it on moral grounds, and the ego, which, because of unhappy experiences, utters a warning against it. Thus, in the transference-resistance the very fact of the transference is utilized as a weapon against the whole analysis.

We see, then, that in the transference a dualistic principle comes into play in the ego: instinct and repression alike make themselves felt. We learn from the study of the transference-resistance that the forces of repression enter into the transference no less than the instinctual forces. Anti-cathexes are mobilized as a defence against the libidinal impulses which proceed from the Ucs and are revived in the transference. For example, anxiety is activated as a danger-signal against the repetition of some unhappy experience that once ensued from an instinctual impulse, and is used as a defence against analysis. Here the repressive forces throw their weight on the side of the transference because the revival of the repressed tendency makes it the more imperative for the subject to defend himself against it and so put an end to the dreaded laying bare of the Ucs.

In order to bring out the twofold function of the transference let me sketch a fairly typical transference-situation such as arose at the beginning of one of my analyses.

A woman patient transferred to the analyst an important object-cathexis from the period of early childhood. It represented her love for a physician to whom she was frequently taken during her fifth year on account of enlarged tonsils. On each occasion he looked into her mouth, without touching the tonsils, afterwards giving her some sweets and always being kind and friendly. Her parents had instituted these visits in order to lull her into security for the operation to come. One day, when she trustfully let the doctor look into her mouth again, he inserted a gag and, without giving any narcotic or local anaesthetic, removed the unsuspecting child's tonsils. For her this was a bitter disillusionment and never again could she be persuaded to go to see him.

The twofold function of the transference from this physician to the analyst is obvious: in the first place it revived the object-relation to the former (a father-substitute), but, in the second place, her unhappy experience with him gave the repressive forces their opportunity to reject the analyst and, with him, the analysis. 'You had much better stay away, in case he hurts you', they warned her, 'and keep your mouth shut!' The result was that the patient was obstinately silent in the analysis and manifested a constant tendency to break it off.

This typical example shews how the ego manages in the transference to rid itself of two different influences, though in the shape of a conflict. For the establishment of the transference is based on a conflict between instinct and repression. Where the transference-situation is intense, there is always the danger that one or other of the conflicting forces may prevail: either the analytic enterprise may be broken up by the blunt transference demands of the patient, or else the repressive institutions in the mind of the latter may totally repudiate both analyst and analysis. Thus we may describe the transference and the resistance which goes with it as the conflict-laden final result of the struggle between two groups of forces, each of which aims at dominating the workings of the ego, while both alike obstruct the purposes of the analysis.

In opposition to this dual influence, the object of which is to inhibit the analysis, we have the corrective influence of the analyst, who in his turn, however, must address himself to the *ego*. He approaches it in its capacity of the organ of perception and of the testing by reality. By *interpreting* the transference-situation he endeavours to oppose those elements in the ego which are focussed on reality to those which have a cathexis of instinctual or defensive energy. What he thus accomplishes may be described as a *dissociation* within the ego.[2]

We know that dissociations within the ego are by no means uncommon. They are a means of avoiding the clash of intolerable contradictions in its organization. 'Double consciousness' may be regarded as a large-scale example of such dissociation: here the left hand is successfully prevented from knowing what is done by the right. Many parapraxes are of the nature

---

[2] It may be doubted whether 'dissociation' is an appropriate term for non-pathological processes in the ego. This point is answered by the following passage in Freud's *New Introductory Lectures on Psycho-Analysis*, a work which has appeared since this paper was read: 'We wish to make the ego the object of our study, our own ego. But how can that be done? The ego is the subject *par excellence*: how can it become the object? There is no doubt, however, that it can. The ego can take itself as object; it can treat itself like any other object, observe itself, criticize itself, do Heaven knows what besides with itself. In such a case, one part of the ego stands over against the other. The ego can, then, be split; it becomes dissociated during many of its functions, at any rate in passing. The parts can later on join up again' (p. 80).

of 'double consciousness', and abortive forms of this phenomenon are to be found in other departments of life as well.

This capacity of the ego for dissociation gives the analyst the chance, by means of his interpretations, to effect an alliance with the ego against the powerful forces of instinct and repression and, with the help of one part of it, to try to vanquish the opposing forces. Hence, when we begin an analysis which can be carried to completion, the fate that inevitably awaits the ego is that of *dissociation*. A permanently unifed ego, such as we meet with in cases of excessive narcissisms or in certain psychotic states where ego and id have become fused, is not susceptible of analysis. The therapeutic dissociation of the ego is a necessity if the analyst is to have the chance of winning over part of it to his side, conquering it, strengthening it by means of identification with himself and opposing it in the transference to those parts which have a cathexis of instinctual and defensive energy.

The technique by which the analyst effects this therapeutic dissociation of the ego consists of the explanations which he gives to the patient of the first signs of transference and transference-resistance that can be interpreted. You will remember that in his recommendations on the subject of technique Freud says that, when the analyst can detect the effects of a transference-resistance it is a sign that the time is ripe for interpretation. Through the explanations of the transference-situation that he receives the patient realizes for the first time the peculiar character of the therapeutic method used in analysis. Its distinctive characteristic is this: that the subject's consciousness shifts from the centre of affective experience to that of intellectual contemplation. The transference-situation is *interpreted*, i.e, an explanation is given which is uncoloured by affect and which shews that the situation has its roots in the subject's childhood. Through this interpretation there emerges in the mind of the patient, out of the chaos of behaviour impelled by instinct and behaviour designed to inhibit instinct, a *new point of view of intellectual contemplation*. In order that this new standpoint may be effectually reached there must be a certain amount of positive transference, on the basis of which a transitory strengthening of the ego takes place through identification with the analyst. This identification is induced by the analyst. From the outset the patient is called upon to 'co-operate' with the analyst against something in himself. Each separate session gives the analyst various opportunities of employing the term 'we', in referring to himself and to the part of the patient's ego which is consonant with reality. The use of the word 'we' always means that the analyst is trying to draw that part of the ego over to his side and to place it in opposition to the other part which in the transference is cathected or influenced from the side of the unconscious. We might say that this 'we' is the instrument by means of which the therapeutic dissociation of the ego is effected.

The function of interpretation, then, is this: Over against the patient's instinct-conditioned or defensive behaviour, emotions and thoughts it sets up in him a principle of intellectual cognition, a principle which is steadily supported by the analyst and fortified by the additional insight gained as the analysis proceeds. In subjecting the patient's ego to the fate of therapeutic dissociation we are doing what Freud recommends in a passage in *Beyond the Pleasure Principle* (p. 18): 'The physician . . . has to see to it that some measure of ascendancy remains [in the patient], in the light of which the apparent reality [of what is repeated in the transference] is always recognized as a reflection of a forgotten past.'

The question now suggests itself: What is the prototype of this therapeutic ego-dissociation in the patient? The answer is that it is the process of *super-ego-formation*. By means of an identification—of analysand with analyst—judgements and valuations from the outside world are admitted into the ego and become operative within it. The difference between this process and that of super-ego-formation is that, since the therapeutic dissociation takes place in an ego which is already mature, it cannot well be described as a 'stage' in ego-development: rather it represents more or less the opposition of one element to others on the same level. The result of super-ego-formation is the powerful establishment of moral demands; in therapeutic ego-dissociation the demand which has been accepted is a demand for a revised attitude appropriate to the situation of an adult personality. Thus, whilst the super-ego demands that the subject shall adopt a particular attitude towards a particular tendency in the id, the demand made upon him when therapeutic dissociation takes place is a demand for a balancing contemplation, kept steadily free of affect, whatever changes may take place in the contents of the instinct-cathexes and the defensive reactions.

We have seen, then, that in analysis the ego undergoes a specific fate which we have described as therapeutic dissociation. When analysis begins, the ego is subject to a process of 'dissimilation' or dissociation, which must be induced by the analyst by means of his interpretation of the transference-situation and of the resistance to which this gives rise.

As the analysis proceeds, the state of 'dissimilation' in the ego is set up again whenever the unconscious material, whether in the shape of instinctual gratification or of defensive impulses, fastens on the analyst in the transference. All the instinctual and defensive reactions aroused in the ego in the transference impel the analyst to induce the therapeutic process of ego-dissociation by means of the interpretations he gives. There is constituted, as it were, a standing relation between that part of the ego which is cathected with instinctual or defensive energy and that part which is focussed on reality and identified with the analyst, and this relation is the filter through which all the transference-material in the analysis must pass. Each separate interpretation reduces the instinctual and defensive cathexis of the ego in favour of intellectual contemplation, reflection and correction by the standard of reality.

However, once the analyst's interpretations have set up this opposition of forces—the ego which is in harmony with reality versus the ego which acts out its unconscious impulses—the state of 'dissimilation' does not last and a process of *assimilation* automatically begins. We owe to Hermann Nunberg our closer knowledge of this process, which he calls 'the synthetic function of the ego'. As we know, this function consists in the striving of the ego, prompted by Eros, to bind, to unify, to assimilate and to blend—in short, to leave no conflicting elements within its domain. It is this synthetic function which, next to therapeutic dissociation of the ego, makes analytic therapy possible. The former process enables the subject to recognize intellectually and to render conscious the claims and the content of his unconsciousness and the affects associated with these, whilst when that has been achieved, the synthetic function of the ego enables him to incorporate them and to secure their discharge.

Since there are in the transference and the transference-resistance two groups of forces within the ego, it follows that the ego-dissociation induced by the analyst must take place in relation to each group, the ego being placed in opposition to both. At the same time the interpretations of defensive reactions and instinctual trends become interwoven with one another, for analysis cannot overcome the defence unless the patient comes to recognize his instinctual impulses, nor put him in control of the latter unless the defence has been overthrown. The typical process is as follows: First of all, the analyst gives an interpretation of the defence, making allusion to the instinctual tendencies which he has already divined and against which the defence has been set up. With the patient's recognition that his attitude in the transference is of the nature of a defence, there comes a weakening in that defence. The result is a more powerful onslaught of the instinctual strivings upon the ego. The analyst then has to interpret the infantile meaning and aim of these impulses. Ego-dissociation and synthesis ensue, with the outcome that the impulses are corrected by reference to reality and subsequently find discharge by means of such modifications as are possible. In order that all these interpretations may have a more profound effect, it is necessary constantly to repeat them; the reason for this I have explained elsewhere ('Zur Dynamik der Bewältigung des

Übertragungswiderstandes,' *Internationale Zeitschrift für Psychoanalyse*. Bd. XV, 1929).

Now let us return to the case I cited before and see how it illustrates what I have just said. The patient's resistance, which began after a few analytic sessions, took the form of obstinate silence and a completely negative attitude towards the analyst. Such meagre associations as she vouchsafed to give she jerked out with averted head and in obvious ill-humour. At the close of the second session an incident occurred which shewed that this silence and repellent attitude were a mode of defence against a positive transference. At the end of the hour she asked me if I had not a cloakroom where she could change her clothes as they were all crumpled after she had lain on the sofa for an hour. The next day she said to me in this connection that, after her analysis, she was going to meet a woman friend, who would certainly wonder where the patient had got her dress so crushed and whether she had been having sexual intercourse. It was clear that, as early as the second session, her ego had come under the influence of the transference and of the defence against it. Of course, she herself was completely unconscious of the connection between her fear of being found out by her friend and the attitude of repudiation which she assumed in analysis.

The next thing to do was to explain to the patient the *meaning* of her defence. As a first step, the defensive nature of her attitude was made plain to her, for of this, too, she was unconscious. With this interpretation we had begun the process which I have called therapeutic ego-dissociation. When the interpretation had been several times repeated the patient gained a first measure of 'psychic distance' in relation to her own behaviour. At the start her gain was only intermittent and she was compelled almost at once to go on acting her instinctual impulses out. As, however, the positive transference was sufficiently strong, it gradually became possible to enlarge these islands of intellectual contemplation or observation at the expense of the process of acting the unconscious impulses out. The result of this dissociation in the ego was that the patient gained an insight into the defensive nature of her attitude in analysis, that is to say, she now began to work over preconsciously the material which had hitherto been enacted unconsciously in her behaviour. This insight denoted a decrease in the cathexis of those parts of the ego which were carrying on the defence.

Some time afterwards there emerged the memory of her visits to the kind throat-specialist and of the bitter disillusionment in which they had ended. This recollection was in itself a result of the synthetic function of the ego, for the ego will not tolerate within itself a discrepancy between defence and insight. The effect of the infantile experience had, it is true, been felt by the ego, but this effect had been determined from the unconscious; it now became incorporated in the preconscious in respect of its causal origin also. It is hardly necessary for me to point out that the discovery of this infantile experience of the patient with the physician was merely a preliminary to the real task of the analyst, which was to bring into consciousness her experiences with her father and especially her masochistic phantasies relating to him.

In overcoming the transference-defence by the method of therapeutic ego-dissociation we were not merely attacking that part of the ego which was using the patient's unhappy experience with the physician in her childhood to obstruct the analysis; we were, besides, counteracting part of the super-ego's opposition. For the defensive attitude was in part also a reaction to the fear that her friend might find out that the patient had been having sexual intercourse. Now she had developed an obvious mother-transference to this particular friend, and the mother was the person who had imposed sexual prohibitions in the patient's childhood. By means of the therapeutic ego-dissociation a standpoint of intellectual contemplation, a 'measure of ascendancy', had formed itself in her mind, in opposition to her defensive behaviour: in that dissociation the 'reality' elements in the ego were separated not only from those elements which bore the stamp of that unhappy experience and signalled their warning, but also from those other elements which acted as the executive of the super-ego.

In the case we are considering, the next result of the analysis was that the positive transference began to reveal itself, taking more openly possession of the ego and manifesting itself in the claims which the patient made on the analyst's love. Once more, dissociation had to be induced in the ego, so as to separate out of the processes of dramatic enactment an island of intellectual contemplation, from which the patient could perceive that her behaviour was determined by her infantile experiences in relation to her father. This, naturally, only proved possible after prolonged therapeutic work.

I hope that this short account may have sufficed to make clear what I believe to be one of the most important processes in analytic therapy, namely, the effecting of a dissociation within the ego by interpretation of the patient's instinctually conditioned conduct and his defensive reaction to it. Perhaps I may say in conclusion that the therapeutic dissociation of the ego in analysis is merely an extension, into new fields, of that self-contemplation which from all time has been regarded as the most essential trait of man in distinction to other living beings. For example, Herder expressed the view that *speech* originated in this objectifying process which works by the dissociation of the mind in self-contemplation. This is what he says about it: 'Man shews reflection when the power of his mind works so freely that, out of the whole ocean of sensations which comes flooding in through the channel of every sense, he can separate out, if I may so put it, a single wave and hold it, directing his attention upon it and being conscious of this attention. . . . He shews reflection when he not only has a vivid and distinct perception of every sort of attribute, but can acknowledge in himself one or more of them as distinguishing attributes: the first such act of acknowledgment yields a clear conception; it is the mind's first judgement. And how did this acknowledgment take place? Through a characteristic which he had had to separate out and which, as a characteristic due to conscious reflection, presented itself clearly to his mind. Good! Let us greet him with a cry of "eureka"! This first characteristic due to conscious reflection was a word of the mind! With it human speech was invented!' (*Über den Ursprung der Sprache.*)

In the therapeutic dissociation which is the fate of the ego in analysis, the analysand is called on 'to answer for himself'[3] and the unconscious, ceasing to be expressed in behaviour, becomes articulate in *words*. We may say, then, that in this ego-dissociation we have an extension of reflection beyond what has hitherto been accessible. Thus, from the standpoint also of the human faculty of speech, we may justly claim that analytic therapy makes its contribution to the humanizing of man.

---

[3] German: '*zur Rede gestellt*'; literally, 'is put to speech'.

Psychoanalytic Therapy

We must admit that the efficacious operation of psychoanalytic therapy will be for many a mystery, the solution of which is hard to find. This is connected with the strange deviousness of the neurotic process which is so foreign to our conscious thinking, and with which we become more intimate only after profound study of psychoanalysis. The theory of the neuroses, which a presentation of psychoanalytic therapy must include, complicates the task of presentation, since one is always in danger of dwelling rather on the preliminary explanation of the theory of neurosis rather than on the explanation of its therapy, a danger which I myself cannot completely avoid. But if patience will perhaps reward us in the end by making one or another component of the "mystery" of analytic therapy more intelligible.

You know that a scientifically minded physician is not satisfied with a therapy if he does not know how it works. The requisite for such knowledge is an understanding of the functions of the organs and of their relationship to one another in health and in disease; he must know therefore physiology and pathology. This is just as valid for the psyche as it is for the soma. In psychoanalysis there exists a particular relationship between knowledge of the normal function, or psychodynamics, and of the therapy applied to the neurotically afflicted mind. For in psychoanalysis the therapeutic procedure was from the beginning the means not only of gaining insight into the structure of the pathological state, but it taught us the mechanisms of the normal mentality as well. The normal state was, of course, at the same time the goal to be attained by the therapy.

Neither is this a complete innovation in medicine. I might mention the pharmacology and pharmacodynamics of the heart, and how these branches of learning point out the path for investigation of cardiopathology and cardiophysiology. If, however, the access to the understanding of pathological and normal states and their dynamics by means of therapy was no

Die Psychoanalytische Therapie. *Almanach*, 1935, 24–47.

new one, it was nevertheless new in regard to the vast extent therapy was used for psychological understanding and investigation in psychoanalysis.

For, and this is the cornerstone of psychoanalytic treatment, investigation and treatment become one in the therapeutic process of analysis; they are identical, and this is due to the specific structure of the neurotic processes and to the dynamic discharge of the forces working within them through the process of "making conscious," which will be explained later.

With the increase of exactness in the research connected with any natural science, the material which is to be investigated appears to become more complicated. If we take as an example the theory of cancer—cancer, as an independent proliferation of the cells within tissue which is apparently normal, furnishes perhaps the best analogy with the neurotic symptom from the field of somatic pathology—if you follow how cancer research had to be extended from local clinical and histological findings to the concept of cancer as a disease of the whole somatic system, if you keep in mind how the influences of cancer upon the chemistry of the body and upon endocrine disturbances was discovered, until at the present time cancer has become a separate branch of medical science, then you can imagine something similar in the fifty years of psychoanalytic theory of the neuroses. These years have brought a wealth of knowledge and of problems into the theoretical structure of this science. But in a didactic presentation such as this it is justifiable to present first the original simple concepts of the pathological process and to a certain degree, historically, to make such emendations as the simple scheme has undergone in the course of psychoanalytic progress.

The fundamental pattern of the psychoanalytic theory on the origin of the neurosis is a well known one. The neurotic symptom owes its formation to the return of repressed mental impulses. These impulses are based on organic instinctual strivings, and have been repressed—that is, they have been expelled from consciousness, from the conscious personality to the unconscious where nothing of them becomes known—because the contents of the instinctual aims, which are of a sexual-incestuous or cruelty-hatred character, cannot comply with the aesthetic and ethical norms of the personality. Of course, in the beginning of psychic development, repression is the effect of an external force, that is, of education; for only the educated individual represses independently and automatically. Repression occurs therefore for the most part at a time when the plasticity of the psyche is most disposed to external influence, that is, in early childhood.

Education at this early stage consists in nothing more than taking the bundle of diffuse and often contradictory strivings after instinctual aims, as which, from the standpoint of instinctual psychology the infant must appear to us in his earliest stages, and uniting, equalizing and suppressing them in order to bring the child into harmony with his environment and with the social norms of the group to which he will belong. The most effective tool for this work of repression is anxiety, primarily the anxiety that the child will lose the person who cares for it, usually therefore, the mother in the early stages of infancy, and later on anxiety because of physical or mental punishments.

Repression of instinctual impulses is the same as flight before them. But it is a peculiar flight, half-doomed to failure, because we carry with us on this flight the somatic sources of the instincts which are integrated with our body and which do not cease to produce the instinctual energy. It is a flight, therefore, in which we carry with us the source of the danger from which we try to flee. Against this danger an inner barrier has to be erected, a restraint imposed upon it so that one does not see it, indeed finds hardly a trace of it, and this insures a safe custody of the repressed. We can see that repression robs us of psychic energy, namely that of the repressed impulse, and costs us an expenditure of psychic energy in the form of the counterforce which we must expend in order to hold the impulse in repression.

In the beginning repression requires a great active effort. Later it operates as an automatic process without any intensive activity on the part of the conscious personality, since it is necessary only to maintain the equilibrium between repressed forces and conscious personality.

Neurotic illness occurs if the equilibrium of repressed instinctual impulse and counterforce, which latter we call countercathexis, is disturbed in favor of the repressed impulse. The repressed impulse then breaks into the conscious personality and this consciousness must yield due to its own weakness against the force of the instinctual impulse. In neurosis, however, the conscious part of the personality is still strong enough to prevent the impulse from obtaining direct gratification; the instinctual impulse does not dare to show itself openly; it must, therefore, undergo an alteration in form, a distortion. The new form under which it makes its appearance is the *neurotic symptom.*

I shall attempt to illustrate this simplified scheme of symptom formation by an example. It is, however, not easy to find a neurotic symptom in an adult person which shows this relatively simple structure. Usually symptoms are of a much more complicated composition, and even in the case I am going to describe to you now it will be necessary to enlarge a little upon our simple scheme.

A young man of twenty-two years caught scabies through sexual intercourse. When he was treated, some of the ointment got on his foreskin where it caused an excoriation that became infected. Lymphangitis was the result, because of which he was obliged to remain in bed for several weeks. When he recovered and again attempted to have intercourse, it became obvious that he was incapable of it because his erections were only partial and later did not take place at all, so that he had become impotent. At the same time, another very troublesome symptom had appeared as well as a general feeling of anxiousness. Whenever the patient happened to be in a public restaurant he had the sensation that his hair was standing on end and that everyone was looking at him because of this. This peculiar feeling caused him embarrassment and anxiety and he had to hurry to the washroom in order to wet and brush down his hair. But the relief lasted for a few minutes only, and soon after his return to the restaurant the disagreeable sensation that his hair was standing on end returned, so that he had to repeat the brushing down six or seven times during the time that he was in the restaurant. The whole situation finally became so great a torment that he avoided as far as possible going into places where he had to remove his hat. Finally he went to a psychoanalyst.

Now we will attempt to apply our theoretical scheme of neurosis to this case. You observe that our patient has repressed his genital impulses; the power of which he is robbed is that of the genital function, which expresses itself in the absence of erection. In his increased anxiousness you may recognize the effect of the counter-cathexis, which attempts to maintain the repression. But at the same time the repressed impulse breaks through. You will have noticed already that the missing genital erection was transferred to the hair, not actually, but only in imagination, an indication of the magical character which we find in every neurotic symptom. The repressed impulse becomes obtrusive, and at the same time incomprehensible to our patient because of its distortion, and is, in addition, in this case a kind of protest, like a contradiction of the real lack of erection, which latter is displaced to the hair and becomes a public performance. I should like to mention also that these are infantile instinctual characteristics which the impulse has taken on in the symptom.

We find already that our simple scheme is not adequate even for this uncomplicated symptom, for, apart from the infantile characteristics which require a particular explanation, there is another striking factor. The repression did not take place with the consent of the patient. It even occurs, in this particular instance, against his will. It is true that during his convalescence he thought, "Now I will give up sex, since it puts me in such a fix," but afterwards he took his intention no more seriously than does the adolescent his resolution to abandon masturbation. Here something stronger in his personality exerted its influence and caused the repression, not only without the consent of his will, but even against it. This unknown factor watches over repression with the eyes of Argus. But some of these eyes sleep occasionally, that is, when we are sleeping ourselves, and then, repressed instinctual impulses may creep into our dreams which we would not allow while awake.

Freud called this power which watches over the repressed and maintains it in repression the *censor*, because it is through this power that the distortion takes place, if the repressed impulse returns to consciousness. Later Freud called it the *Super-Ego* because it is an institution erected in the Ego which watches over the latter, criticizing and judging it as to what is good and what is bad, therefore nothing else but *conscience*. It is strange enough, and only intelligible in the light of its origin that conscience extends further than consciousness and is more severe as we see in our case. But this is connected with the fact that the wishes of our patient were more evil than he himself knew.

I must give here some further details about the origin of his symptom. During his illness his mother had nursed him, and had made compresses for his infected lymphatic glands; it was unavoidable that on these occasions she should see his genitals. Exhibition of his genitals had played an important part in his early childhood. As a little boy he was very proud of his penis, and had often shown it to his younger sister to compel her admiration. This is nothing particularly abnormal, since we often observe similar behavior in children. But these exhibitionistic pleasures were directed especially towards his mother since she was the person who was always with him, and who had nursed and washed him. The exhibitionistic pleasure had been forbidden him repeatedly and energetically, and not only with regards to his genitals, which will explain another aspect of his symptom. As a child he had been very proud of his long blond hair, which was for him another object of exhibitionistic pleasure until he was five years old, when his father, with the idea that he was too big to have such long hair, had it cut off. It happened that, at this time, he heard the story of Samson and Delilah and of how Samson had lost his virile strength when his hair was cut off. Even as a child he had grasped the symbolism of this story only too well and too deeply.

Another incident happened while he was ill in bed. He read the drama of Don Carlos to his mother. The choice of the play did not occur to him without an unconscious understanding of the hidden significance of the drama, with which he was already familiar. In this tragedy by Schiller the son desires the mother, not directly, but with a slight distortion, since Elizabeth of Valois is the step-mother of Don Carlos, but is, all the same, his father's wife. It is known how Don Carlos is destroyed thereby. If

Schiller atoned for his open display of unconscious wishes by a severe inhibition of his dramatic production—and you must understand the significance of this for a poet of such productivity as Schiller—and wrote only philosophical and aesthetic essays for seven years, overcoming his inhibition only when his own father died and he himself became a father, it is then little wonder that our patient in the critical situation in which he was placed, atoned for his incestuous temptations and wishes with an inhibition of his genital function.

But enough of this. I am afraid that you may already have formed the impression that I am going into so much detail to avoid explaining to you the process of psychoanalytic therapy. But this is not so. I have already described it to you. The discovery of all those factors which were operative in determining the symptom is precisely psychoanalytic therapy. To seek out the unconscious sources of the symptom, further, to make them conscious, and still further, to cause them to be experienced emotionally during the course of the treatment is the precise exercise of psychoanalytic therapy. I have already stated that in psychoanalysis investigation and treatment are the same. But I have still to tell you how the work is done and why it is effective, and I am willing to admit that this is by far the most difficult part of my task.

We introduce the patient to analytic therapy by giving him the opportunity to talk, from time to time by putting questions to him about what he is saying; more rarely we make a comment. Most of the time we are only listening to him. The situation during a typical analysis is perhaps somewhat unusual, since the patient lies on a couch and we sit behind him so that we are out of his sight. He has only to observe one rule, namely, to say everything that comes into his mind, without criticism, and despite his own moral, aesthetic and intellectual objections. This requisite we call the *fundamental rule* of psychoanalysis. Obedience to this fundamental rule is almost the only task for the patient, and it remains in force throughout the whole analysis. There is nothing done in analysis but talking, as far as possible by the patient, less by the analyst. And here an old question arises: "How can one be cured through talking?" I think that I can make the answer to this question clear to you by the following explanation.

This fundamental rule was the result of years of intensive research done by Freud with neurotic patients. Originally Freud had started the treatment by examining the neurotic symptom itself, with the assumption that the patient must know a great deal about it, but that the knowledge was merely not accessible to him, and that a certain pressure on him would re-activate the forgotten paths of symptom formation, the interrelationships of which could then be conjectured. Later, chiefly due to the insight that the repressing factors in the personality operated without the knowledge of consciousness, the technique of psychoanalysis had to be changed. Our explanation will become too complicated if we do not explain two new terms, one of which I have already used. We call the whole complex of instinctual impulses in their totality the Id. The Id is therefore the seat of origin for the organically based instincts. It is the seat of all violent and forbidden desires. All psychic processes originate in the Id, and in the ultimate analysis derive their energy from there. These processes strive to express themselves in instinctual actions, but before they have access to motility they have to pass that inner censor about which we have already spoken. The access to motility is controlled by the Ego, as are the expressions of emotions, although not so completely. The Ego is the organized part of the psychic personality, that part which we mean when we speak of ourselves as "I." It is relatively integrated and takes consideration of reality. Consciousness is bound up with the Ego. It is the Ego which defends itself against the forbidden instinctual impulses, by withdrawing its attention from them and thus repressing them. From the Ego proceeds the counter-cathexis, which keeps the repressed material from becoming conscious and from breaking through into motility. In the Ego, for the most part unconsciously to be sure, that critical institution is operative, the function of which is our conscience, and which we have called the Super-Ego.

If we describe our patient's symptom in this terminology, we shall say that a part of his repressed Id impulses had broken into his Ego. This repressed instinctual impulse, to be sure, had, even after its eruption into the Ego, to respect the critical institution and submit to disguise and dilution through displacement of the genital erection to the hair. The Ego then no longer recognized the instinctual impulse as such, partly because of the powerful addition of earlier repressed and long forgotten material preserved from the earliest years of childhood.

You must not imagine that the separation between the Ego and Id in the normal person is always so definite. In the state of psychic normality the rejected impulses are maintained safely in repression; apart from this the communication between the Ego and the Id is relatively unhindered and free, and this is what guarantees the psychic freedom and being at ease of the normal individual. In the state of neurosis, the attempt to separate the two provinces becomes stronger. The Ego becomes more suspicious of the Id, the Id on the other hand more obtrusive and violent against the Ego, as we have seen in the case of our patient.

The symptom, however, is only an excessive exacerbation of a general permeation of the Ego by the insufficiently repressed impulses of the Id, and the efficacy of the fundamental rule in psychoanalysis is based upon this general permeation of the Ego by Id impulses. The repressed impulses exert considerable pressure and tension since they have preserved their dynamic power, so that if the Ego is unable to hold them completely under repression, self-betrayal of what is forbidden but desired permeates the individual "through every pore," as Freud says in his "Psychopathology of Everyday Life."

There are in addition to these certain particular psychic formations which deviate from the Ego's relationship to reality and reveal strong influence by the Id, although here again only in distorted form. These are fantasies and daydreams, parapraxes and dreams during sleep, which the Ego is eager to put aside and disregard because of their treacherous and evil content. The fundamental rule, therefore, which obliges the patient to tell all his associations without criticism, has the effect of granting instinctual impulses of the Id more free play in the Ego than they have in the rigid, purposive, logical and unobjectionable methods of thought and judgment. The Ego senses this effect of the fundamental rule immediately and reacts to it with anxiety; and anxiety is always a sign that the Ego is afraid of violent instinctual impulses and does not feel strong enough to control them.

If the fundamental rule for the most part sets aside conscious criticism of the associations, the counter-cathexis is thereby diminished to some extent and the Id consequently granted more freedom to influence the associations and psychic processes in its own way. Thus our possibility of recognizing what is going on in the deeper layers of the psyche, or at least what would like to go on is increased. Freud has worked out a specific technique for the recognition of the Id impulses in the material provided by the associations, namely *interpretation* of the associations, which means that in addition to their conscious meaning as Ego processes, the modifying unconscious influence of the Id must be recognized, in the associations. With this technique as with any other a certain talent for the work is necessary for its correct application.

But the associations are not the only manifestations by which we recognize the subterranean, many-branched network of unconscious material from which the symptom is pushed up to the surface like a mushroom. The partial liberation of the Ego through the operation of the fundamental rule manifests itself also by another very peculiar phenomenon, of which you will certainly already have heard, and that is the *transference*.

The instinctual impulses which have been repressed in early childhood were, for the most part, bound up with certain objects, persons near to the child. The most important objects of childhood are the father and the mother, as the individuals central in infantile experience, and the siblings; they are, in the unconscious, intimately bound up with the repressed instinctual impulses. And, strangely enough, with the more intense permeation of the Id impulses into the Ego, which as we have seen, has been partially relaxed through the operation of the fundamental rule, these childhood objects re-enter present experience. This repetition takes place in such a manner that the analyst becomes the object of the repressed infantile instinctual impulses. It is this phenomenon in psychoanalytic therapy which is the most difficult to clarify. Perhaps, however, an observation which has been frequently made will be helpful. Many people show in their love relationships, if these are repeatedly formed and then dissolved again, the peculiar trait that these relationships all follow a certain course which is typical of the individual concerned. Often the schematic recurrence is only recognizable to close attention to it, because slight changes make it unclear. Such people, for example, experience the same disappointment in their love objects over and over again, or they always attain the object under the same conditions. There is something of a compulsion to repeat experiences in their behavior. If I give an example of such repetitions, I should like to choose it from the field of artistic productions, because the general accessibility of such material and the general acquaintance with it facilitates conviction. I could hardly demonstrate, even in a clinical case, so many repetitions of the same behavior as in the following literary example.

In the music-dramas of Richard Wagner we find a leitmotiv which is not a musical one, but concerned with the plots of the operas. We may call this a repetitionally conditioned leitmotiv in Wagner's own life because it played an essential role in his own love relationships as well. The motif is that of ravishing the bride. In all his music-dramas, from the first to the last, someone, as a rule a tenor, takes away from another, usually a bass or baritone, the bride, beloved or wife. Thus the Flying Dutchman from Eric the hunter, Manfred from Nurredin, Tannhauser from Wolfram, Lohengrin from Telramund, Tristan from Marke, Stolzing from Hans Sachs, Sigmund from Hunding, Siegfried from Wotan, and Parsifal, in the last and most sublime form, frees Kundry from Klongsor's evil influence. Wagner himself twice in his own life realized his own love fantasy, which we see as bound up with the condition of an injured third. He fell deeply in love with the wife of his friend Wesendonck and he finally married his own friend Buelow's wife. There is hardly another man in whose love life I could point out so clearly the compulsive repetition of certain prescribed conditions, both in fantasy and in reality. With people who display such undisguised repetition compulsion in their love lives, one has the impression that the love is not fixed upon the object but upon the conditions which surround the object. These people carry their object relationships with them and bring them into conscious experience if they find an external object whose circumstances fulfill the conditions of love they carry within. The real love object is only the recipient of the pre-formed object relationship and is therefore easily interchanged, if the conditions change, for a new external object upon which the pre-formed object relationship is displaced. If one analyzes these series formations in behavior, one discovers that some behavior or a wish dating back to early childhood furnishes the pattern for all the subsequent repetitions. And only through the discovery of this original behavior is it possible to free the individual from this spell of compulsive repetition, if it is disturbing and harmful to his personality.

Through the widening of the sphere of influence of the Id, caused by compliance with the fundamental rule, repetitions of early affect relationships to objects occur, which otherwise could not exert so much control over the Ego that the latter would permit such compulsive repetitions. These object relationships which rise out of the deeper layers of the repressed have less relationship to reality than those on the surface. Their capacity for displacement and their minimization of reality values is so intense that the strange occurrence now takes place that the analyst, as the person who helps to lift the repressions, becomes the object of these repressed impulses, so that they are repeated with him. We enter here a fantasy world, and with more complete understanding of it we may realize that the Ego which must maintain the relationship with the external world, is unable to tolerate this world of fantasy and therefore refuses to have anything to do with it. If this magical, unreal and most violently passionate instinctual world, pregnant with past experience, breaks into the Ego in the form of a neurotic symptom, heavy damage results.

The analyst, then, becomes the object of the instinctual impulses which he is trying to bring out of the Id into the Ego, or better, he is experienced as a repetition of the original object of these instinctual strivings. This happens because of the psychoanalytic situation, in which the analysand does not see the analyst and does not know him at all, or very little, so that the object experiences, brought up from the depths of the unconscious to the surface, are projected onto the analyst as though onto a blank screen. The conditions under which these repetitions appear are reduced to a minimum, to a suggestion if the analysis is occupied with these deeper layers, if only the process of their coming to the surface is not disturbed. Therefore, it is necessary that the projection screen represented by the analyst should be as clear as possible; the clearness is to be attained through the relatively impersonal attitude of the analyst. This impersonal and restrained behavior is necessary too because the analyst has to give back to the patient the emotions which are directed toward him. In so doing he sould give as little as possible of his own personality. It is as though he were only a ferment in the analytic process, a catalytic agent which does not enter into the final formula.

The transference of earlier object relationships to the analyst also occurs because the instinctual impulses have a powerful tendency towards repetition, particularly if through repression they have been shut off from participation in the growth and maturation of the rest of the personality. This tendency toward repetition is in general hindered, through repression, from becoming expressed in reality. I have already spoken about the occasional exceptions which occur in love life. During psychoanalysis the Ego becomes more lenient toward repetitions of Id impulses and early object relationships, because it gradually learns through the analytic training to govern Id impulses and because it has the insurance of psychic help which the analyst guarantees. We find therefore in analysis that infantile experiences and object relationships are repeated with the analyst, and this phenomenon we call transference.

In these repetitions, projected onto the analyst, we have one of the most important means of recognizing the object relationships of early childhood and the way in which they worked themselves out. While the associations that emerge under the influence of the fundamental rule involve a conscious intellectual working through of and control over psychic fields which have hitherto been inaccessible, the transference involves a widening of the affective experience over hitherto inaccessible instinctual processes. The transference, that is to say, the repetition with the analyst not only of real experiences but also of fantasied emotional contents, is, by reason of its repetitional character, a cardinal means of recognizing the forgotten past with its instinctual foundations.

But transference has also serious drawbacks. For it is not the ultimate therapeutic task to bring about the repetition of early childhood experiences but rather to extinguish their efficacy in the psyche, to remove the infantile elements which cling to the instinctual life and prevent it from being incorporated in the conscious personality, in the Ego. It is therefore necessary to strip the repetitive character from the instinctual impulses which are repeated in the transference, to free them from the infantile fixation and to give their dynamic energies to the conscious personality, so that it can employ them for its own manifold purposes. I shall speak about the accomplishment of this task later. There is another drawback to transference which I cannot explain before I have spoken of a dynamic factor which must necessarily play a great part in psychoanalytic therapy, namely *resistance*. It was from meeting with the resistance which he had to overcome while trying to free repressed material that Freud first began to recognize the whole dynamics of neurosis, and further, the dynamics of instincts and repressions in the entire personality. I should like to clarify the function of the resistance through a comparison which Freud made in one of the lectures that he gave in 1907 at Clark University in Worcester, Massachusetts at the invitation of the president, Dr. Stanley Hall. Freud said there:

"Perhaps I can make the process of repression and its necessary relation to the resistance of the patient more concrete by a rough illustration, which I will derive from our present situation.

"Suppose that here in this hall and in this audience, whose exemplary stillness and attention I cannot sufficiently commend, there is an individual who is creating a disturbance, and, by his ill-bred laughing, talking, by scraping his feet, distracts my attention from my task. I explain that I cannot go on with my lecture under these conditions, and thereupon several strong men among you get up, and after a short struggle, eject the disturber of the peace from the hall. He is now 'repressed', and I can continue my lecture. But in order that the disturbance may not be repeated, in case the man who has just been thrown out attempts to force his way back into the room, the gentlemen who have executed my suggestion take their chairs to the door and establish themselves there as a 'resistance', to keep up the repression. Now, if you transfer both locations to the psyche, calling this 'consciousness', and the outside the 'unconscious', you have a tolerably good illustration of the process of repression." A little further he continues, "Remember that with the ejection of the rowdy and the establishment of the watchers before the door, the affair is not necessarily ended. It may very well happen that the ejected man, now embittered and quite careless of consequences, gives us more to do. He is no longer among us, we are free from his presence, his scornful laugh, his half-audible remarks, but in a certain sense the repression has miscarried, for he makes a terrible uproar outside, and by his out-cries and by hammering on the door with his fists interferes with my lecture more than before. Under these circumstances it would be hailed with delight if possibly out honored president, Dr. Stanley Hall, would speak with the rowdy on the outside, and then turn to us with the recommendation that we let him sit in again, provided he would guarantee to behave himself better. On Dr. Hall's authority we decide to stop the repression, and now quiet and peace reign again."

In the first part of this image, when after the repression the disturbing fellow is outside the hall and the men are sitting against the door to prevent him from returning, you will have recognized the counter-cathexis as a dynamic resistance against the return of the repressed material. But besides the intra-psychic function of the counter-cathexis as an expenditure of energy to prevent the repressed from returning, we have to speak about the relationship of this counter-cathexis to the analyst, who is trying to lift the repression, that is to say, about the function of the counter-cathexis in psychoanalytic therapy. For this purpose we shall have to enlarge a little upon the image of the lecture hall used by Freud. Freud says, "On Dr. Hall's authority we decide to stop the repression, and now quiet and peace reign again."

But in reality there are difficulties connected with our decision, for to begin with the authority of the analyst is not so overpowering that his mere effort at reconciliation would suffice to bring about peace and quiet. This effort at mediation must direct itself toward two areas: first, to the lecturer and audience, as representing the unit of the conscious personality, which is not so ready to believe in the now good behavior of the disturbing fellow, and secondly to those gentlemen sitting against the door, who, away from the center of consciousness, are not aware of all that has been going on in the meantime, who don't recognize the authority of our president, who refuse to relinquish their function of hindering the return and now offer resistance to the president when he insists that the disturber be allowed to come back to the hall. And there is still another thing to be done: the disturber has to change, has to give up his childish behavior and rise to the level of the audience, so that he can be assimilated with it. The most important task, however, is the mediation with the guardians at the door or, to translate the process into psychoanalytic terminology, the subjugation and overcoming of the unconscious parts of the resistance. For these gentlemen by the door are hard-bitten reactionaries who will regard anyone who tries to establish communication with the repressed as bitter enemies. We should not forget that the bulk of repression occurs in early childhood, and that antiquated fears, prohibitions which have long been inapplicable to the adult, anxieties and fantasies of the child and frequently faulty educational processes are still operative in these guardians of repression. We have already mentioned that education has to form the first repressions. During our attempt at partial undoing of the repression in analysis, the usual occurrence is that the relationship to the repressing educator is also repeated with the analyst and appears in the transference. Transference and resistance then coincide, if the transference is made from the repressing educator to the analyst. Since educator and love object are usually the same in childhood, it often happens that contradictory emotional attitudes are transferred to the analyst. Instinctual wishes and anxiety defenses, tender feelings and hate resulting from disappointment along with similar contradictory emotional states are regular characteristics of certain phases of transference in analysis.

You see what complicated mechanisms coincide in transference. But the fact that a repetitional character clings to these experiences, which often recur in form of slight allusions only with the analyst as object, makes them exceedingly valuable for our depth psychological investigation. For one can discover, during the transference to the analyst, the origin of the contradictory attitudes, of the instinct and the defense formed against it. A repetition of the history of childhood occurs during transference, often however through reversing a sequence of events, or in cross-sectional layers, but always easily recognizable to the experienced analyst.

As an analyst one observes the phenomena of the transference quietly, making interpretation without reacting emotionally to the patient's affective manifestations. But interpretation in the case of transference has a meaning different from that of the interpretation of associations and dreams where interpretation is more or less intellectual recognition and explanation, and the drawing of conclusions through insight imparted on a conscious level. During the transference the Ego is under the influence of the repetitional strivings of the instincts, or antiquated defenses against them. To interpret the transference means to oppose the repetitional experiences with the analyst with understanding, to maintain a standpoint of dispassionate observation against the demands of both instincts and defenses and to lead the primacy of intellect and self-control against violent emotions. This is a difficult task which requires a long time and must meet violent instinctual or anxiety conditioned impulses with much patience and often with untiring repetition.

In the interpretation of the transference the continuously applied comparison between *then* and *now*, between the unreality of the infantile tendencies and reality, between child and adult plays the greatest part. Through effective interpretation, however, the instinctual impulses are detached from the person of the analyst and their desires are recognized as caused by the forgotten past. The Ego then becomes able to assimilate this past, as we can see by the emergence and widening of early childhood memories. The dynamic factors of the instinctual impulses which have been repressed up until now pass over into the Ego, which appropriates them for its manifold purposes. The symptoms are thus deprived of their sources of psychic energy and disappear. Through the transference and its dissolution the Ego learns to accomplish renunciation of instincts, which, until this time, was possible only through repression, by way of other means. One of these is sublimation, which means diverting the desire for gratification to ethically higher and more social aims; another is true renunciation without repression of instinctual tendencies which are incompatible with the personality. To one portion of the instinctual strivings which were held back from satisfaction because of the infantile condition, the adult Ego of the normal individual can allow gratification that is free of anxiety, in which respect the genital impulses are of first importance.

The very fact that the object of the instinct and the person who was the source of repression unite in the repetitional experiences of the transference in one person, namely the analyst, is of cardinal importance for the cure of neurosis through psychoanalysis. For with the analyst as mediator a reconciliation can take place between the conscious personality and the instinctual forces, that is to say between the Ego and the Id. Through the transference of the early object relationships onto himself the analyst holds in his hand the torn threads of the past, and it is his task to unify the personality through bringing these together and to resolve the conflicts of the dynamic tension from which the neurotic symptom drew its sustenance or at least mitigate these to the point where they lose their pathogenic effect. This task makes great demands on the experience, intuition and ethical responsibilities of the therapist.

I should like finally to point out one factor which I am inclined to consider very important in psychoanalytic therapy. The analyst must remain undisturbed by the patient's manifold affect reactions, to which he is exposed in the transference, by endeavoring tirelessly to recognize their repetitional character, by pointing it out to the patient until the latter can assimilate the instinctual stirrings into his Ego and consciously work them through. But the indefatigable interpretation and the analyst's freedom from affect alone cannot have this desired effect upon the patient. As in the early education of the child's instincts, so in the corrective re-education of the adult by psycholanalysis, the task can be accomplished only if the patient, despite his emotions of love and hate, above and beyond his attempts at repetition of pleasurable or disappointing and injurious experiences, is convinced that he is in the hands of an understanding sympathetic person.

Throughout his abundant affect experiences, the patient must always be conscious that the therapist, in spite of his necessary reserve, has only the interest of the patient at heart, even though he cannot prevent him from experiencing certain disappointments on his way to adult reality.

In his final classification of instincts, Freud distinguishes between love instincts and destructive instincts. If we ask what kind of instinctual forces the analyst uses for his therapeutic work in psychoanalysis, we may answer: in order to overcome the patient's resistance, his contradictory emotional attitudes, and for the separation in the patient's Ego during the course of the analytic treatment, he has of course to apply aggressive energies; but to unite, to balance, to reconcile the neurotically separated parts of the personality, to dispel anxiety, in the final analysis to *heal*, that we can do only with the help of the love instinct, of the Eros.

On Criteria Of The Libido

Bernfeld concerns himself in the paper, "Uber die Einteilung der Triebe" (Imago, Bd, XXI, 1935) with the classification of the instincts and the vicissitudes of this classification in the course of development followed by the psychoanalytic theory of instincts. He gives detailed consideration to the *criteria* of the libidinal processes and finds a number of criteria postulated by Freud for the libidinal processes not tenable, thus the relationship to the somatic source and to the goal, the chemical criterion, the physiological criterion; finally only one criterion remains valid, which he calls the "psychoanalytic" one. According to Bernfeld's "psychoanalytic criterion," the sexual instincts embrace all that is meant by sexuality in the usual usage of the term, all pleasureful activities concerned with erotogenic zones, and finally all that derives therefrom after analytic work.

Bernfeld cites examples for his psychoanalytic criterion. "If in the course of an analysis the instinctual action in question betrays its origin from a masturbation fantasy, if through repression it has become separated from a sexual-orgastic experience with which it was originally united, if it fulfils the same function in the mind which earlier (or 'normally') was fulfilled by a sexual affect or a sexual action, it will then be reckoned in one and the same class, namely that of the sexual instincts."

If we examine more closely the co-ordinating principle which Bernfeld calls the "psychoanalytic" criterion, we will then observe that it does not seem to be constructed from a unified point of view and that it does not itself constitute a unity. For in this psychoanalytic criterion there is a popular aphorism, "Everything that has to do with sexuality in the bad sense of the word," united with a characteristic of pleasure psychology, "all pleasureful activities concerned with erotogenic zones and what derives therefrom."

Freud, as Bernfeld shows, has avoided a definition of the term *sexual*. Even in the lecture, *The Sexual Life of Man*, from the first series of

Uber Libidokritchrien. *Imago*, 1936, 22, 371–378.

Introductory Lectures on Psychoanalysis, Freud avoids giving the content of the term *sexual*. In order to shed some light on what is meant by *sexual*, he breaks away first from the sphere of what we ordinarily designate as sexual, and causes the perversions to pass before us as an impressive spectacle which he himself compares with the visions of St. Anthony in the *Tentations* of Flaubert, and there must indubitably be termed sexual in accordance with the emotional connotation of speech usage. He is of the opinion that "In general we are not without orientation as to what men mean by sexual." We see here that the emotional connotation of the word *sexual* functions as a kind of guiding principle, as it does for Bernfeld. It is now for us to investigate what processes are designated as sexual in our ordinary speech, wherein we are not on the whole without orientation as to what is to be considered as sexual. According to my opinion, our orientation as to what is sexual derives from empathy and our criterion is the emotional phenomenon of *sexual pleasure*.

The co-ordination between pleasure and sexuality can be established by a comparison of definitions in Freud's writings. If we consider the classical definition of the concept libido from *Group Psychology and the Analysis of the Ego*, we find that it rests upon the use of the word *love*: "Libido is an expression taken from the theory of the emotions. We call by that name the energy (regarded as a quantitative magnitude, though not at present actually measurable) of those instincts which have to do with all that may be comprised under the word *love*. The nucleus of what we mean by love naturally consists (and this is what is commonly called love, and what the poets sing of) in sexual love with sexual union as its aim. But we do not separate from this what in any case has a share in the name *love*—on the one hand self-love, and on the other, love for parents and children, friendship and love for humanity in general, and also devotion to concrete objects and to abstract ideas.

We are of the opinion, then, that language has carried out an entirely justifiable piece of unification in creating the word 'love' with its numerous uses, and that we cannot do better than take it as the basis of our scientific discussions and expositions as well." (Group Psychology and the analysis of the Ego, p. 37f.)

If in addition to this we consider what Freud has said about love in "Instincts and their Vicissitudes," we come to the conclusion that the corresponding *pleasure* is the criterion of what is sexual. "When the object becomes a source of pleasurable feelings, a motor tendency is set up, which strives to bring the object near to and incorporate it into the Ego; we then speak of the 'attraction' exercised by the pleasure-giving object, and say that we 'love' that object." (Collected Papers, IV, p.79.)

So the word "to love" becomes shifted ever further into the sphere of the pure pleasure-relation existing between the Ego and its object and finally attaches itself to sexual objects in the narrower sense, and to those which satisfy the needs of sublimated sexual instincts."

Love is found, therefore, where the object is a source of pleasure. Because "love" is simultaneously the basis of the concept libido-sexual energy, pleasure also appears in this equation as the criterion of the sexual. It is easily intelligible in this connection that pleasure-principle and sexuality are coordinated by Freud, such as in the two following quotations from his paper, "The Economic Problem in Masochism": "The pleasure principle represents the claims of the libido," and "It is not difficult to infer what force it was that effected this modification (the Nirvana-principle of the pleasure principle). It can only be the life instinct, the libido, which has this wrested a place for itself alongside the death instinct in regulating the processes of life." (Collected Papers, II, 256f.)

If we examine the two classical works on libido theory among Freud's writings, the "Three Contributions to the Theory of Sex" and "On Narcissism: An Introduction" on the basis of their understanding of libidinal processes, we find in them our assumption that sexual strivings are recognizable through their pleasure values confirmed in the course of our investigation. In the "Three Contributions" the investigation proceeds from the manifest pleasure experiences of the perverts, beginning with the homosexuals. It is demonstrated in further analogies with the behavior of the child. Chapter 7 of the first contribution is called, *Reference to the Infantilism of Sexuality*, and leads to the second contribution, which is entitled *Infantile Sexuality*. Central in this contribution is the investigation of *pleasure-sucking*. As the determinant factor in the latter the following is established: "It is, moreover, clear that the action of the thumbsucking child is determined by the fact that he seeks a *pleasure* which he has already experienced and now remembers." (Basic Writings, p. 586.) The same identifying trait is advanced for the other infantile sexual manifestations.

In "On Narcissism: An Introduction" the significance of *pleasure* as a criterion of the sexual, also of the narcissistically sexual, is clear. It says there, "The word Narcissism is taken from clinical terminology and was chosen by P. Näcke in 1899 to denote the attitude of a person who treats his own body in the same way as otherwise the body of a sexual object is treated; that is to say, he experiences sexual pleasure in gazing at, caressing and fondling his body, till complete gratification ensues upon these activities. Developed to this degree, narcissism has the significance of a perversion, which has absorbed the whole sexual life of the subject;

consequently in dealing with it we may expect to meet with phenomena similar to those for which we look in the study of all perversions.''

"Now those engaged in psychoanalytic observation were struck by the fact that isolated features of the narcissistic attitude are found in many people who are characterized by other aberrations, for instance, as Sadger states, in homosexuality, and at last it seemed that a disposition of the libido which must be described as narcissistic might have to be reckoned with in a much wider field, and that it might claim a place in the regular sexual development of human beings.'' (Collected Papers, IV, p.30).

Proceeding from the pleasure value in the perversion of narcissism, this pleasure value is established in the course of normal development and in this way gives justification for the formation of narcissism according to the libido theory.

If pleasure is actually the criterion of what is sexual, it must also be of interest to us from the therapeutic practical standpoint how we detect this criterion in the individual case, and what can help us verify our assumptions that a mental phenomenon is of a sexual nature. We approach this through derivation of principles of libido theory from practical analytic experience.

In the final analysis and in the strictest sense the verification of our assumption that a mental process is of a sexual nature is only possible where the individual who is the vehicle of the process and who produces it recognizes the pleasure value himself and either experiences sexual pleasure in connection with the process under investigation, or else remembers the experience of sexual pleasure in connection with this process.

This is actually the case in strictly worked-through analytic treatments. Through the lifting of repression those mental constellations in the formation of which libidinal instinctual forces are involved are consciously experienced by the analysand as accompanied by sexual pleasure, or else by the conscious memory of it. The libidinal components of a psychic formation, such as a symptom, a symptomatic action, or the product of a sublimation are in the strictest sense established analytically only if their connection with sexual pleasure is experienced or remembered in the Ego of the person concerned. This experience of the connection of a mental process or formation with sexual pleasure is the most important path of knowledge in libido theory investigations. In any case the therapeutic result is always bound up with this experience, which Freud has put in the neat formulation of Moliere, *Il y a fagots et fagots*.

A short example might be helpful in demonstrating what has been said above. In one patient an intensely experienced sympathy with animals was striking. This sympathy was so strong that the patient could not stand the sight of raw meat when it was lying in the butcher's shop window, with the result that she made a wide detour around such shops with a phobic avoidance. For a long time it was not clear in the analysis what libidinal impulse was at the bottom of the affect and the neurotic avoidance. After numerous resistances had been overcome, the following occurred one day: The patient was sitting in the waiting room of her dentist with anxious excitement, because she was very afraid of the dentist. While she was waiting she was reading a sportsman's periodical that was lying there, and hit upon the following passage: "What a feeling of elation for the hunter, when, after having wounded the deer he sees it spring into the air and fall again." At this moment she felt a powerful and very pleasant genital sensation to which she was otherwise quite unaccustomed. Thereby the masochistic-libidinal components of her sympathy with animals was demonstrated. Her avoidance was based upon this all too strong identification with the tortured creature. As her memory soon made accessible, it was connected with childhood fantasies, in which, with great feelings of pleasure, she identified with cattle, which, as she had observed, had their legs drawn together by a rope when they were being slaughtered, so that they fell down heavily and usually broke a horn. It was not too difficult to trace more deeply repressed sadistic pleasure experiences on the same basis, and to make them conscious.

This example seems to me to provide the most convincing proof of the libidinal basis of a psychic formation, clearly indicated, and just through the experience of a connection between the phenomenon under investigation and sexual pleasure. The direct experience of the connection can also, of course, be substituted for by the memory of this connection. In both cases the union of the formation to be examined with sexual pleasure in the *Ego of the person concerned* as an experience or as a memory is the essential criterion of what is libidinal. The analytic-therapeutic result seems to have a general dependence upon this strict condition.

The second more facile method of theoretical libidinal examination consists in the fact that one turns away from the experience of this connection *in the Ego of the person under examination* and contents oneself with the fact that this connection is produced through empathetic observation of foreign psychic material in the Ego of the investigator.[1]

---

[1] *Libido theory* is here used in the sense of the *programmatic* content of the term 'libido theory' as Freud repeatedly formulates it in his writings, and as it is derived from a condensed compilation of Freud's remarks on it, something like the following: "The libido theory attempts to explain all manifestations of the normal and pathological (perverse) sexual life from the first day of life until old age, as well as the manifestations of the neuroses and psychoses, as well as many phenomena in the field of general psychology, through the observations and theories made by psychoanalysis about the sexual instinct, its dynamics and development, and to express all of this in terms of the libido theory. The procedure of the

This more facile second method, which turns aside from the experience of the connection in the Ego of the person to be examined and contents itself with the establishment of this connection in the Ego of the investigator, is repeatedly legitimized by Freud. I would like to recall something from the classical analysis of the "Rat-man", and the description of an important compulsive fantasy by the patient, who says,

" . . . the criminal was tied up . . . a pot was turned upside down on his buttocks . . . some rats were put into it . . . and they . . . bored their way in." Freud then says further, "At all the more important moments while he was telling his story his face took on a very strange, composite expression. I could only interpret it as one of horror at pleasure of his own of which he himself was unaware" (Collected Papers, III, 304f.)

Here the possibility of pleasure was read in the face of the patient, that is, through empathy with the play of the features it was grasped, and thus the connection of the compulsive symptom with anal-sadistic sexual pleasure was felt by the *investigator*. The connections remain unconscious to the person who produces the fantasy, and it is only the defense which becomes conscious. It is a necessary feature in a therapeutic analysis that through the removal of resistances the patient becomes capable of experiencing this pleasure. For the purposes of investigation and proof in libido theory it is sufficient to develop empathy with the psychic situation of the patient, therefore here the feeling which makes its appearance with the falling away of the resistances against the pleasure experience is assumed. This second and more facile method of procedure in the investigations of libido theory naturally admits of a considerably greater possibility of error than the first and stricter method.

This is the point at which to deal with the criterion "emotional-verbal connotation of the word sexual" which criterion is to be found in Bernfeld *expressis verbis* in the "psychoanalytic" criterion, and in Freud in the lecture on Human Sexual Life. I believe that instead of emotional one could say here *empathetic*, whereby the *pleasure* of the other is felt by empathy. Such empathy is possible on the basis of one's own sexual experiences of the present and of the past. Indeed, the more accessible the memory of events which have at one time been experienced with sexual pleasure is to consciousness, the greater will be the possibilities for empathy

libido theory is therefore not dissimilar to the process of the natural sciences, in that it proposes relatively simple rules and laws for the genetic explanation of the complicated abundance of phenomena (From the author's *Handbook of Psychoanalysis*). The libido theory therefore traces the libido in all mental impulses, and is concerned with its transformations and elaborations. Or, considered from the standpoint of mental phenomena, it attempts to explore the libidinal components in mental phenomena is concerned with the origin of these components and the fate which has caused them to be applied *to the particular phenomenon in question.*

with the sexual life of others. The opening up of the polymorphously-perverse impulses of childhood for the memory, as occurs in analysis, increases this capacity for empathy to a considerable degree. This is one reason among many others why it is required of an analyst that he subject himself to a careful and deep analysis. Further, the extension of the capacity for empathy with regard to the sexual which is the result of his own analysis considerably enlarges the realm of the sexual for the analyst, which he is able to grasp through his intensified capacity for empathy. Great portions of the extended sexual realm which the analysis has mapped out for him are therefore felt by the analyst with complete empathy. The criterion "verbal term sexual" is much more widely applicable for the analyst than it is for the non-analyst.

The points of view of Bernfeld in the "psychoanalytic" criterion which seem to divergent are thus considerably unified, and the criteria "designated as sexual" and all pleasureful activities in the erotogenic zones, by means of the possibility of grasping through wider empathy on the part of the analyst become to a great degree coincident.

There is a third method of investigation in libido theory which consists in the transferring of such results as derive from the first two methods mentioned, of a connection between experiences and of empathy, by the path of analogy with other objects of investigation in the same way that in other sciences the results of some specific investigation are taken as sufficient basis for establishing general validity. Thus libidinal quantities in formations are derived *per analogiam* without there being a verification of the libidinal quantity in each case through the experience of pleasure or through empathy.

If one compared the programatically considered libido theory with a criminology of the libido, a comparison from which Freud is not far off, when he speaks of "hiding places of the libido," or of the fact that the analyst "traces," then the first method of procedure, which has as its content the experience of the connection in the Ego, has a parallel with a confession, the second method of empathetic observation parallels the incriminating evidence of a witness, and the third method of analogy and indirect conclusions has a parallel with circumstantial evidence. Sometimes the possibility of error is thereby indicated.

The standing connections between the libido and its derivatives in various areas are derived *primarily* by way of experience and by empathy, and are verified by the criterion of pleasure. The third method is naturally impossible without the first and the second. To put it succinctly, without the analysis of neuroses "Leonardo da Vinci, a Psychosexual Study of an Infantile Reminiscence" could never have been written.

The postulation of the death instincts led to another point of view with regard to the sexual instincts. From this standpoint the latter are regarded as independent of the pleasure that accompanies them in its intention, tendency, and perhaps most clearly in their effect. And indeed in its effects of or tendencies toward constructiveness, union, assimilation, combination; the sexual, as equivalent to the libidinal would be anything which aims at an effect, which is opposite to destruction. Bernfeld designates this criterion "physiognomic." The places in which Freud indicates the physiognomic criterion with particular clarity are quoted:

" . . . The libidinal, sexual, or life drive, best summarized as Eros, the intention of which it would be to form living substance into ever greater unities, and thereby to preserve the continuation of life, and to lead it into higher developments (from Psychoanalyse und Libidotheorie, Handwörterbuch für Sexual-Wissenschaften, edited by Max Marcuse, Ges. Sch. XI, 223)."

"Libido as the energy of the instinct to preserve living substance and to combine it into ever greater unities." (Civilization and Its Discontents)

" . . . the erotic instincts, which are always trying to collect living substance together into ever larger unities . . . " (New Series of Introductory Lectures).

Bernfeld is correct in his assumption that both criteria, the "psychoanalytic", in which we are of the opinion that the factor of experiencing pleasure is the essential one, and the "physiognomic", characterized by its tendency and effect—constructiveness—are, because of their essential differences, completely independent of one another, and nevertheless are not contradictory. We might, however, give thought to the fact that the most intense manifestation of the libido, which serves us as a prototype, namely sexual union in the sex act, reveals a union of both criteria very convincingly: pleasure is intensified to the maximum, and there is the effect of *union* in the form of the most intimate connection between two individuals, as well as the constructive effect in the begetting of a new being.

Critique Of The Theory Of Transference

It is certain that the transferecne is the most impressive and the most important process in psychoanalytic therapy. The development of the transference, but primarily the regularity with which it developes, required an explanation from the beginning, and numerous explanations have been given for it in the course of analytic research. Before we make a critical approach to these explanations, we want first to define the phenomenon of transference unequivocably, in accordance with its nature. A definition of the term by Freud in "Fragment of An Analysis of a Case of Hysteria" will furnish us with the first orientation, toward a sufficient foundation. It runs,

> "What are transferences? They are new editions or facsimiles of the tendencies and phantasies which are aroused and made conscious during the progress of the analysis; but they have this peculiarity, which is characteristic for their species, that they replace some earlier person by the person of the physician. To put it another way: a whole series of psychological experiences are revived, not as belonging to the past, but as applying to the person of the physician at the present moment. Some of these transferences have a content which differs from that of their model in no respect whatever, except for the substitution. These, then—to keep the same metaphor—are merely new impressions or reprints. Others are more ingeniously constructed; their content has been subjected to a moderating influence—to *sublimation*, as I call it—and they may even become conscious, by cleverly taking advantage of some real peculiarity in the physician's person or circumstances

Zur Theorie der Ubertraugung. *Imago*, 1936, 22, 456–470.

and attaching themselves to that. These, then, will no longer be new impressions, but revised editions. (Collected Papers, III, p.139)

This is by no means the first place in which Freud speaks of the phenomen of transference. Already in the "Studies of Hysteria" there is a wide recognition of its significance, (1895), where in the paper "Toward the Psychotherapy of Hysteria" the disturbed relationship to the analyst is mentioned as the most serious obstacle to the cathartic cure, an obstacle which is met with in every serious analysis. The disturbance of the relationship to the analyst can be conditioned by (1) personal estrangement (2) by the fear of becoming so attached to the person of the analyst that personal independence is lost and one falls into a sexual dependence on the analyst, (3) (literally) if the patient fears that he will transfer painful ideas which appear in the content of the analysis to the person of the analyst. This is a regular occurrence in many analyses.

We come upon the word 'transference' repeatedly in Freud in other connections, primarily in the presentation of the psychology of dream processes, where the displacement of psychic intensities from some elements to others is designated as the transference of these intensities. We will examine these different uses of the same term in regard to the identity of the things themselves which underlie it.

In general we know, therefore, what we have to understand by 'transference' during the analytic cure, namely the reanimation of past object relationships and the displacement of recent object relationships of such kind that the person of the analyst is substituted for the object, and the relationship is therefore experienced with the analyst. Through the transference a current cathexis of the analyst with an object relationship that was at first entirely independent of his person takes place. The analyst is substituted for the original object of instinctual impulses, attitudes towards objects, wishes and fantasies, and in the typical case, this substitution remains unconscious to the analysand. The change of object, therefore, occurs in the layers of the unconscious.

We recognize such changes of object of psychic strivings from our metapsychological investigations in all possible areas. There can be no doubt for us that transference in analysis represents a special case only of a general capacity for displacement which can be ascribed to a number of psychic tendencies. We know that such displacement is particularly characteristic of those psychic processes which are subject to the primary process, which, therefore have not participated in the development to the higher form and order of the secondary process, and we connect this capacity for displacement with the unbound character of the psychic energy in the system Ucs. It must remain outside the framework of this investigation to characterize more nearly and deeply this displacement of psychic intensities according to their essential nature. We must in connection with our theme content ourselves with having characterized transference as a special instance of displacement. As early as 1909 Ferenczi very clearly and unequivocably showed the connection between transference and displacement. We therefore take it as established that transference is a special case of displacement, and that such displacement mechanisms concern particularly the unconscious processes. We know thereby that the information about displacement yielded by metapsychological investigation is also valid for the transference. Nevertheless the general remarks about displacement are not sufficient for us. We want to have a more exact knowledge about transference than a transplanting of the knowledge gained about displacement to its special instance of transference can yield us. The reason is obvious. We meet this special instance of displacement regularly and, one may say, under experimental conditions, namely in analytic therapy. There the transference is our most important means of gaining insight, as well as, on the one hand, the most powerful motor force of the treatment, on the other, the strongest bulwark of resistance. It stands therefore at the center of our analytic interest, from the standpoint of therapy and that of research.

I have mentioned in the beginning that the regularity with which the transference makes its appearance has provoked authors to an attempt at explaining it. The first of such attempts is found in Freud, in the "Studies in Hysteria." In the addendum to the passage previously quoted, in which the term 'transference' was first defined by Freud, it says, "The transference occurs through a false connection." And further,

"It happened in the following way: First the content of the wish appeared in the consciousness of the patient, without any memories of the surrounding circumstances which could allocate the wish to its place in the past. Through the compulsion to associate prevailing in consciousness the now-present wish bound itself up with my person, with which the patient was allowed to concern herself, and through this misalliance, which I call a false connection, the same affect was aroused which the patient had suppressed upon the banishment of this forbidden wish. After I have once experienced this, I can assume from each familiar claim made upon my person that it again represents a transference and a false connection. In a strange manner the sick person becomes each time the victim of the deception."

An indication of what Freud means by the term "false connection" follows in another place, in the *Studies in Hysteria*, and reads:

"There seems to exist a need to bring psychic phenomena of which one becomes conscious, into a casual connection with the rest of consciousness. Where the real use of the perception is withdrawn from consciousness one unthinkingly tries to establish another connection in which one believes, although it is false. It is clear that a splitting of the content of consciousness must be present, which gives the greatest impetus to such "false connections."

The first explanation, therefore, that of Freud, calls transference a false connection, something like what Jones later called rationalization. We can see from the last sentence of the passage quoted that Freud himself is not satisfied with his own explanation, when he says, "The patient strangely becomes a victim of the deception each time." Freud could not have found the regularity with which the phenomenon occurred strange, if he had already given the real explanation for its occurrence.

The next explanations proceed from the structure and dynamics of the mental apparatus. Thus Ferenczi, in his paper *Introjection and Transference* attempts to derive a general theory of the behavior of neurotics from the phenomenon of transference during the analytic cure. The strength of repression wards off cathexes from the original ideas, and converts them into *free-floating libido*, the presence of which in the mental apparatus, however, is difficult to tolerate. In order to bind this libido, and at the same time to divert it farther from its original object, the neurotic, who, in accordance with his repressions, disposes of a great abundance of such free-floating libido, turns to other objects and cathects them with this libido. This is the *mania for transference* of the neurotic. Ferenczi attempts to explain the disproportionate love and hate and the exaggeration of the neurotic by this mania for transference. The neurotic to a certain extent convulsively incorporates the greatest amount possible of the external world in the Ego. Ferenczi imagines this a kind of process of attenuation which he gives the name *introjection*. (It is unnecessary to call attention to the fact that the content of the term introjection as it is now used is only partially covered by Ferenczi's definition of it.) The transference is, therefore, according to Ferenczi, an introjection, i.e., an incorporation of the external world, in the sense of an object cathexis, for the purpose of attenuating the free-floating libido that proceeds from the repressed impulses. Dynamically, therefore, the transference would be the result of repression. We cannot, however, accept this dynamic explanation of Ferenczi on the basis of repression as valid, because obviously the patient in transference *does not* detach himself from the original object, but on the contrary brings this object with him into every new relationship and covers every new object with it. In this sense the transference could be at the most the result of a repression which failed. But there still remains the fact to be explained that the lifting of the repression in the analytic cure regularly leads to the transference.

In addition to this explanation for the general transference of the neurotic, Ferenczi felt the need of giving specific explanation for the transference in analysis, without thereby completely separating it from the rest of the transferences. He proposes an explanation for the transference during the analysis which then appears repeatedly in analytic literature. It is the explanation of the *status nascendi*.

The presence of the analyst at the appearance of the unconscious wish impulses in consciousness is taken to be the reason why these wish impulses are transferred from earlier objects onto the analyst. "The impulses which have been repressed, and which gradually become conscious confront *in statu nascendi* the person of the physician, and attempt to fasten their unsatisfied valences on the personality," says Ferenczi. This explanation, with which we incidentally make a critical approach to the repetition compulsion, reminds us of the first one given by Freud, namely the compulsion to associate with which it has in common the factor of making an appearance out of the unconscious.

The explanation of the *status nascendi*, however, has something further in common with those explanations that make the *object hunger of the Id* responsible for the transference. The "unsatisfied valences" of Ferenczi mean nothing else. Because the instinctual wishes in the Id exist in a state of extreme tension, they attempt to overpower each new object, with the hope that through this object they will finally attain to gratification. Thus Nunberg finds one of the most powerful motives of the transference in the object demands of the Id (H. Nunberg, Probleme der Therapie, Int. Zeit. f. Psa., Bd. XIV, 1928). One must of course imagine that the conservative nature of the instincts and their being blocked from any development through repression is the reason for the fact that the analysand is not hungering after a new object in the transference, but after his old object. For it is just the reactivation of the *old* relationships with a new object that is the essence of the transference.

In the literature of psychoanalysis, the original meaning of the word *transference* is not always preserved. In general any relationship to the analyst is called transference. We must investigate whether the transferences can be separated from the abundance of these relationships or whether any relationship—to the analyst, and perhaps every relationship besides this one is not essentially a transference. If the latter were so, the lack of a distinction between the content of the term *relationship* and that of *transference* would not be justified. We shall consider this problem later.

The object hunger of the Id, which is only an expression of its longing for gratification, serves us as a manifold criterion in the explanation of the transference. It explains primarily the regularity with which the transference makes its appearance, because we must in every analysis be confronted with an Id which is demanding gratification. But we cannot recognize anything in this explanation which is specific for the transference; we cannot thereby distinguish the transference from other object relationships; which leads to the problem which will be handled later, of distinguishing between transference and other object relationships.

The next explanation of the transference in the analysis comes from Freud; it was discovered by him, and called the *repetition compulsion*. We know that the repetition compulsion proceeds from the conservative nature of the instincts, which expresses itself in its drive to reinstate previous conditions. If the resistances of the Ego against this reinstitution is pushed back and set aside, then this early condition is reproduced, and also earlier object relationships, in which the analyst appears as a representative of the object of the infantile instinctual wishes. The faithful reproduction of the past in the transference is to be ascribed to the repetition compulsion. Through it the experiences and attitudes in the transference become, in Freud's words, *a mirror of the forgotten past*. (Beyond the Pleasure Principle.) The explanation by means of the repetition compulsion is thoroughly in accord with that through the object hunger of the Id, since through the repetition compulsion forgotten *instinctual demands* are faithfully reproduced in the transference. But the repetition compulsion does not furnish us either with a distinction between the transference and other object relationships. In fact the powerful irruption of the repetition compulsion during the cure by no means influences the relationship to the physician alone, but in a similar manner embraces all other object relationships in its scope. Freud says about this in his paper, *Recollection, Repetition and Working Through* the following: "We soon perceive that the transference is itself only a bit of repetition, and that the repetition is the transference of the forgotten past not only onto the physician, but also onto all the other aspects of the current situation. We must be prepared to find, therefore, that the patient abandons himself to the compulsion to repeat, which is now replacing the impulse to remember, not only in his relation with the analyst, but also in all other matters occupying and interesting him at that time, for instance, when he falls in love or sets about any project during the treatment."

Among the numerous transferences which we observe that the patient makes during the cure, therefore, that toward the analyst is only one among many others which are conditioned by the repetition of object relationships, and which are occasioned through the object hunger of the Id—strivings that succeed in entering the Ego. The *status nascendi* of the instinctual impulses which appear therefore is valid not only for the transference onto the physician, but for all new object relationships and for the modifications of object relationships already in existence, which take place during the cure. Therefore the *status nascendi* cannot be considered a basis for the distinction between the transference and other object relationships. Our investigation obviously narrows down to a focussing of the various explanations of transference on one problem, where numerous questions converge into one: can a theoretical distinction be made between transference and object relationship? And if not, what is it that so emphasizes the transference to the analyst among the numerous object relationships during the cure, and which makes it the outstanding one during the analysis? A penetrating investigation of the possibilities of distinction between transference and other object relationships is found in Freud's paper *On Transference Love*. It is true that Freud here treats only one detail of the transference phenomena, namely the erotic transference to the analyst in the form of being in love with him; but nothing speaks against the consideration of what is there said about transference love as applicable to the totality of transference phenomena in all their rich diversity. Freud formulates the question as follows: "Can the love which is manifested in analytic treatment not truly be called real?" And his investigation, primarily the comparison between the actual observation of the character of love during the treatment with love as observed in daily life, leads him to the clearly formulated conclusion: one has no right to dispute the *genuine* nature of the love which makes its appearance in the course of the analytic treatment. (Collected Papers, II, 388).

In contrast to this, L. Jekels and E. Bergler attempt to differentiate theoretically, that is, on the basis of the psychology of instincts, between love and transference. We cannot avoid a critical examination of their arguments.

The authors begin their arguments with the problem of object cathexis, which, while they call it a *miracle*, they nevertheless attempt to explain. Their explanation is based entirely upon Freud's latest theory of instinctual dualism, Eros-Thanatos. The point of reference from which they want to explain their miracle is the Super-Ego, which they understand to be a neutralized zone between two neighboring lands. The battle between Eros and Thanatos, according to the visually dramatized presentation of the authors, is waged chiefly around the neutralized zone. "As in war," both "opponents" make all efforts to claim the neutral region between them. One root of the Ego ideal consists in the attempt of the Ego "to divert the aggression of the death instinct, which is directed towards the Ego to objects, whereby the latter become dreaded." This act of the destructive instinct is "parried" by the Eros, through incorporation of the anxiety arousing object in the Ego, where it becomes a subject of the individual's own narcissism. The second root of the Ego ideal is said to be the compromised preservation of the infantile feeling of omnipotence in the form of narcissistic cathexis of the Ego ideal. This latter would thereby become a libidinal reservoir. But "the Thanatos does not give itself up, but rather dents the weapon which the Eros has forged in that a desexualization takes place." Thus the Ego ideal becomes alternately the prey of the one and the other, according to their predominance, and then bears the colors of the current victor. "Through utilization of the Ego ideal for its own purposes the daemon mobilizes the Eros against itself, attacks it with its own weapons and in such a manner defeats the intentions of the Eros which the latter followed through upon the erection of the Ego ideal.

But the Ego is further involved in an unremitting effort to engage the thrusts of the Thanatos in order to parry them. The aggression directed against the Ego, because of projection, is experienced as coming from the external world, for the purpose of sparing the individual's narcissism. Finally the Eros becomes aggressive in wit, in comedy, in humor, and in mania, which formations represent attempts to "wrench its tool" from the daemon, as these authors call the destructively cathected Super-Ego, with which the daemon can torment the Ego. These, according to these authors, are the conditions relative to the Super Ego.

But now these authors apply their conception of the struggle going on within the psyche for an explanation of *love*. They base their assumption upon Freud's statement that the lover has erected his ego ideal in the object. They mean, namely, that *love is also an expression of the struggle between Eros and Thanatos* in such a way that love is concerned with a disarming of the daemon so that the "instrument of torture"—the Super-Ego—is taken away, and the neutralized zone of the Super-Ego joined to the erotic striving. The indifferent energy with which the authors identify the Super Ego is applied to the intensification of the erotic striving, while the loved object and the Ego ideal are identified. These authors assert that love is regularly preceded by tension between the Ego ideal and the Ego, without giving any evidence to support this. Love serves thereby to renew the Ego ideal, which in its form up until now was inadequate against the aggressions of the daemon. The essence of love, however, is said to be first the *re-introjection* of the projected Ego ideal into the Ego, and it returns strengthened into the Ego. Therefore the Thanatos or daemon, respectively, that is, the strong cathexis of the Super Ego with destructive energy forces the individual to love. Love thereby is taken to be the result of guilt feelings. Just as in the case of the provident warrior against his enemy, the lover attempts to wrench the weapon of the Ego ideal from the Daemon at the latter's first approach, before the latter has complete mastery of it. So far, therefore, are the conditions in love.

In contrast to these is the transference, "an act of despair arising out of panic fear." For in the transference not only the Ego ideal originating from the Eros is transferred, but the whole Super-Ego, therefore the Daemon as well. In this way the analyst is taken to be not only a love object, but also an ar object. The evidence of these authors for this theory of an essential qualitative difference between transference and love seems scarcely valid to me.

The authors support this differentiation by the *aspect*, as they describe it, of the lover and the individual making a transference. They find between the two "an almost grotesquely amusing contrast: on the one hand the neurotic who can hardly do more than pass the years without initiative in deeply passive behavior on the analytic couch in the 'in-between-realm' of the transference, on the other hand the lover with the entire armor of his activity and his initiative: projection of the Ego ideal, courtship of the object which is to realize his Ego ideal, his unflagging attempts to remodel this object in the sense of wish fantasies, as well as to wrest from reality the most and the best for this apparently realized Ego ideal.

Entirely otherwise is the neurotic, who as one disarmed and already defeated still attempts through numerous unsuccessful compromises like a desperado to follow the identical road of the battle against the daemon."

It is not difficult to contradict the authors in this. If one observes the neurotic who passes years without initiative on the analytic couch rather than in his love life, it appears as nothing else but his transference. And can these authors never have had the experience in their analytic work that an analysand with a craving for love has projected her Ego ideal onto them, has paid court to them as an object and has attempted untiringly to remodel this object in the sense of the wish fantasy, in such a way as to wrest from reality the most pleasure possible for this apparently realized Ego ideal, therefore everything which they consider as "pathognomic" for love. What the authors describe is the pathological-pregenital type of love in serious neuroses on the one hand, which, naturally, is also seen in the transference, enforced with destructive tendencies and with anxiety, and the love approaching to normal, which similarly we meet in the transference in our analytic work on the other hand. The representation of the facts as if the one neurotic type of love occurred only in the transference, while the other normal type occurred as an object relationship outside of the analysis, is not true representation of the real conditions. It does not, therefore, seem justifiable to me to make a distinction between transference and love on these grounds.

We cannot pass over the work of Jekels and Bergler without a consideration of one particular characteristic which they define as a difference between love and transference. Through discussion of this characteristic we make a connection with the problem of the transference which still confronts us. This characteristic is, according to the authors, "the infallibility with which the transference makes its appearance, accompanied by, or even in spite of lack of choice in relation to the object, the complete freedom of the choice, which takes place with an impetuous setting aside of age and sex, and without consideration for personal qualities or the lack of them."

The authors see in this characteristic of the transference a clear indication that it is "an act of despair, which results from a feeling of panic." In the same sense they interpret the 'impetuosity' of the transference, its "headlong tempo," so to speak. To a less prejudiced observation the characteristic of the infallibility of the appearance of the transference is by no means to be taken for granted, nor is the appearance of it so precipitate as the authors assume for their distinction between transference and love. It is just the assent from the "practical experience of the creative analyst" of which the authors cannot be certain in reference to their pronouncements. Let us hear what Freud has to say about this:

"The first goal of the treatment remains that of attaching the patient to the cure and to the person of the physician. One need do nothing more than allow him time. If one arouses serious interest, carefully sets aside the first resistances which appear and avoids hitting certain wrong notes, the patient institutes such a relationship by himself and puts the physician in place of the imago of one of those persons from whom he was accustomed to receive love."

This attempt of the analyst to bind the patient to himself, and to set aside the resistances to this union which arise was what Freud had in mind when he spoke of love induced by the analytic situation as *provoked* love, and advanced this provoked origin as one of the few features which give transference love a special classification. (Observations on Transference Love, Cool. Pap.II.) Also, when a few lines later he says that the analyst "has evoked this love by undertaking analytic treatment in order to cure the neurosis" (II, 388), and similarly, "We open the transference to the patient as a play ground, on which he is permitted to conduct himself with complete freedom."

Nunberg attempted to discover the libidinal sources of the transference in his excellent work "Problems of Therapy." He found several such sources: the helplessness of the sufferer, who attaches himself to the analyst because the latter promises him help, the belief in magic and in the omnipotence of the analyst, the narcissistic gratification of the patient through talking, the conclusion that it is love, when the analyst devotes his attention to him; briefly, the patient has opportunity enough to form a tie to the analyst, to make him "an image of those persons from whom he was accustomed to receive love," if the analyst behaves accordingly. But in the course of the treatment the patient has also occasion just as frequently to hate the analyst, to be anxious because of him, briefly to run the whole gamut of his affects, which actually appear in the transference, and of which transference love is only one, if the most important one for the progress of the cure.

The precipitous onset of the transference, which sometimes occurs before the patient has seen the analyst, which again Jekels and Bergler consider a pathognomic distinction between transference and love, does not seem to me to require an explanation through the Daemon. One need only remember with what anticipations and hopes men who are under strong instinctual tension enter a new situation, what fantasies they bind up with objects which they encounter for the first time, and one will be able to understand how transferences "already begin in the waiting room," and not only in the case of analysts. Every distinction between transference and other object relationships seems, as we attempt to get a better grasp of it, to slip through our fingers.

We must consider still another factor which Freud mentions as a distinction between love and transference. The transference "is to a high degree lacking in reality, is less sensible, less concerned about consequences, more blind in its estimation of the person loved than we are willing to admit of normal love." One observes, from the caution with which Freud formulizes, that we do not willingly admit these as characteristics of normal love. For he himself considerably weakens the argument for such a distinction in the following sentence: "We should not forget, however, that it is precisely these departures from the norm that make up the essential element in the condition of being in love." (Coll.Pap. II 388)

The liberation of a greater abundance of affect, and the decreased regard for reality in the analytic object relationship seem to me to be considerably conditioned by the specific characteristics of the analytic cure. We are assiduous in our attempts to dispense with many of the otherwise valid considerations for the appearance of affects during the cure. We promise the patient's Ego "rewards and advantages, if it will give up its resistance." (Inhibition, Symptom and Anxiety, p. 147). We promise the Ego that we will support it, if the affects produce too much anxiety; we advise the Ego to venture into unreal affects. It is therefore little wonder if the Ego permits the formation of affectual relationships in the analysis, which have less justification in reality.

The repetition compulsion, which can certainly not be ascribed to the consideration of reality, according to Freud, could not find expression until "the work of the treatment coming to meet it has loosened the repression." In the widening of the realm of the Ego, which is involved in the loosening through the fundamental rule and obedience to it, the repetition of old affectual processes appear which the Ego would not have ventured upon without the assurance of psychic help. More unreality clings to those object relationships which have been more deeply repressed, and which therefore originate in earlier layers, than to the surface relationships; displacement and disparagement of the values of reality is more intensive in them than it could be without such a transformation of the Ego. It is also true that during the training of the analytic experience, the Ego gradually learns to master Id impulses, and in accordance with such experience, can give increasingly more room to hitherto repressed object impulses.

And we should not forget that the *resistance* uses the transference for its own purposes, "it is greatly intensified by the resistance" (Coll. Pap. II, 388), and makes use of this exaggeration in order to demonstrate to the Ego the necessity of new repression. This influence of the resistance upon the object relationship to the analyst is a further explanation of much of the deviation from other object relationships to the transference.

The striking characteristics which distinguish the transference relationship from other object relationships can, therefore, be explained by the specific situation of the analytic cure, and by the dynamic conditions under which the transference makes its appearance and pursues its further development. *But in its essence the transference is an object relationship like any other.*

We have arrived at the point where our problem capsizes on the way to its solution and poses a new question: "Are there object relationships which are not transferences?" We must content ourselves here with illuminating this problem by sidelights. From the standpoint of a very generally accepted formulation we may say: just as there are no current impulses in which something of the past is not mingled, so there is no important object relationship of the adult in which past object is not used to screen an infantile one. The memory traces of the first and vastly important object relationships of childhood constitute the *cliche*, to use Freud's excellent designation, upon which all future object relationships are patterned.

In his paper "Introjection and Transference," Ferenczi calls the first object love and the first object hate transferences, whereby he understands that thé first love and hate are a transference of the autoerotic pleasure and unpleasure feelings onto the objects which cause those feelings. In general, however, one will do well to distinguish between object relationship and narcissistic relationship, to which latter pseudo-object relationships of the purified pleasure-Ego belong. Let us therefore modify our question and ask up to what point in time new object relationships, which are not transferences, are developed. Only in Ferenczi have I found an approximate given time. In "Introjection and Transference" he writes: "It has been proved that in every individual the child who wants love and who is thereby fearful and anxious, continues to live, and that all later loves, hates, and fears are only transferences, or, as Freud calls them 'new editions' of currents of emotion which were acquired in early childhood (before the completion of the fourth year), and which were later repressed."

The problem in child analysis, why children in the earliest years of life produce no transference in the analysis seems directly deducible from Ferenczi's remarks. But if we consider on the other hand, that transferences already play a significant part in the first great object relationships of childhood, that often, particularly in the individual evolution of the great framework of phylogenetic experiences, what has been experienced and observed with distant objects is transplanted, we may well say transferred to the first great object relationships, we will see that also in these 'cliches' no completely pure and primal experience with the object can be discovered. Must we not rather assume the fulfillment and re-experience of the phylogenetically inherited scheme in the ontogenetic individual as the pattern form for all transference? It might therefore well be difficult to delimit the point in the course of childhood at which the development of independent object relationships no longer occurs. We may hope here that more extensive experience, particularly that of child analysts, will provide us with a solution.

Two Cases of Fetishism

Fenichel has emphasized the closeness of the relationship between fetishism and transvestitism in his paper on The Psychology of Transvestitism. In both conditions there is an overvaluation of woman's clothing, and both perversions are founded upon an adherence to the idea of the phallic woman.

It is Fenichel's opinion that the transvestite differs from the fetishist in that he makes an additional identification with the woman, expressed in wearing feminine apparel in order to reduplicate the phallic nature of the woman. In the first instance, the transvestite is a woman with a penis under his clothes, in the second place the woman's clothing carries a phallic significance as a fetish, and is used for exhibitionistic purposes in this sense. The material here to be presented deals with two cases of fetishism which seem to show that Fenichel's formula, which he regards as a specific one for transvestitism, can also be extended to cover certain types of fetishism. The discussion of the specificity of the definitions of the two perversions will be postponed until after presentation of the material.

Case S. (analyzed by Sterba) was a man of thirty, in the employ of a bank, who came to analysis because of a feeling of general embarrassment. In the first analytic hour he confessed that his embarrassment was intimately connected with his sexual secret: he was "both sexes." By this odd term he wished to express this: that his sexual object was a rubber apron. He stole these rubber aprons from laundresses or fishwives, and the stealing itself was a necessary prerequisite for the satisfaction of his perverse gratification. When he was naked he took his fetish, spread it out on the bed or on the floor, sat on it, drew one corner up between his legs, like a diaper, so that it was firmly pressed against his genitalia, and then had an orgasm. After his orgasm, he was beset by a strong sense of guilt and by hatred against the fetish which he often threw away, only to fetch it back now and then when he needed it. The patient's sexual activity was completely spent in this fetishistic act. His shyness had never permitted him to approach women, but they figured in his fantasies as love objects, and there was a strong and therapeutically useful tendency toward normal sexual contacts with women.

The interest in the piece of rubber began in his early childhood, in fact, in his fourth year. Soon after birth the patient was taken away from his mother, who was a servant girl and could not keep her illegitimate child with her. Until he was seven he lived with foster-parents whom he loved very much. He was particularly attached to the foster-mother. He was then boarded in a place in which he was not well cared for and where he was made very unhappy by the sternness and hard-heartedness of the woman. Half a year later an aunt took him to live in her home, where he stayed until he entered analysis. This aunt was an unfriendly, quarrelsome, stingy person who shrank from sex. He constantly strove to leave her but was nevertheless inwardly bound to her.

When he was four years old his beloved foster-mother had a baby, a girl. Now he often had the opportunity to see the child changed, and on these occasions a rubber sheet was used. Soon the smell of the rubber excited him, and he began to notice pleasurable sexual sensations when he smelled or touched the rubber. It was during the latency period that he first purloined a rubber cloth in the house and brought it into contact with his genitalia in order to obtain sexual pleasure, so that he developed his perverse practice very early. He continued with this fetishistic practice until puberty, when orgastic emissions became connected with this sexual act, with which feelings of guilt were associated from the very beginning.

Because of external circumstances it was impossible to prolong the analysis until the deepest layers had been worked through, but enough material was available to cure his fetishism. During the same period when the little girl suddenly appeared in the home of his foster-parents and he had ample opportunity to observe her penislessness, it happened that he was frequently sent to church by his Catholic foster-parents. There the crucified Christ began to awaken his lively interest and to excite him sexually. He thought that the Velum Christi was wrapped about the loins of Christ to arouse voluptuous feelings, just as he later acted it out with the rubber sheet. Also, the smoothly painted surface of the velum of the wooden statues reminded him of rubber. Consequently he acquired his fetishism by means of an identification with the crucified Saviour.

But his fantasies about the crucifixion were founded upon observations of parental intercourse which he had interpreted sadistically: the menstruation of his foster-mother confirmed him in the belief that the penis was taken away from the woman during the sexual act and that a bleeding wound resulted. The crucified Christ represented to him the woman masochistically suffering and bleeding during the sexual act. However, the veiling cloth (Schamtuch) over the genitalia had to him the meaning of that which is covered up, the genital (Schamteil), the penis. In this way his fetishistic act constituted an excellent denial and contradiction of the penislessness of the woman which caused him so much fear and anxiety.

The first part of his perversion indicated the true circumstances: when he stole the rubber apron from the women, a truly active procedure, it signified "the man robs the woman of her penis." This meaning was refuted in the second part of his activity, in which he passively carried out the real perverse act with which sexual pleasure was connected; the woman retains the thing between her legs, the penis, even in the masochistically conceived passive situation of intercourse. For during the fetishistic act he was himself the woman in the passive masochistic situation, but on the one hand he had not only his own penis, of which he was particularly aware because of the pressure upon it, but also the fantasied one, the velum—the rubber cloth. A dream showed the phallic significance of this fetish in an impressive manner: "I pull an elongated object larger than my finger out of an old box.[1] It gets bigger. I put it on the floor. It turns into a rubber cloth. I sit on it and have a pollution." The box was really a tin can and reminded him of an old alarm clock belonging to his aunt. The alarm clock had only one leg instead of two because the other one had been broken off. It soon became evident to him that the old box stood for his aunt who, moreover, had severe rheumatism in her one leg and limped (the one leg of the alarm clock is missing). In this dream it is clear that his fetish signifies the penis of the woman. His fetishistic act, which shows him masochistically identified with the woman, makes sexual satisfaction without anxiety possible for him, since he demonstrably retains his penis even in his passive feminine situation. In this connection it is unnecessary to discuss the anal determinants of his fetish (the smell of the rubber; being swaddled when dirty).

The second case K. (analyzed by Kronengold) concerns a twenty-four year old student, who came to analysis because of compulsive masturbation and an aversion for women. He preferred the company of men and became sexually excited whenever he saw them roughhousing.

His masturbation was dependent upon certain conditions: he fettered his ankles together with a rope which he then passed up between his thighs, beside his penis, and up to the nates. Frequently he also bound his arms

---

[1]. "Alte Schachtel" = old maid.

and hands. By stretching his legs he exerted pressue on his penis by means of the rope, and achieved an orgasm. The force necessary to pull on the rope was so great that welts were raised on the body. He usually masturbated in front of a mirror, nude, except for his carefully polished shoes. He powdered and rouged his face, and spread a handkerchief over his penis. A modification consisted of hanging by a strap from the hinge of a door, bound, and head downward and then gaining satisfaction by pressing his penis against the door. Although he repeatedly tried to dispose of the ropes and straps he would then steal new ones from his mother. He wanted to spend his feelings of guilt by frequent churchgoing and confessions, but at the sight of the young men who assisted the priest he became sexually excited and had to avoid the church, plagued by pangs of conscience.

He was the only member of his family who was devout, and he became so at the age of ten. He built an altar at home, dressed up as a priest by tying covers about his body, and chose a youg cousin as ministrant. During puberty he bound up the same cousin, and gained sexual satisfaction by pressing his penis against him while they were scuffling. He made his first attempt at fettering upon his brother, who was four and a half years younger. The patient had been very much fixed upon his mother, and the birth of his brother was a severe trauma. Thereafter he refused to sleep in his own bed. He slept with the mother, beside the brother, helped her take care of him, and even adopted her pet names for the child. Later he showed a lively interest in sewing and crocheting, and played with dolls like a girl.

He preferred to go to those churches where the priests wore the cingulum in plain sight. In a dream, old women took the place of the priests who were celebrating high mass. The women were naked and carried spittoons in their hands instead of chalices.

Although the analysis could not be completed in this case either, it nevertheless yielded material that makes his perversion comprehensible. He identified himself with his mother as a defense against the threat of losing her when his brother was born. In this way the mother swaddling the child was regarded as phallic, and the swaddling itself was conceived as a castration of the brother, which complied with the patient's hatred of the newcomer. In a dream pertaining to this situation the younger brother was in bed. The patient would have liked to fetter him. The mother was there too and he wanted her to go away so that he could put his penis into the hole his brother had in front. As this dream shows, priests represented phallic women to him. The patient himself designated them as "women in masculine clothing." The penis was not only hidden under the vestment (he covered the penis with a cloth during the masturbatory act) but was coincidentally represented exhibitionistically by means of the cingulum, substituted for by the rope used in masturbation. In the drawing made by the patient himself, the rope passing over his genitalia is clearly recognizable as a penis symbol. This narcissistic identification with the phallic mother covers the underlying masochistic identification with the suffering mother. In corresponding coitus fantasies the woman was crushed to death. The blood stains he saw in his mother's bed he equated with his own diarrhea. He participated in the suffering of the woman in childbirth in the fantasies underlying the perverse act.[2] In a dream the mother was carrying a knapsack on her back. It was hard for her to carry[3] because she only had one strap on. A second dream during the same night signified: "I am in my analytic hour. My loose front incisor is to be replaced by a firm tooth." The patient succeeds in satisfying his masochistic wish by fettering himself, but in the process he demonstrably keeps the penis.

In both cases there is a question of fetishistic perversion. The fetishistic act, even if superficially viewed, as in these cases a passive feminine, outspokenly masochistic experience. In the case of S. there is a distinct identification with the foster-sister whose rubber sheet became his first fetishistic object. This identification is intensified by the Christ fantasy in which the velum corresponds to the fetish, but the suffering Saviour represents the mother as the passive partner in his sado-masochistic conception of intercourse. In K.'s case the superficial picture of the fetishistic procedure already demonstrates its masochistic character. The fettering which leaves welts behind, is open to no other interpretation. Here, too, we observe the identification with the mother who suffers masochistically during intercourse, as is clearly shown by the dream of the mother with the knapsack, and the subsequent dream in which he is to lose a tooth. Freud has pointed out the phallic significance of the fetish[4]. It is clear in both cases. In case S., by the equation rubber cloth-velum, in which the veiling cloth (Schamtuch) takes the place of that which is to be covered up, the penis; as well as by the dream which shows the development of the fetish from the penis-like structure which falls out of the box—aunt. This dream also makes it evident that it is the woman's penis which becomes the fetish. In the case of K. the phallic significance is apparent in the fetish itself. The cingulum of the priests, that knotted rope which ordained priests wear over their habits and secular priests under it, with

---

[2] The German word entbinden has the double meaning of "giving birth" and "unfettering" (loosening of bonds).
[3] Tragen—be pregnant.
[4] Fetishismus. Ges. Schr. XI.

the two ends hanging down from the middle of the body, leaves no doubt of its genital symbolism. Indeed Catholic priests are often devaluated as men and turned into women by the unconscious, because of their symbolic attributes such as celibacy, the tonsure, and their womanish skirtlike garments. The patient K. consciously thought of them as women, but the cingulum gave them the value of phallic women. In both cases this identification with the woman who suffers masochistically during the sexual act, but nevertheless obviously keeps her penis, serves the purpose of denying the penislessness of the woman.

In the theoretical sphere, the analytic findings in the two cases of fetishism entirely comply with the formula for transvestitism proposed by Fenichel. The fetishistic act has the significance of an identification with a woman who keeps her penis despite her masochistic role. In both cases, the penis was twice represented in the manner which Fenichel considered specific for transvestitism. On the one hand, the penis is particularly felt in the fetishistic act of pressing the fetish against the genital region, so that its existence is clearly proven to the possessor; on the other hand, the fetish, which becomes connected with the body during the act, itself represents a penis. It has frequently been observed elsewhere that, as in this instance, duplication serves the purpose of a vigorous denial of a deficiency. In both of the cases the same formula may be applied which Fenichel has adopted for transvestitism, but the patients are, nevertheless, pure fetishists without a transvestitic component. Therefore, we believe that Fenichel's formula concerning the denial of the penisless condition of the woman by means of a reduplicated emphasis of her penis should not be confined to transvestitism, but should be extended to include cases of masochistic fetishism like ours, in which the person acts out on himself an identification with the woman, using an attribute of phallic significance (clothing, fetish) for this purpose.

The Psychic Trauma And The Handling Of The Transference (The Last Contributions Of Sandor Ferenczi To Psychoanalytic Technique)

In the last years of his life, Ferenczi, the most productive, vital, and many-sided of the apostles of psychoanalysis, involved himself anew with the technical problems of analysis, and with an unusual freshness of approach reopened paths which had been abandoned in the progress of analysis which, in his opinion, could furnish a new therapeutic yield, or, as he himself figuratively put it, "to come upon new veins of gold in the previously abandoned shafts."

He devoted himself to these efforts as a result of the formulation of his own "active technique." The active technique concerned itself with bringing about an increase in tension through the compulsion not only to recognize deeply buried impulses, but also to *act these out* before the physician. This experience of repetition before the physician was intended to make these impulses more accessible to consciousness and thus to bring them under the control of the latter.

The danger which was involved in this technique lay in the resistances of the Ego, which thereby came into conflict with the analyst, and Ferenczi was forced, at the Homburg Congress to take back some of his suggestions on the "active technique." Ferenczi's therapeutic effort, as his master has called it in his obituary his "overwhelming need to heal and help," caused him to shift quickly to the other side of the analytic attitude.

At the Innsbruck Congress, in his lecture, "The Problem of Terminating

Das psychische Trauma und die Handhabung der Ubertragung. (Die letzten Arbeiten von S. Ferenczi zur psychoanalytischen Technik.) *Internationale Zeitschrift fur Psychoanalyse*, 1936, *22*, 40–46.

the Analysis," (Int. Ztschr. f. Psa. XIV,1, 1928), Ferenczi made a demand for the "unshakable goodwill" which the analyst must maintain toward the patient, no matter now extreme the latter may become in his behavior and utterances. This good will must be honest and unfeigned, must be so unshakable and unlimited that all attempts of the patient "to test the extent of the analyst's patience" must fail. On the basis of this good will, the correction of childhood takes place, as well as that of the reactions corresponding to it, which includes the neurotic ones. The comparison between the behavior of the analyst and the unreasonable affective behavior of the educating person in childhood furnishes the patient with the possibility of making more or less rapid alteration in a favorable direction.

And in the analysis itself the attitude of the patient alters after the ineffective explosion of provocative aggressions. Buried demands for tenderness and love appear with a "naive candor." This naivete in utterance of needs for tenderness, the childlike form in which these demands were couched, was something very striking to Ferenczi, who attempted to induce it in his patients. For this purpose he employed a technical means which was directed toward the Ego of the patient, namely the demand for *relaxation*, i.e., for complete surrender to the entirely spontaneous appearance of inner impressions, tendencies, and emotions.

At the basis of the relaxation principle there lies a tendency towards increased emotionality in the analysis, a tendency which we can already designate here as one regressive to catharsis.

For the attainment of this maximum emotionality in the analytic process, however, according to Ferenczi, something more than merely this purely receptive goodwill is necessary. Because in such dramatic-emotional moments the Ego of the patient sinks to a deeply infantile level, and the relaxed adult attitude of the analyst becomes disturbing. It causes the emotional springs to run dry, i.e., it occasions new repression. The analyst as well as the patient, therefore, must sometimes regress to the infantile level which corresponds to the emotional experience in the Ego of the regressed patient. The analyst must participate in the return to childhood if he does not want to disturb that return in the patient. Ferenczi calls this technical artifice, "Play analysis." If the infantile game between the analyst and the patient is not to be broken off brusquely and detrimentally, the questions which must furnish details and provide stimulation for the production of further material must remain entirely on the level of the regressed patient. Ferenczi made an astonishing and novel impression with his lecture on the 75th birthday of Sigmund Freud in the Viennese Psychoanalytic Society when he reported the following about a patient of his who was at the height of manhood:

"Once, in the middle of a conversation he put his arm around my neck and whispered in my ear, 'Grandpapa, I'm afraid I'm going to have a little baby.' Then I hit upon, as it seemed to me, the happy idea of saying nothing to him at first about transference and the like, but rather in the same whispering voice posed the counter-question, 'Yes? Now why do you think that?' One could not, while listening to this report, fail to be moved by the warmth and sympathy which lay in the tone of the counter-question. The lecture was entitled, "Child Analysis with Adults." One could have called it, "Child Analysis With Adults Regressed Through Relaxation."

There are, therefore, two technical novelties which Ferenczi suggests to us in his last works, relaxation and play analysis, to which are added as auxiliary measures intensified suggestion and the encouragement of fantasy formation.

But good will, relaxation and regression with the patient to the infantile level are not sufficient technical aids to the analyst for the achievement of a deeper Ego regression in the patient. There is still another disturbing factor which the analyst has to conquer in himself. He must completely dispel the "nominal confusion between adults and children." In their trace states, about which I shall speak in the second part of my paper, the patients attain to an astonishing clairvoyance about the wishes, tendencies, moods, sympathies and antipathies of the analyst, whether these are consciously known to the analyst or not. The criticism of these emotional attitudes and the aggressive reaction to them are repressed by the patient because of anxiety, and identification with the analyst is substituted for them. Because these processes, as a result of the similarity in the behavior of the analyst and that of the educating person in childhood, take the form of a repetition of the pathogenic process, the analyst must also dispose of this last hindrance to a different kind of reaction in the patient, must let fall the mask of "hypocrisy of professional activity," and must admit to the patient all impulses of a negative nature and all passagere indifference. This does not result in a negative reaction, by any means, but on the contrary, a "remarkable relief." Indeed, the whole equilibrium of the personality seems to be established thereby, as it says in Ferenczi's last work.

If we consider what the new technical implement of Ferenczi and his prescriptions for behavior mean for the analyst, we must say that it implies an almost superhuman participation with, adjustment to, agreement and sympathy with the patient, one might even say an acting out with him. Ferenczi himself describes his process as a kind of *pampering*, and in another place calls it *the principle of concession*. There is only *one* comparison which can be made, which Ferenczi himself chooses, that with the loving mother "who does not go to bed at night before she has talked over with her child all the unresolved great and small cares, anxieties, bad intentions, and scruples, and dispelled them in a calming way." (Int. Ztschr. f. Psa. XVII, s. 170). But Ferenczi's concern about the patient goes further than that of the tender mother often can, it means at least to go so far that he himself once said in the Viennese Psychoanalytic Society, half in earnest and half jokingly, that he could really have only one patient.

My next task is to demonstrate what, according to Ferenczi, the effect of applying this technical principle of maternal pampering is.

We have already spoken of one effect. It results from the request for relaxation and means a regression of the patient's Ego to an infantile level, that regression in which the analyst in "play analysis" must participate in order not to disturb the reactions of the patient. The patient, conscious of the watchful solicitude, well-wishing sympathy and readiness to sink with him in regression on the part of the analyst, trusts himself to sink into the past and to reproduce experiences from it. The manifestations of the patient soon become more naive and childish. Among the thoughts and pictorial ideas, little expressive movements and sometimes passagere symptoms appear more frequently. Finally, made possible by the atmosphere of trust and through the feeling of complete freedom in the analysis, states of withdrawal make their appearance, "trance states," as Ferenczi calls them with predilection, in which the patient acts out and the analyst has to act out along with him in order not to disturb the process. Paraesthesia, cramps in particular parts of the body, powerfully expressive movements, slight hysterical attacks, sudden shifts in the focus of consciousness, dizziness, clouding of consciousness accompanied by amnesia, and finally almost threatening comatose states can all be observed in these trances.

Ferenczi understands these manifestations to be physical memory symbols, so that in these trance states entire portions of the past are reanimated. In the trance state the physician forms the only link between the patient and reality. It remains possible for him to ask questions, and also to preserve information about parts of the personality which have been split off. He stands, therefore, in direct contact with the unconscious, which fact enables him to take the lead in an infantile conversation.

If we consider the processes described as taking place in the patient in their totality, the comparison with catharsis strikes all of us. Ferenczi does not hesitate to consider the trance reactions of his patients as *neo-catharsis*, and to describe them thus. Among his technical measures all the requisites for the introduction of a hypnotic-cathartic occurrence are given, thus in the maternal-hypnotic attitude of well-wishing, in the enticement into a return to the infantile, in the physical contact on a tender basis, such as holding the hand, stroking the head, etc. Ferenczi wishes first of all to establish an enormous difference between catharsis and neo-catharsis. It is his opinion that palaeo-catharsis leads only to fragmentary irruptions of emotions and memories with merely temporary efficacy. In neo-catharsis, on the other hand, the final remains of neurosogenic elements are brought into experience, to a recognition of their real nature and to acting out. Therefore this *regress* to catharsis really represents an essential *progress* in therapy. In the last work published during his lifetime, "Sprachverwirrung," Ferenczi was gradually forced to take back part of this distinction, because the relieving effect of acting out in the trance state did not appear, and powerful anxiety developed which nullified the result or at least made it questionable.

Ferenczi, however, did not waver, and advances the final technical demand for relinquishment of the hypocrisy of professional activity which copies and repeats the situations of childhood too closely. This relinquishment should consist in making clear just this contrast between the infantile situation and the repetition in neo-catharsis, through the confidence which the attitude of the analyst inspires in the patient, and thus makes a repetition of the infantile repression impossible. Here Ferenczi's work breaks off. Death took him before he was able to communicate more prolific and longer observations on the results of his latest technical discoveries.

And now finally as to the theoretical results of these procedures. They can be summed up in one phrase: *trauma redivivum*.

Ferenczi declares that through the memory material advanced or confirmed by the neo-catharsis the *original traumatic* factor in the aetiological equation of the neuroses once more attains to intensified significance. One even forms the impression from Ferenczi's last works that Ferenczi would like to elevate this factor to a primary, almost exclusive importance. Thus the sentence in the "Sprachverwirrung" that, "the trauma, particularly the sexual trauma, cannot be given emphasis enough as a factor in the cause of illness." One experiences in his works how much he himself is shaken by this conclusion and touched by it affectively. The trauma does not rest upon the traumatophilic sensibility of the child who is disposed to neurosis, which sensibility according to the opinion of analytic theory, experiences otherwise harmless and normal forces as traumatic and therefore irruptive, but consists rather of *real* unjust, unenlightened, capricious, tactless, or even cruel treatment by adults. The *tendency to incest*, masked as tenderness, of the adults, the manifestations of which operate upon the child as a trauma, immediately eclipses the neurosogenic significance of the Oedipus Complex in the child.

Ferenczi has new material on the direct effect of the trauma on the child.

The first impulse is one of rejection, of hate, of disgust, of powerful defense. But the horrible anxiety over the more powerful attacker forces the child to subject himself with complete passivity to the will of the former. This occurs primarily through a complete identification with him. In this manner even before the formation of the Super Ego guilt feeling developed in the child's psyche, namely along the path of introjection of the guilt feeling of the adult after the sexual attack. The effect of this shock experience is always a passagere psychosis, i.e., a turning away from reality associated with negative hallucinations of what has been experienced and with positive hallucinatory compensations of a pleasureful delusory character. The neurotic amnesia, perhaps also the usual childhood amnesia, is traceable to a psychotic splitting off of a part of the personality which occurs under the influence of the shock. This split off portion of the personality continues to live a hidden life, and it is possible in neo-catharsis to enter into a relationship with it, just in the form of the infantile conversation mentioned in connection with play analysis.

The significance of the trauma so overshadows everything else in Ferenczi that the instinctually conditioned components of the neuroses are relegated completely to the background. On the basis of this primary significance of the trauma to which he is so partial, Ferenczi makes a further scientific regression which leads him far back into pre-analytic times: he arrives at the theory of the innocence of the child. Trauma and seduction become to a considerable extent identical for him. The child is said to have, even when his play with adults takes on erotic forms, the consistent tendency to remain at the level of tenderness. It is the adult who first introduces the wishes of the mature sexual person to the child, and thus brings sensuality into play. "Genuine sensuality is foreign to the child," is the remark of one of Ferenczi's pupils in the Viennese Society. The consequences of the technical discoveries of Ferenczi extend this far.

The result of Ferenczi's new technical discoveries is, therefore, for him and his pupils, a new theory of neuroses, or more exactly, a reanimation of an abandoned portion of the theory of the neuroses, the theory of the trauma, and primarily of the infantile sexual trauma. From a broader standpoint of observation, beyond the pros and cons of this new theory *one* connection seems to me worthy of particular notice, a connection the significance of which Freud recognized very early.

The relationship between theory and technique was the subject of a prize essay awarded by Freud at the Berlin Congress in 1922. On the basis of this early insight of Freud that a reciprocal relationship exists, it can scarcely be wondered at that a renewed application of the cathartic method must lead to a reanimation of the traumatic theory of the neuroses. A more exact knowledge of the results achieved, which Ferenczi has not left us, would necessarily have much to say about this reciprocal relationship.

One might well expect that further works by Ferenczi's pupils, still under his direct influence or posthumously guided by his spirit will furnish us with details of this process and of its results, will make more accessible and extensive the understanding of Ferenczi's last struggles with the depths of the human mind, and will make us more certain in the critique of this last therapeutic contribution to analysis.

Aggression In The Rescue Fantasy

The increasing recognition of the significance of the aggressive tendencies in normal and above all in neurotic psychic processes, has in recent years led to a revision of the findings of psychoanalytic research with the result that in different psychic productions a new significance has been discovered. It has been seen that they are no longer to be considered as containing only positive libidinal tendencies but, almost without exception, negative destructive ones as well.

We investigate here the rescue fantasy for its aggressive content although the life-preserving, love-affirming attitude of the individual producing the fantasy towards the object to be rescued appears to contradict the presence of any aggressive intention.

Freud devoted some paragraphs to the rescue fantasy in his paper, Contribution to the Psychology of Love.[1] He showed there that the rescue fantasy primarily expresses the wish to *give back* to the parents the life which one owes to them, by rescuing one or both of them from danger of death. Where the mother is concerned, we find tender emotions mixed with the longing to be big and independent at the origin of the fantasy. If the son rescues the father in his fantasy there is an attitude of defiance expressed in it, a denial of the fact that one has to thank one's father for one's life. In what Freud said, we find the first indication of a *negative* component in the rescue fantasy which has not been elaborated in analytic literature.

The content, 'rescuing', expresses only a part of the complex fantasy, for the object to be rescued must first have been brought into the danger from which the producer of the fantasy is to save it. The adolescent who fantasies saving the king or the president from the danger of a murderous attack, only undoes the crime in his unconscious fantasy of having brought

---

Aggression and the Rescue Fantasy. *Psychoanalytic Quarterly*, 1940, 9, 505–508. Also in: Die Agression in der Rettungsphantasie. *Internationale Zeitschrift fur Psychoanalyse*, 1940, 25, 397–399.
[1] Freud: Coll. Papers, IV, p. 200.

the father substitute into danger. Clinical analytic investigations show us most clearly the unconscious aggressive content of the rescue fantasy.

A first example is taken from the analysis of an eighteen-year-old homosexual girl. The great difficulty in her analysis was her absolute refusal to give up the hope of becoming a boy. One day she was told that it would be necessary for her to accept her female anatomical constitution. The reaction was a protestation which one can only call grandiose. That evening she went out with a young man who was courting her and let him deflower her. There was severe bleeding which continued for four days, and she was therefore referred to a gynaecologist. He could find only a small erosion not important enought to account for the continuous bleeding and declared this to be psychogenic. It did not cease for a week and then menstruation began a week before the expected time (this patient had always had a regular period every twenty-eight days). The menstruation was prolonged from the usual three, to eight days. When it ceased, the patient had an attack of nosebleed during the analytic hour, which recurred during the two following hours. After this show of hostility against me, for such it was—reminding one of the superstitions of the Middle Ages when it was believed that the victim's wounds would begin again to bleed at the approach of the murderer—the patient told me the following dream.

> At a trial, the analyst is condemned to death. The execution finally depends on whether some women agree to it or not. An endless row of women pass by the judge's table, strange thin veils streaming from their heads. The situation is such that the women when they are asked if they agree that the analyst is to be beheaded, are compelled to say, 'I do'. At our patient's turn, she is the only one who dares to say, 'No', thus saving the analyst's life.

The dream is obviously a fantasy of rescue. Analysis however shows that the saving is merely a façade and the happy ending of a lie. The court has sentenced the analyst to death and the women are in favor of the execution. The patient's 'no' has another significance. The women with veils who are compelled in the dream to agree as they pass the table, are women at the wedding altar where the situation necessitates saying 'I do.' (The altar is called in Latin *mensa* which means 'table'.) This saving dream, then, shows itself in its deeper content to be a combination of protest and spiteful revenge. The aggression in the rescuing is obvious here.

Two minor examples illustrate the same. A patient, at a time when she feels rebuked by the analyst, produces the following fantasy of rescue.

There is a war and the analyst is badly wounded. The patient, a field nurse, finds him, a poor wreck of a human being, blind, without legs and arms. She saves him from further dangers which menace him and takes care of him. He could not have survived without her help and finally he sees how much she loves him and is grateful to her to the end of his life.

Here an interpretation is superfluous. Cruelty and revenge are too clearly expressed.

The next example is a slip of the tongue of a patient who begins to relate a rescue fantasy with the words: 'Doctor, I have had a rescue fantasy against you', instead of 'about you', thus betraying the aggressive content even before relating it.

Two further examples are given, the first from the analysis of a woman, the second an item found in a newspaper.

During puberty, a girl had seriously evolved the plan, in order to rescue him from military service, of creeping into her older brother's room while he was sleeping and quickly cutting off one of his fingers. She was greatly astonished at her father's anger when she related to him her plan.

In the New York Times of July 20, 1940, there appeared the following:

'A sleep-walking farmer killed his three-year-old daughter while dreaming he was saving her from a mad dog. He often walks in his sleep and is subject to nightmares. During a nightmare he dreamed that a dog was attacking his children, leaped from bed and snatched up his little daughter. When he swung her out of the dog's reach, the authorities said, her head struck the staircase and her skull was fractured. Then he went back to bed, still asleep. The farmer was not held and no charge was filed against him.'

These examples have been chosen from many. In my experience it is justifiable to look for some aggressive content in every rescue fantasy and I am convinced that it is to be found.

The Dynamics Of The Dissolution Of The Transference Resistance

In addition to the interpretation of the content of the unconscious, a considerable amount of the work in therapeutic analysis is required for the interpretation and dissolution of the resistances. Only through the dissolution of the resistances is it possible to interpret the content of the unconscious and to reconstruct the past.

We seek here to investigate the dynamics of the dissolution of a specific group of resistances called transference resistances. Transference resistances are of a peculiar importance, as they can be observed throughout the course of analysis and are very often the common ground on which other types of resistances find the possibility of expressing themselves.

Before we can approach the dynamics of the dissolution of these resistances, it will be necessary to acquaint ourselves with the dynamics of the development of these resistances. Let us repeat what Freud wrote about the origin of the transference resistance in his paper, The Dynamics of the Transference:

> 'Now as we follow a pathogenic complex from its representative in consciousness (whether this be a conspicuous symptom or something apparently quite insignificant) back to its root in the unconscious, we soon come to a place where the resistance makes itself felt so strongly that it affects the next association, which has to appear as a compromise between the demands of this resistance and those of the work of exploration. Experience shows that this is where the transference enters on the scene. When there is anything in the complex-material (the content of the complex), which can be at all suitably transferred

to the person of the physician, such a transference will be effected and from it will arise the next association; it will then manifest itself by the signs of resistance—for instance, a cessation in the flow of associations. We conclude from such experiences that this transferred idea is able to force itself through to consciousness in preference to all other associations, just *because* it also satisfies resistance. This type of incident is repeated innumerable times during an analysis. Over and over again, when one draws near to a pathogenic complex, that part of it which is first thrust forward into consciousness will be some aspect of it which can be transferred; having been so, it will then be defended with the utmost obstinacy by the patient.'[1]

The development of the transference resistance occurs, according to Freud's description, in this way: out of the material lying near to the preconscious, that part which is suitable for transference pushes itself forward into the consciousness and takes possession of the analyst. However, whether the analyst becomes a hated, a loved or a feared person in a particular situation, depends upon which relationship is favorable for the resistance, that is, for the prevention of the appearance of unconscious material.

In order to facilitate an understanding of what follows, it may be advisable to illustrate with a case history how the transference is established as a *resistance* against the investigating work of the analysis. The case I am now going to report is especially adapted to our investigation because a particular transference resistance formed the main obstacle to the progress of the treatment for a long period of the analysis. The patient was dismissed, free of his symptoms and with his character favorably changed after a two-year analysis.

This patient was a twenty-seven-year-old bank employee. When the analysis began he was out of work. He wanted to be treated for depression, general inactivity and headaches which were very painful at times. The principal symptoms were, however, difficulties with eating which had led to a considerable loss of weight. He had to chew every mouthful of food for a long time; fibrous meat and the skins of fruit he had to spit out, for when he tried to swallow them he became terrified that he would choke. For a long time after this symptom had made its appearance—fifteen months before the beginning of the analysis—he had lived only on milk

[1] Freud: Coll. Papers, II, 346

and chocolates. At the same time, he developed a sexual disturbance in the form of ejaculatio praecox. The patient was often constipated and had suffered from pruritus ani since his neurosis had broken out.

Characterologically the patient belonged to the group of passive feminine personalities; he was very submissive, very obedient to everyone and very fearful that he might injure somebody. He was extremely cowardly; sometimes however, though not very often, he would display an outbreak of blind hatred against persons of whom he was afraid, particularly against his superiors, but only when these persons were not present. In these attacks of rage and hatred, at a safe distance from the person causing his displeasure, he would express his emotions in the most violent manner, but the next time he encountered the person, he would behave as submissively and humbly as ever.

His symptoms were developing gradually when the patient's father became ill with angina pectoris two years before the analysis started; he died seven months before the beginning of the analysis. Following this event the symptoms became greatly intensified. The patient began to suffer from painful thoughts about death; he would imagine himself lying in his grave and every person he saw, even those sitting opposite him in the street cars, made him conjecture how long this person still had to live. The headaches and the depression increased greatly.

Subsequent to his father's death, he had lost large sums of money through bad speculations and loans. It was plain that he had an instinctual tendency to lose money and that money played a central rôle in his life. His every thought was directed towards making money and his fantasies were largely built around this theme. Money was also the central theme of a series of symptomatic acts which occurred in the latter part of his puberty. These consisted in stealing money from his mother in order to visit houses of prostitution. This money, however, his mother had secretly taken from his father who was very miserly, and who sometimes did not give her sufficient for household expenses. This act of stealing money with its attendant symbolism very soon came into the centre of the analytic situation.

The patient showed towards me the same servile and submissive attitude that he expressed towards everyone. He always said when talking about the analysis, 'I let myself be analyzed because . . . ' This description was the direct opposite of one used by a woman patient who was very masculine and narcissistic. When she spoke about her analysis, she always said, 'I am doing an analysis because . . . '

The patient was extremely anxious to follow the basic rule of analysis, but after a few weeks thoughts occurred to him which were tormenting. He tried very carefully to avoid them because they could have been considered as gibes and taunts at the analyst. For instance, when he saw my hat hanging in the hall, he thought, involuntarily, 'H'm, I don't like this hat', but he became very frightened by this thought because he knew the hat belonged to me and he felt he ought not to think anything bad about me or my things. Such associations occurred rarely at the beginning of the analysis, but later they occurred frequently. He became frightened of them and of the analysis, that is, of the analyst. This anxiety became so intense that his associations began to be blocked and the progress of the analysis was stopped, as he developed almost a prohibition of thinking. He had to avoid very carefully all references to me and my surroundings. When sitting in the waiting room, for example, he did not trust himself to look around as he was afraid that something in the room might strike him unpleasantly and this might be followed by a hostile thought about me.

This period was initiated by the following dream: he was being hunted by the police because he had embezzled money; he was very frightened. This was to be interpreted as a transference dream, the analyst being represented by the police. It soon became clear that he developed this anxiety due to a transference from the father to the analyst. The anxiety made it impossible for him to obey the fundamental rule because it blocked all associations which were directed against me. It hindered bringing into consciousness one of the most powerful emotions of his psyche—his hatred of his father. One can easily observe how the transference serves the resistance. This resistance is composed of the repression resistance, the resistance caused by the unconscious guilt feeling, and the resistance from the repetition compulsion. His fear of his father was the center of his neurosis. The fear of being choked while eating was closely connected with his fear of his father, for in this symptom the patient experienced an identification with the dying father as a punishment for the death wishes directed towards him. The father's fatal illness was an angina pectoris with attacks of choking, particularly during eating. Deeper down, however, the oral symptom was found to be an expression of defense against a libidinal relationship with the father, in which the patient was identified with his mother on a passive masochistic basis.

The analysis of the libidinal part of the symptom led us back to a childhood observation from his fourth year. The father, personally, used forcefully to stuff food into the geese which were owned by the family. Once the little boy was present when a goose choked in his father's hands during this cruel process. In the anxiety of being choked while eating solid foods, it is apparent that his castration fear was displaced to the oral zone as a result of putting himself in the passive feminine position, an identification with the choking goose (mother).

This patient's strong anxiety was thus brought into the analysis from the very beginning. The result of the development of this anxiety in which the analyst was made the father surrogate was to prevent the confession of just those emotional impulses as a result of which the anxiety originally developed. In many instances the result of a psychic action must also be considered as its motive. It becomes evident that fear of the analyst transferred from the father has been developed for the purpose of resistance. Moreover, we find a very similar reliving of an infantile fear during the transference, such as is described by Freud in the History of an Infantile Neurosis. There he writes:

> 'The first "transitory symptom" which the patient produced during the treatment went back to the wolf-phobia and to the fairy tale of "The Seven Little Goats". In the room in which the first sittings were held, there was a large grandfather clock opposite the patient who lay upon a sofa facing away from me. I was struck by the fact that from time to time he turned his face towards me, looked at me in a very friendly way as though to propitiate me, and then turned his glance from me to the clock. I thought at the time that, in this way, he was showing his eagerness for the end of the hour. A long time afterwards, the patient reminded me of this piece of dumb show and gave me an explanation of it; for he recalled that the youngest of the seven little goats hid himself in the case of the grandfather's clock while his six brothers and sisters were eaten up by the wolf. So what he meant was: "Be kind to me! Must I be frightened of you? Are you going to eat me up? Shall I hide myself from you in the clock-case like the youngest little goat?"'[2]

The fact that the recollection and reconstruction of this pantomime in the wolf-man's analysis took place only 'a long time after' it had been acted out indicates, although Freud does not point it out directly, that the transference of Freud's patient was at that time of a resistance character. We know from the duration of the analysis and from the supplement to the analysis by Ruth Mack Brunswick that the resistances of this patient were unusually strong and that they yielded finally only to the pressure of a fixed time limit. It is understandable from the ubiquity of the castration fear that anxiety often plays a most important rôle in the transference resistance.

---

[2] Freud: Coll. Papers, III, p. 511

Every infantile attitude against which the ego has necessarily to defend itself, may appear in the transference to serve the resistance. This is particularly true of the erotic tendencies of the positive and the negative oedipus complex, sadistic aggression, the pregenital instincts, and so on. Because the transference serves the resistance, the patient acts out infantile experiences to avoid conscious remembrance of them. This leads on the part of the ego to a defense which is directed against the analysis because the analyst has become, in the transference, the representative of the emotional tendency against which the ego has to defend itself. The transference thus serves the repression which the analysis aims to abolish. When our patient makes a father image of the analyst—acts towards him as he would towards his father—he has created the relationship in order to avoid remembering forbidden emotional trends towards the father. Freud writes in Recollection, Repetition and Working Through, 'The greater the resistance, the more extensively will expressing in action (repetition) be substituted for recollecting'.[3] By acting them out in the analysis, resistances, no matter from what source, become tranference resistances.

The analyst's task is to overcome this transference resistance which hinders the progress of the psychoanalytic process. The analyst thereby finds himself in a difficult situation, for he is the object of the emotional repetition operating in the patient in order to hinder the recollections for which the analyst asks. So the analyst has to contend with a vicious circle into which it is necessary for him to break. The analyst's only weapon is the interpretation of the resistance. An understanding of this acting out has necessarily to precede the interpretation of the resistance. The fact that the acting out, since it forms the transference resistance, contains the material against which the resistance arises, makes it possible for us to gain the understanding of the resistance which is necessary for the interpretation. In the manner of expression of the acted out psychic tendencies, in their temporal connection with certain accessory circumstances reported innocently by the patient, possibilities of understanding and recognition lie open to the analyst. Often transference dreams shed light on the particular infantile object and on what will be repeated in the analysis to serve the purpose of the resistance.

In this case, the transference became comprehensible very early. The symptomatic act which was reported in the fourth analytic hour—of stealing during puberty his father's money from his mother in order to visit prostitutes—and the dream of a few weeks later of the police wanting him on a charge of embezzlement, made the transference situation and the defense

[3]Coll. Papers, II, p. 370

against which it was developed immediately clear. This was so much clearer because the hatred which the patient directed against capitalists extended also to the police whose protection of the capitalists made him furious. His ego was defending itself against making the discovery of his own hostile wish to castrate his father. This defense took the form of anxiety because following the dream of embezzlement, the patient developed the fear that some hostile thought about the analyst might occur to him. He repeatedly found himself thinking he could steal some merchandise from a wholesale merchant who had befriended him by giving him large sums of money. He became greatly frightened over this thought because it was exceedingly painful to him to confess it in the analysis. He had frequently in his associations linked the analyst with this merchant in various dreams.

Soon after these connections were recognized, an interpretation of his transference resistance was made to the patient. It consisted of explaining to him, illustrated by the corresponding material, that he was acting towards the analyst as he had towards his father and that he was doing it, although unconsciously, in order to hinder the further progress of the analysis. The analyst tried to make it clear to him that the hostility towards his father, which to some extent was still not conscious, could not be analyzed if he developed the unconscious hostility and consequent anxiety towards the analyst that he formerly had for his father. His attention was drawn to the fact that his fear of hostile thoughts towards the analyst was a result of his inner inclination to such thoughts and proof of unconscious hostility to the analyst.

When an analyst interprets the transference resistance, he opposes the ego of the patient, as the organ controlling reality, to the instinctual activity reënacted in the transference. During the transference, the patient's ego is influenced by instinctual strivings of the id to which, in our case, it reacts with anxiety. The analyst assists the ego, attacked by the id, offering it the possibility of an identification which satisfies the reality testing needs of the ego. This identification of the reality testing parts of the patient's ego is made possible by the fact that the analyst continuously observes and interprets to the patient the psychological situation without prejudice.

The invitation to this identification comes from the analyst. From the beginning of treatment, comments are made by the analyst about the work they will have to accomplish in common during the cure. Many phrases such as, 'Let us recall what you dreamed, or thought, or did there', used by the analyst contain this invitation to identification with him as it is implied every time the analyst uses 'we' to refer to the patient and himself. This identification with the analyst is based first on the patient's wish for recovery and second on the positive transference. The latter plays the most important part. On the other hand however, unconscious parts of this libidinal factor can interfere with the therapeutic process.

In our patient, acceptance of the father's authority contributed much to the readiness for the identification, but the unconscious passive feminine attitude with the resulting danger of castration increased anxiety to a point where the positive transference operated in the direction of the transference resistance. This identification is based finally on a narcissistic satisfaction resulting from the participation in the intellectual work of gaining insight during the analysis.

The analyst therefore tries by means of interpretation to separate those parts of the patient's ego that face and assess reality, from another part which functions in carrying out the unconscious instinctual wishes, or works to suppress those wishes which create the anxiety reaction. By interpretation, the analyst keeps the reality testing parts of the ego from being flooded by the material reënacted from the past in the transference situation. The dynamics for this purpose are obtained by the analyst from the identification of the patient with himself. Through the interpretation the analyst tries to strengthen the ego, even if temporarily, against the instinctual acting out. The possibility of identification with the analyst—so necessary for the interpretation—is a *conditio sine qua non* for analytic treatment.

Separating the part of the ego occupied by the unconscious from its reality testing function cannot be accomplished with one interpretation but by long repetition. The interpretation may be strengthened in the meantime by the convincing power of newly emerging material. The identification grows through stronger support from the intellect, or becomes more efficacious through a libidinal reinforcement of the identification. Often the separation of the ego from instinctual activity in the beginning of the analysis lasts only a short time—perhaps only one analytic hour or a portion of an analytic hour—and acting out of instinctual drives immediately afterwards reasserts its dominance over the ego. In these short phases however in which acting out is interrupted with the aid of identification with the analyst, to this brief dynamic effect of temporary identification, a topographical change may be added: to the acted out material some recollection may rise to consciousness. With this topographical change the temporary strengthening of the ego through identification with the analyst becomes a permanent strengthening owing to the enlargement of the ego's control over hitherto inaccessible parts of the unconscious.

Comprehension of the analysis of the transference was not very great in the beginning with our patient. His ego was too greatly occupied with the defenses against the instincts and with the defense against anxiety. Interpretation, however carefully made, increased his anxiety and his submissiveness. Later he came to recognize the paralled between the feared father and the analyst and to recollect instances of fear of his father which to a great extent he had forgotten.

First he remembered the anxiety he had felt immediately after his father's death. He failed to arrive in time for the funeral—the father died abroad—although he could easily have been present, since he had known beforehand of the father's serious illness and approaching death. Next he remembered the first night he spent at home after his father's death and how, because of his fear, it was impossible for him to sleep alone. Finally, he recalled the terrible attack of anxiety he had when in going through his father's clothes he held in his hands the trousers which his mother told him his father had last worn. In horror he threw the trousers into a corner of the room and for twenty-four hours did not dare to reënter the room. He then related a strange event which had occurred during his puberty. He had masturbated since his fifteenth year, often with conscious fantasies about his mother. One day, when he was seventeen, he had a headache, went to bed and masturbated to get rid of it, but the headache grew worse and he felt miserable, dizzy and numb. He became feverish during the night, and the doctor called in the morning and declared the illness to be influenza.

The father was greatly distressed about this illness of his son whom he so much loved, and on the following day had a fainting attack with convulsions and foamed at the mouth. This was the first of a short series of attacks which the doctor diagnosed as epilepsy related to cerebral arteriosclerosis. Our patient attributed his own illness to the masturbation and had been afraid that the doctor in examining him would make the discovery. His reaction to the father's attacks was one of intense anxiety and a bad feeling of guilt, for unconsciously he connected the father's attacks too with his own masturbation through which he considered he had become ill, thus causing his father's excitation and worry. The temporal connection between his masturbation and the father's first epileptic attacks was taken as a manifestation of magic and owing to his constant death wishes, he identified the epileptic with the cardiac attacks. After this he refrained to a great extent from masturbating and also from stealing money. The father's attacks of angina pectoris he identified with the epileptic ones, thus connecting the death of his father with masturbation. Subsequent to the father's attacks of angina pectoris he ceased entirely to masturbate and it was then that the first neurotic symptoms appeared in the form of depression, fear of suffocation when eating, constipation and pruritus ani.

Through the repeated interpretations of the transference resistance, a first step was taken towards bringing the unconscious to consciousness, for the patient remembered his fear of his father. He did not however lose his fear of the analyst, but the process of controlling this anxiety was initiated by the fact that, through the interpretation, a part of the acted out material was transformed into recollection and thus the original object of the anxiety became distinctly recognized as such. Simultaneously the patient's feeling of hatred increased, not against the analyst towards whom he had become on the contrary more servile, but against capitalists and against the Christian race to which the analyst belonged and towards which the Jewish patient always felt hostile and at the same time fearful. It was not difficult to show him that he had displaced his hatred from the analyst to capitalists, and partly satisfied it by his racial hatred.

One day after he had had another outbreak against capitalism and in his rage had expressed the opinion that things could not be better until two hundred company directors had been hanged, he had the following dream: the analyst is standing beside his desk. He hurriedly sees and dismisses one patient after the other, talking to them in Czech. He earns a great deal of money.

The writing desk the patient recognized as that of his former director. He had always hated the Czech nation and my name is of Czech origin. The capitalist is to him a substitute for his own father, for the latter possessed the money the patient was obliged to steal in order to go to prostitutes (mother). The money in this case has the typical significance of the penis—the potency of the father.

A dream he had much later in his analysis confirmed this symbolic significance of money and merchandise in a most striking fashion. Following an outbreak in which he dared to insult the analyst quite openly, he dreamed that a police officer was handling him very roughly. The following day in the dream, he went to the same place to deliver some merchandise and as he handed over the goods from his sample case, he saw that they were all male sexual organs. This dream represents the development of his passive feminine character. It was possible for the patient to take the servile attitude which enabled him to eliminate every direct manifestation of hate because this attitude gave him a libidinous satisfaction which in the past he had obtained by the passive feminine surrender to his father and which was relived in the transference.

In comparison with the dream in which the patient is wanted by the police for embezzlement, the other dream in which the analyst standing at his writing desk is earning a great deal of money, shows the progress from anxiety to manifest hatred that is only hinted at first in dreams. This inner change caused by the continuous influence of the interpretation became much clearer in a symptomatic act which occurred in the sixth month of the analysis.

One day as the patient was leaving the analytic hour, he was accosted in the street by a man who wanted to sell him silk stockings at a very low price. The patient was sure that they were stolen goods, but depite or rather because of his, he went into a doorway with the man and bought six pairs of the stockings from him. Immediately afterwards he was afraid that I might have seen him from my window. In his unconscious, stealing and receiving stolen goods were identical; the neighborhood of my house and the time the incident had occurred which was just after the analytic hour, made the action appear to him as though it had been committed against me. On the same day he imposed on himself a punishment, a kind of symbolic castration. Then he discovered that the man had only given him three pairs of stockings instead of six, and that they were of very inferior material. Soon after he had given the stockings to his fiancée for whom he had bought them, he broke an object which he liked very much. He avoided for weeks afterwards going through the street where the incident had occurred—my apartment being also accessible from another street—because he was afraid the police might have seen him and arrest him for receiving stolen goods.

The patient repeats in the transference a symptomatic act of his puberty, the symbolic castration of the father, followed by anxiety and self-punishment. The progress from development of anxiety to acted-out manifestations of hatred and the active castrative wish corresponds to a dissolution of anxiety accomplished by two factors. First, the interpretation of the anxiety in the analytic transference serving the resistance. Consciousness of his fear of his father and the strengthening of the ego connected with it, made possible the dissolution of anxiety through recognition of the difference between reality and infantile fantasy. Second, the absence of any affective reaction on the part of the analyst is of important significance for the dissipation of the anxiety. The reaction of increased anxiety and passivity to the initial interpretation is related to the patient's expectation that the analyst would react with anger and retaliation to the discovery of the hatred which the patient felt for him. When this did not occur and when his increasing hatred against capitalists and the revelation of the fact that this hatred too was directed against the analyst and had merely been displaced, was also not followed by any rebuke or withdrawal of interest from the psychological situation—the objective observation and explanation still being carried on by the analyst—the patient was able to recognize that some of his anxiety was irrational. The interpretation was now able to be effective because infantile material was recollected and recognized as belonging to the suppressed and displaced hatred. The very lack of emotional reaction on the part of the analyst made it easier for the patient's ego to observe the transference in identification with the analyst on a reality basis. The analyst's objectivity showed that he considered the patient's hostility belonged not to the actual situation, but to the forgotten infantile past. We know however that just this lack of emotional reaction on the part of the analyst may afford an opportunity for the development of severe transference resistances. It serves excellently to establish a continuous reaction of disappointment in a patient. If this kind of disappointment had been experienced in childhood by the patient, it would often be repeated in the analysis, with the analyst as object, to serve the purpose of the resistance. It could only be overcome through the interpretation of the resistance character of the repetition by strengthening the ego through identification with the analyst.

The time required for the dissolution of resistances was discussed by Freud in his paper, Recollection, Repetition and Working Through.[4] There Freud speaks about the slight effect of a single interpretation of the resistance and about the necessity for repetition over a long period of time. This repetition is the 'working through' of resistances and is compared with the 'abreaction of quantities of affects.' When the analyst draws the patient's attention to his repetitive acting-out in the transference, the effort has often only a very momentary effect; the quantitative effect is a very slight one in comparison with the powerful mass of resistance. If we imagine the quantity of energy involved in a single interpretation in comparison with the enormous quantity of transference resistance, we can apply to the situation the physical principle of energy in the following formula: work = energy $\times$ distance. According to this formula the work of the dissolution of the resistance by means of the slight effect of our interpretation can only be accomplished when the distance is correspondingly great; therefore the distance, in our case expressed in time, for the 'working through' of the transference resistance is necessarily a long one.

The quantity of the transference resistance is to a great extent dependent on the quantity of other resistances. Resistances have the tendency to accumulate wherever there is a favorable opportunity to withstand the analysis. In most cases the transference offers the best opportunity. In the case used for illustration, for example, we see that the resistance coming from the compulsive repetition, from the unconscious feeling of guilt and from the resistance by repression, takes part in building up the transference

[4]Freud: Coll. Papers., II, p. 366

resistance. Freud speaks of the transformation of resistances into negative, hostile transferences;[5] it is on account of this transformation that the dissolution of the transference resistance so often becomes the chief task of the therapeutic work. In the case of our patient, the analysis finally showed the development of anxiety in the transference to be castration anxiety which had arisen from infantile masturbation with accompanying incestuous wishes towards the mother and the hatred and castration wishes towards the father. In the analytic situation, the same castration anxiety developed which had been the reason for the repression of the infantile masturbation. Thus this infantile masturbation is the last determining factor in the development of anxiety in the analysis. If the resistance resulting from this anxiety is augmented by the addition of other resistances, then the final resistance in the analysis cannot be considered as an index to the amount of the genuine infantile anxiety: for the anxiety resulting from infantile masturbation, on account of its particular capacity for being used as a resistance in analysis, becomes the nucleus of crystallization or the basis for the addition of all the other resistances. In a footnote to his paper The Dynamics of the Transference, this idea was alluded to by Freud. The footnote I shall quote belongs to the following sentence in the text: 'Over and over again, when one draws near to a pathogenic complex, that part of it which is first thrust forward into consciousness will be some aspect of it which can be transferred; having been so, it will then be defended with the utmost obstinacy by the patient.' The footnote says: 'From which however one need not infer in general any very particular pathogenic importance in the point selected for resistance by transference. In warfare, when a bitter fight is raging over the possession of some little chapel or a single farmhouse, we do not necessarily assume that the church is a national monument, or that the barns contain the military funds. Their value may be merely tactical; in the next onslaught they will very likely be of no importance.'[6]

The dissolution of the transference resistance means then not only the dissolution of the resistance resulting from the genuine infantile castration anxiety but also a liberation of the supporting resistances which often can only later be separately dissolved, because during the phase of the violent acting-out in the transference these resistances are not accessible to interpretation and dissolution. I have the impression that the supporting resistances do not cause an increase of the anxiety, though they do make it more refractory to dissolution in the analysis. The problem of quality will have to be the subject of a further examination.

[5] Freud: *Introductory Lectures on Psycho-Analysis*. Allen & Unwin. 1922, p. 379.
[6] Coll. Papers, II, p. 317.

The Relaxation of the Analyst

It is possible that the title of this paper may give the misleading impression that it is about the problem of the mental and physical hygiene of the analyst in his free time. However this is not so; it deals with the mental relaxation of the analyst during the analytic hours and with a certain psychic attitude which I regard as indispensable to the analyst in the analytic situation; it is therefore of a technical nature and is concerned with the theory of psychoanalytic therapy, more particularly with what may perhaps be called the theory of the "counter-resistance." I would like to point out from the beginning that what I have to say is not new; I am going to repeat and emphasize things so well known to psychoanalysts that they are often too easily forgotten.

The first publications on the subject of relaxation in psychoanalytic therapy appeared eleven years ago; they were the work of Ferenczi and dealt with a certain state of relaxation which, according to his own description, was so profound that it led to auto-hypnotic conditions and violent acting-out of early infantile traumatic material. Ferenczi's *neocatharsis*, brought about by the profound relaxation which he induced in his patients, had to be rejected by psychoanalysis, since psychoanalytic therapy is based first and foremost on self-mastery through objective self-observation and better instinctual control upon the part of the Ego, and only to a minor degree upon the cathartic discharge in the analytic situation.

In my report on Ferenczi's last technical papers at the Vienna Vierländertagung—Four nations meeting—in 1935,[1] I expressed the critical attitude of psychoanalysis towards his last therapeutic attempts, and yet

---

†Read at the forty-third annual meeting of the American Psychoanalytic Association 5 May 1941, at Richmond, Virginia.
The Relaxation of the Analyst, *Psychiatry*, 1941, *4*, 339–342.

[1] Das psychische Trauma und die Handhabung der Uebertragung. Die letzten Arbeiten von S. Ferenczi zur psychoanalytischen Technik [The Psychic Trauma and the Handling of the Transference. The Last Contributions of Sándor Ferenczi to Psychoanalytic Technique.] *Internat. Zeitschr. f. Psychoanalyse* (1936) 22:40–46.

I found that the study of these and my own earlier personal contact with Ferenczi had left stamped upon my mind a deep impression of the intensely human quality in his relationships to his analysands. Anyone who had once heard Ferenczi talk about his patients, or had come to him personally for advice, was always greatly affected by his friendliness and sincerity, by his complete freedom from tension and by the naturalness with which he came to the help of those who sought it. It was not only his kindliness which charmed; perhaps more than anything else it was his calm and the inner security which one felt to be expressed in his behaviour. Without these qualities he would neither have been able to induce nor to endure the profound relaxation of his patients—a relaxation so profound as to enable them to regress sometimes almost to psychotic manifestations during the analytic hour.

Ferenczi's therapeutic successes are indisputable; there is no doubt he was one of the most brilliant therapists in psychoanalysis. In my opinion much of his therapeutic success was due to his own personal constellation, the essential elements of which can and should be attained in some degree by every capable analyst. The principal element in this personal constellation is expressed in what I call "the *relaxation* of the analyst." This relaxation is based on a complete freedom from anxiety on the part of the analyst in regard to his patients and particularly in regard to the manifestations of their unconscious.

In order to understand how essential it is that the analyst should have a relaxed, tension-free attitude towards those of the patient's manifestations which are directed against him, we must again make clear the function of the analyst in analytic therapy. The most important factor in the patient's relationship to the analyst is what we term the *transference*, which as we know means the repetition of emotional experiences of early childhood, with the analyst as substitute-object. The transference is, of all the factors in the analytic situation, the most valuable source of knowledge to the analyst. In a paper entitled *The Fate of the Ego in Analytic Therapy*,[2] which I read at the Congress at Wiesbaden in 1932, I demonstrated that is is the analyst's aim to create a division in the analysand's Ego. This division or dissociation is established by means of the following process: that part of the patient's Ego which is concerned with testing reality is brought into identification with the analyst in order to observe objectively, in cooperation with the analyst, the other elements of the Ego which are cathected—laden, or charged—with instinctual or defensive energy. It is

---

[2] Das Schicksal des Ichs im therapeutischen Verfahren [The Fate of the Ego in Therapeutic Procedure]. *Internat. Zeitschr, f. Psychoanalyse* (1934) 20:66–73. The Fate of the Ego in Analytic Therapy. *Internat. J. Psychoanal.* (1934) 15:117–126.

mainly through the establishment of this therapeutic cleavage in the Ego that the analyst is able to induce the patient to recognize the transference phenomena as what Freud calls "a reflection of a forgotten past."[3]

The objective, observant attitude of the analyst, free from all affective reactions, is therefore an essential condition in the therapeutic process. In this paper I want to say something against this attitude, nothing which will attack it in principle, but rather which will restrict it and lessen the element of hardness in it. Scientific progress, as we know, very often takes place in this dialectical way.

The objective attitude of the analyst can easily be carried too far and the consequences to the analysis may then perhaps be graver than the occasional acting-out of the analyst in an incontrolled counter-transference. I have observed this in my own experience of patients who have come to me after having already been analyzed by someone else. From these analysands one can, in my opinion, learn a great deal about the various analytical techniques and about the difficulties we analysts have to overcome in ourselves in dealing with our patients.

There are some analysts who, no matter what may be the manifestations of the patient, always maintain the same interpretative, observant attitude. They are not interested in the person and his emotional conflicts, but only in the manifestations of his unconscious for which they are tirelessly on the lookout. Their interpretative zeal, their constant eagerness to interpret, hardly allow for the emergence of an infantile instinctual impulse in the transference, since any material which appears in the analytic situation is immediately choked by interpretation. Such analysts are not unlike cats lying in wait at the mouse-hole, and this attitude certainly leaves no possibility for a study of the free behaviour of the infantile impulses.

Another form of, let us say, defense on the part of the analyst against the infantile material which is emerging and being established in the transference, does not express itself in the action of immediate interpretation, but rather in the analyst's whole attitude, which can best be described as "keeping the patient at a distance." Through this attitude, every impulse which, in the transference, is directed against the analyst is, from the outset, instinctively thrust aside, as though the analyst's entire Ego were protesting against the instinctual manifestations directed against him. This attitude is not expressed in the words used by the analyst, for often what he says may seem to be in agreement with the patient's manifestations and yet the latter feels, by intangible signs, the defense the analyst is inwardly setting up against the unconscious material. One European analyst who,

[3] Freud, Sigmund, *Beyond the Pleasure Principle;* London, International Psycho-Analytical Press, 1922 (90 pp.); p. 18.

as a matter of fact, subsequently became psychotic, developed this kind of defense to such a degree that one of his female patients could not help being aware of his shrinking back each time she mentioned her positive feelings for him and her pleasure sensations. His repeated response, "This is no pleasure couch," confirmed this and forced her to repeat her infantile repressions. Any allusion she made to the analyst's body seemed to affect him as though it were a personal sexual attack. No wonder the analysand abandoned this analysis in a more neurotic state than when she had begun it. This extreme and pathological case shows in grotesque exaggeration what is manifested by some analysts in a lesser degree, namely, a lack of relaxation which can only have a detrimental effect on the analysis. A tense, defensive attitude on the part of the analyst represents an exact repetition of the attitude of parents and of adults in general to infantile sexuality, and therefore compels the patient to repeat his infantile repressions. Freud says in his *Introductory Lectures:* "The decisive part of the work is carried through by creating—in the relationship to the physician, in 'the transference'—new editions of those early conflicts, in which the patient strives to behave as he originally behaved, while one calls upon all the available forces in his soul to bring him to another decision."[4] But we shall have to admit that the analyst whose attitude is not relaxed, owing to inner tension through defense, is not psychically capable of forcing the patient to change his attitude towards his own instinctual demands.

I have noticed that, strangely enough, behaviour such as I have described, does not usually result in a negative attitude on the part of the patient towards the analyst, but that, on the contrary, the transference in such a case grows beyond all bounds, the analyst looms as big and important as the parents were, or appeared to be during that childhood period when the main repressions took place. The above mentioned patient was, after three years of analysis with the "repressing analyst," so imbued with his personality, he was a figure of such vast importance to her that when she came to me she was deeply disappointed because my attitude did not afford her the opportunity for as much worship and awe as she had been able and was indeed obliged to develop towards her analyst in her first analysis. A tense, unrelaxed attitude on the part of the analyst is bound to release anxiety in the patient, making it impossible for him to lessen his defense and to transform the ethical norms of his childhood to the reality of the world of adults.

The establishment of the therapeutic cleavage of the Ego by means of the attitude of observation introduced by the interpretation is only a part

[4] Freud, Sigmund, *A General Introduction to Psycho-Analysis;* New York, Liveright, 1935 (403 pp.); in particular, p. 395.

of the work of handling the transference, which is, as psychoanalysts know, one of the most difficult tasks in analytic therapy. Each time an interpretation of an infantile impulse is made, it is bound to have the effect of a frustration because the infantile wish is confronted with the impossibility of its fulfillment in the world of reality. The attitude of the analyst should give the patient the possibility of changing the infantile instinctual aims to real ones in the outside world; he must for a time permit free play to the repetitive infantile tendency, he must be able to endure being the temporary object of this infantile impulse.

Freud says: "We admit it into the transference as to a playground, in which it is allowed to let itself go in almost complete freedom and is required to display before us all the pathogenic impulses hidden in the depths of the patient's mind."[5] But we can only offer the patient the freedom of this playground if we ourselves are relaxed in our attitude towards him, if anxiety does not compel us to defend ourselves against his instinctual claims and if we are able, on the contrary, temporarily to adapt ourselves to them. We can extend Ferenczi's demand for elasticity of analytic technique to a demand for considerable elasticity in the analyst's attitude.

Relaxed behavior, however, is also necessary from another standpoint in the therapeutic process of analysis. We have already mentioned that the analyst has to act as mediator between the objects of the infantile desires and the adult world of reality. The patient tries to compel him to play the part of the infantile object in order to obtain instinctual satisfaction as well as help for his instinctual defense. Since the analyst has to try to guide the patient's tendencies towards reality, he must not merely *preach* reality, he must *represent* and *be reality*. I am of the opinion that within the limits of the classical analytical technique it is legitimate and indeed indispensable that the analyst should not content himself with being impersonal, but must sometimes behave as a very real human being to his patients. It may be necessary occasionally for the analyst to show the patient a part of his own real world, because this will allow the patient to see that the analyst is not a superman but a fallible being like himself, who also meets with personal difficulties against which he has to struggle and which cannot be made to vanish by magic.

The patient's over-estimation and aggrandizement of the analyst must

---

[5] Freud, Sigmund, Further Recommendations in the Technique of Psycho-Analysis. Recollections, Repetition and Working Through. *Collected Papers;* London, Hogarth Press (1933) 2:366–376; in particular, p. 374. The original German of Sigmund Freud might well be translated to read: "We offer the transference to the patient as a playground for his repetitive tendencies, where he is allowed to let himself go in almost complete freedom and is required to display before us all the pathogenic impulses hidden in the depths of his mind."

inevitably be reduced. This is a painful process to the patient; it may also sometimes cost the analyst an effort to restrain his own narcissism sufficiently to reduce to normal the patient's oversize image of him, and many of the patient's instinctual demands will become more urgent once the analyst appears as a human being like himself. Here too, the analyst's freedom from anxiety is an essential condition in the treatment of the transference—it should indeed be certain that when anxiety does come up in the analytic situation the analyst is not the one to develop it. This is indispensable, not only in order to obtain the best results from our therapy, but also if we are to preserve from stultification the analytic findings in regard to the origin of neurosis and particularly Freud's discovery of the importance of the instinctual forces in childhood and neurosis.

We know how intimate is the relationship between analytic technique and theory and how Freud himself considered this relationship so important that he offered a prize for the best study on the subject. If the analyst, for reasons within himself, has to set up a defense against the recognition of the instinctual processes in the patient, he will rationalize this defense by changing his theoretical conception of the neurotic process. The paths that are then taken are usually "old ways of non-psychoanalysis," to which we can apply what Freud said about the theories of Adler and Jung in his *History of the Psychoanalytic Movement:* " . . . they have caught a few cultural" and we may add sociological, "overtones from the symphony of life, but once more have failed to hear the most powerful melody of the impulses."[6]

I think that we who are followers of Freud are all conscious that even in our own ranks we have to struggle to preserve the integrity of Freud's findings. The most important weapon in this struggle is the re-discovery of Freud's findings in the analyses we ourselves are accomplishing and which we help others to accomplish. Our duty seems to me to be to acquire the relaxed therapeutic attitude which alone can enable us to accept, and to help our analysands to accept the truth fought for and won by the genius of Freud.

---

[6] Freud, Sigmund, The History of the Psychoanalytic Movement, Brill, A. A. [ed.], *The Basic Writings of Sigmund Freud;* New York, The Modern Library, 1938 (vi and 1001 pp.); pp. 933–977—in particular, p. 974.

The Abuse of Interpretation

In this paper I shall attempt to deal with the unconscious reasons for the practice, to be found particularly among more inexperienced analysts, of interpretation outside of psychoanalytic situations. Such extra-analytic interpretation usually serves no useful purpose whatsoever. On the contrary, it often results in damage of one sort or another. It would seem beneficial therefore, to investigate the nature of the motivations leading towards such behavior: an understanding of these motivations may, on the one hand, help some of those who are guilty of such conduct to bring their behavior under better control; and, on the other hand, some understanding of these matters might assist those who are the victims of such irresponsible interpretation to avoid certain of the evil effects which it is apt to occasion.

From the viewpoint of method, the essential thing about psychoanalysis is that it attempts to discover hidden meaning behind the manifest phenomena of the mind: it is an *interpreting* process. It follows from this that the most important task of psychoanalytic therapy lies in the interpretation of manifest thinking and behavior in terms of the hidden, unconscious meaning latent in them. Accordingly, technical interest was very early directed towards facility in interpretation and towards an understanding of the effect of interpreting. The beginner in psychoanalysis was given careful suggestions along these lines; in fact, Freud himself, from his rich clinical experience, gave advice designed to instruct the beginner as to the proper use at the proper time of this most important of psychoanalytic instruments.

One of the most indispensable of these counsels is to the effect that an interpretation should not be given until the ego of the analysand is in a condition to endure it, to accept it and to make some use of it, at least in the sense of working it over in his own mind. The necessity for a state of *rapport* with the ego of the patient has become one of those things which

†Read at the forty-second annual meeting of the American Psychoanalytic Association 19 May 1940, at Cincinnati, Ohio. Translated from the German by William V. Silverberg.
The Abuse of Interpretation, *Psychiatry*, 1941, 4(9), 9–12.

we take for granted, especially now that the psychology of the ego has assumed so important a rôle in psychoanalysis.

If we make the attempt to get into closer contact with some unconscious tendency which has become known to us through certain of its derivatives in the patient's productions, we begin to feel resistance to our efforts: this resistance is the self-defense of the ego. The fact that this resistance is for the most part unconscious and that therefore it enters into the analytic situation without the conscious awareness of the patient, was what led to the recognition of unconscious parts of the ego, as Freud described in *The Ego and the Id*. As a result of this recognition, our knowledge of the psychology of the superego and its repressive function was enormously enriched.

An appreciation of these facts has the logical consequence that, in our therapeutic attempts, our first effort must be to draw the patient's attention to this resistance, of which he is not aware, and to place it before him as a problem for conscious consideration. This first step leads the patient inevitably to the question as to what he is defending himself from, and thus points the way to the second step of the therapeutic process; namely, the uncovering of the unconscious id tendency which has all along been the object of defense; and, as we proceed farther, the discovery of what the origin and vicissitudes of this tendency have been in the early stages of the patient's life.

It may thus indeed be said that psychoanalysis has recovered from its own case of measles, which consisted in trying to interpret the unconscious directly, without first analyzing the resistance set up by the patient's ego. Careful training in the various institutes is helping the beginner to omit, in his ontogenesis as a psychoanalytic therapist, the phylogenetic stage of 'wild' id interpretation through which psychoanalysis passed in its beginnings. The student analyst is, from the onset of his training, encouraged to consider first and foremost the ego side of the analysand and to apply his interpretations with great circumspectness.

It is therefore all the more striking that a number of psychoanalysts are inclined to neglect this consideration for the ego of another in their daily lives, outside the analytic situation. We can all think of young analysts, and perhaps a few not so young, who, outside the analytic room, drop completely that hesitancy to rush in with interpretations which is demanded by consideration for another's ego and its defenses. Such 'wild analysts outside the analytic situation,' if I may be permitted this expression, interpret in their own families, among their friends, in society and to the public. Wherever they can make an interpretation, they do so, under the spell, as it were, of a *furor interpretandi*. The harm they do is almost incalculable. In order to grasp this we must understand thoroughly the deeper effects of interpretation.

In the first place, interpretation in analysis has the effect and, indeed, the purpose of awakening in the patient a mistrust of himself. This self-mistrust constitutes one of the most effective means of bringing the patient to an attitude of mind favorable to therapy. It is a prerequisite for self-observation, for that cleavage in the ego which forms the basis for the therapeutic process. The result of this self-mistrust in the therapeutic situation is a focusing upon those neglected derivatives of the unconscious which would otherwise be quickly dispelled from the periphery of consciousness. In therapy this self-mistrust leads to the discovery of the infantile sources of various drives, as well as the corresponding infantile defenses, and towards a synthesis within the ego in which the repressions of one's past life are incorporated into one's present consciousness. When an analyst outside the analytic situation gives interpretations of some individual's behavior or verbal productions—be the interpretation right or wrong—a source of self-mistrust is created in this person; and, since he is not in an analytic situation, he cannot be given the opportunity to make that synthesis which would heal this cleavage, an opportunity which would later on be available to a patient under analysis. The result is apt to be a disturbance of the individual's naturalness—he is apt to become too aware of his own behavior—and for this he will take revenge in the form of hostile impulses of one sort or another towards the interpreter, unless he finds an outlet in elaborating the interpretation in a masochistic manner—that is to say, by regarding the interpretation as a sadistic attack upon him and reacting to this with masochistic enjoyment.

A second effect of interpretation results quite often in even more profound disturbance. This depends upon the fact that every interpretation of an unconscious mechanism signalizes a frustration. Unconscious tendencies, as is well known, stand in sharp antithesis to the conscious ego. If interpretation endeavors to bring the unconscious tendency into the view of the conscious ego,—and this is indeed the purpose of interpretation—then one of two things must happen: either the ego must undertake vigorous defensive measures—defenses familiar to us in analysis as resistances,—or else, if there is a too great submissiveness towards or dependence upon the interpreter, the ego must turn against the impulses thus brought into awareness by interpretation and suppress any expression of these impulses. This instinctual frustration, which results from every interpretation, must bring about a serious disturbance in the relationship of the individual to the analyst interpreting in this wild and dilettante fashion. Anyone who has undertaken the analysis of one of the victims of this extra-analytic *furor interpretandi*—and I have repeatedly seen such victims among patients from psychoanalytic circles—knows what psychic misery and impotent hatred such irresponsible interpretations bring about, no matter how accurate they may be.

The fact that so many analysts show such a striking want of psychoanalytic common sense—or, indeed, of any common sense whatever—that they cast this, so to speak, to the four winds, should be a matter for serious thought. This lack of restraint in interpreting is often observable in analysts when they address lay audiences or write for the general public. In such circumstances they are often defective in that 'psycho-diplomacy' which they have so readily at their disposal within the analytic situation. If a surgeon were to use his scalpel upon those about him in so indiscriminate, so gratuitous and so unnecessary a fashion, it is obvious what measures the public would have to take with regard to him. A similar abuse of psychoanalytic interpretation not infrequently results in hostile rejection by the outside world, exactly as if the interpreter were an aggressor. This reaction is more violent than what we should regard as the public's 'natural' opposition to the facts of psychoanalysis, because, in addition to this, the public is reacting to the attitude of the analyst himself. One common result of this is the limiting of the social circle of many analysts to their own analytic group, as no one else will have anything to do with them.

Such an attitude, which unquestionably damages the individual analyst as well as the whole psychoanalytic movement and which is counter to all reason, must be traceable to unconscious motivations. As a result of our experience with such behavior and with psychic processes in general, we should expect that the attitude described would be the resultant of a combination of motivating forces. The first and most superficial of these is easy to determine. It is a displacement or substitute satisfaction for an attitude in which, on the basis of our training and our knowledge of the psychology of the ego, we cannot permit ourselves to indulge in the analytic situation. All analysts know how difficult it is sometimes, particularly at an early stage of training, to restrain ourselves from making interpretations: we are in the position of the child who has suffered pain at the hands of the dentist or the doctor and seizes the first opportunity to repeat upon others in an active form what has been experienced passively. This the child will do, whether such behavior is appropriate to the external circumstances or not. The joy of discovery, the pleasure of rediscovering what Freud has described, often brings in its train an eagerness to communicate this to others which may with difficulty be restrained. It requires a good deal of energy for the beginner to refrain from 'wild' interpretation within the analytic situation itself. The familiar mechanism of displacement results in a tendency on his part to indulge in aggressive interpretation in the outside world as soon as his therapeutic conscience no longer places upon him the obligation of self-restraint.

As a second motivating force for the tendency to interpret outside of analytic situations we may mention the strong feeling of superiority which characterizes many analysts. There can be no doubt that an accurate comprehension of psychoanalytic concepts can confer upon the individual a certain advantage over those who do not possess this insight. There is a primitive joy in 'knowing better' and in displaying this which forms part of the motivation of 'showing off' in the form of extra-analytic interpretation. It may indeed be doubted whether it is actually an accurate and profound insight into others that leads to this practice of unconsidered interpreting outside the analytic situation. Insight that is deep and true ought to make us wise, and if insight does not give us wisdom, then the fault lies in deeper emotional factors.

So I come to a third motivating force, the most important one in determining this reckless and dangerous behavior. It has become more and more common for students of psychoanalysis to return, after a time, for some revision of the original training analysis. It is in such revision-analyses that the experiences have occurred which have given me insight into this third type of motivation. Astonishing as it may sound, this motivation is of *a religious nature*. A dream of a young analyst who showed a marked tendency towards extra-analytic interpreting, and who, after a period of psychoanalytic practice, came to me for some post-analytic work, demonstrates very clearly the religious motivation for such behavior. The dream consisted of a single picture: he sees the Angel of the Lord bringing the glad tidings to the shepherds, but the scroll, instead of the words *Gloria in excelsis*, bears the device *Interpretation*.

At this point the special subject of this paper impinges upon a general problem which psychoanalysis, like all the other sciences, has to face. We should like, so far as this is practicable, to be able to confine ourselves to the special field of abnormal behavior and its concomitants. But Freud, to a greater degree than any of his scientific predecessors, has applied the keen blade of psychological investigation to many religious concepts: he has been uncompromising in his 'scientific agnosticism,' as I once heard him term his attitude towards the problems of religion. Like scientific concepts in general, psychoanalytic concepts stand in sharp antithesis to religious doctrines. This conflict appears in every individual analysis and may be resolved in any one of a variety of ways; or, not infrequently, it is not resolved and continues to exist as a conflict. It is especially true of the analyses of students training for psychoanalysis that these analysands must pass through a stage at which their egos are exposed to a painful conflict between conscious or unconscious religious convictions of an emotional character and their scientific knowledge. This struggle sometimes terminates in a repression of the religious emotions and convictions. We should then not be at all surprised to find the repressed religious factor returning in precisely that form of activity which had brought about the repression; namely, in the work of interpreting in psychoanalytic therapy. Thus we find the self-confidence of the young analyst magnified into the fanatical self-assurance of the religious sectarian, as he hurls interpretation like a burning firebrand among the infidels. We may then regard the effect of this attitude—the fanatical analyst's segregation to his own professional group—as an indication of the motivation that leads to the assumption of the attitude. The group thus receives the character of a secret society in which interpretation is the abracadabra known to all the initiates while outsiders are regarded as ignorant infidels.

And finally, we cannot help regarding the damage caused by such behavior as one of its motivating factors. This is the way in which the inadequately analyzed person revenges himself upon analysis and its founder for the disillusionment that analysis has occasioned him in many spheres, not least of these the religious.

The death of Sigmund Freud has delegated to his pupils a grave and difficult task. They have the obligation of maintaining and handing on not only the knowledge they have through him, but also the cleanness, the agnostic sincerity of his scientific attitude. The manner in which each one of us solves the conflict between religion and science is, ultimately, his own affair. We know that there are various possible modes of solution, among which the mechanism of isolating the conflict within the ego is the most important. But the training analysts among us have the obligation to safeguard so far as lies within our powers, our training analysands from the pitfall of an unsuccessful solution to this conflict: repression, with a return of the repressed in the form of interpreting activity which can only damage them, their analysts and the cause of psychoanalysis in general.

The Significance of a Missed Diagnosis

The following segment of an analytic case history seemed worthwhile reporting because of its professional interest. The deepest motives of the patient's symptoms were not recognized until long after they had disappeared. The patient, a physician, had developed such a personal interest in psychoanalysis and had so recognized the importance of further analysis for the understanding of his own patients and for the development of his personality that he contined his analysis to the end, although the symptom which had forced him into analysis had practically disappeared during the first year of treatment. He stayed in analysis for two years more. Only at the very end of his third year of analytic treatment was much of the material connected with the formation of his symptom brought to consciousness.

The patient came to analysis because he had recently suffered from anxieties which disturbed him to such an extent that he could hardly carry on his practice. Any of the more difficult problems with his patients, any complicated diagnosis, minor operations and particularly an obstetrical case threw him into a panic. He had to seek the mental help of physician friends, avoided patients with whom he expected difficult problems and thus saw his practice shrinking. This condition had lasted for half a year when someone advised him to undergo an analysis.

The incident leading to the outbreak of the neurosis was a professional negligence of which he had been guilty. He had been called to see a child who had a high temperature. He examined the boy, but neglected to look at his ears. He could find no cause for the child's condition, made a diagnosis of influenza without symptoms and medicated him accordingly. The following day the mother called up the physician and told him that she had gone to an ear specialist because the child had complained of pains in his ear. The specialist had found an acute infection of the middle ear and had punctured the ear-drum. Quantities of pus had come out of the ear, the child was relieved of the pain and the fever fell soon after. The mother sounded reproachful and did not ask the doctor to come again. He knew that he had lost the family as patients. He felt extremely guilty, reproached himself bitterly for his negligence, called himself a poor doctor, expected to lose all his patients and from then on developed increasing anxiety.

It was easy to recognize from the analytic material that the patient's anxiety arose mainly from the unconscious part of his relationship to his father, and not to this single professional slip. But the analytic discovery of this relationship met with great resistance. We are used to meeting resistances when we try to undo the repression which has taken place in early childhood. This repression was established for good reasons. These reasons are of an emotional kind and consist in painful experiences, anxieties and feelings of guilt and shame which the child goes through while growing up. These painful experiences are, after all, the same means that we use in education when we try to make our children give up undesirable activities and tendencies. Originally caused by the parental authorities, these painful affects are soon produced automatically when the moral demands of the surroundings have been incorporated into the mind through the process of super-ego formation and they continue the educator's influence on the child. These unpleasant memories and feelings are re-awakened in psychoanalysis when we try to bring back to consciousness the unwanted desires which have been checked by them. They cause resistances against the progress of our uncovering therapeutic work during analysis.

The most intense strivings of childhood are the desires of the Oedipus complex, consisting of sexual yearnings for the parent of the opposite sex and hostile, destructive wishes against the parent of the same sex. In the male child these are repressed mainly through anxieties which are connected with his sexual organ. The Oedipus tendencies find their physical expression in infantile masturbation. When the parents find out about this masturbation they are very much concerned about it and try to make the boy give it up as quickly as possible. The means they use for this purpose is the arousal of anxiety again by threats uttered against the little boy's penis, such as that they will cut it off or that it will rot away if he continues to masturbate. The little boy estimates his organ very highly on account of its pleasure value, approximately as highly as we adults value our eyes, and he makes great efforts under the influence of this castration anxiety to give up his masturbation and his Oedipus wishes. Castration anxiety is one of the most important pathogenic factors in the neurosis of the male individual. It is often psychologically enforced by traumatic experiences during the Oedipus phase, as, for example, operations, accidents, or observations of cruel and destructive acts.

Castration anxiety was the main source of the resistance in our physician's analysis. It could be recognized in the intensity with which he avoided the issue that hostility against his father was one of the most important motives of his neurosis. This castration anxiety centered around an accident which had occurred when he was five years old. He had been struck on the head by his father's horse and had been knocked unconscious.

On the other hand, guilt feelings also contributed much to this resistance. The father had been an extremely kind man who had always worked very hard in order to provide for his family, which consisted of his wife and seven children. The patient was the second child, with a sister several years his senior. All his memories of his father were of a pleasant kind; the father had twice almost sacrificed his own life in order to save the son when he was in mortal danger. One incident he remembered very clearly. At the age of three he was in his father's carriage when the horses ran away. The father was almost run over by the horses when he threw himself in their path in order to stop them and to save his son. For a long time no antagonism against the father could be discovered because his guilt feelings and anxiety prevented this. The father had died of a cerebral hemorrhage some time before the outbreak of the neurosis.

It required extreme patience on the part of both analyst and patient to allow the hate of the father to come to full expression in the analysis. It was possible to recognize this hate or, rather, to infer it indirectly from the material which he related after half a year's analysis. At the beginning of the neurosis he had developed extreme hatred against one of his colleagues, who had the same first name as the son of his older sister. For some time the hatred seemed merely to be caused by jealousy of his sister's child, but gradually it was seen that this hostility was an expression of his unconscious hatred of his father. The jealousy flared up particularly when he discovered that the other physician had an obstetrical case. It could easily be inferred that the jealousy was in reference to his own mother's children, begotten by the father. But only toward the end of the second year of his analysis was he able to express a more open aggression against this father substitute. He once met this colleague in the hospital, where the latter had just delivered a woman of a baby. He could hardly refrain from expressing his rage that "the son of a bitch" should have another obstetrical case. But he had to counteract immediately his own outbreak of rage against the father substitute: he dreamed the following night that he shook hands with his father; this was the first time that his father appeared undisguised in a dream. About this time the patient dreamed of "many dead Rhônian rabbits in an alley", thus expressing his death wishes against his younger siblings. His family came to this country from a little village on the Rhone river in France. He was unable to display any further open hostility toward his father for several months.

The dream about shaking hands with the father occurred at the beginning of the third year of the analysis. It demonstrated the patient's difficulties in bringing out his hatred of his father. Even when this hatred was directed against a substitute figure he was obliged to atone for it by a dream in which he expressed friendliness toward his father. Finally, a dream occurred which showed his resentment against his father, although still in an indirect fashion. He dreamed "that he was pushing a boat with two women in it upstream, so that they should glide away and land at a safe place." The analysis showed that this dream referred to his very early childhood. The father had come to this country when the patient was only six months old. His mother had remained behind with the children in Europe until the father had made enough money for his wife and children to come to America. The patient was two and a half years old when the family joined the father and the little boy resented very much the father's intrusion into his love relationships with his mother and sister. The dream shows his tendency to save the women from the father: he pushes the boat to a safe place and at the same time back against the current of time.

The final revelation of his patricidal tendencies was brought out only at the very end of his analysis when the patient had decided to apply for a commission in the army. Shortly before he left for the army he dreamed that he "thrust a bayonet repeatedly through a wooden door which was stuck full of rifle shells." The assumption was that there were soldiers tied on the inside of the door. When the door was opened he saw that he had killed an old man who lay in a pool of his own blood. The analysis showed by the associations to the dream that it referred to nightly observations which he made after he and his mother and sister had come to this country and joined the father. Since he had lived in poor conditions he had slept with his parents until he was six years old and had every opportunity to observe parental intercourse. He also observed his mother's menstruation and her pregnancies. He understood the parental intercourse as nightly attacks on the part of the father against the mother. He thought that the father injured the mother as well as the children in her abdomen through intercourse (the bloody bayonet, the soldiers tied to the inside of the door); he reacted with violent hatred against the father, which was early repressed through guilt and anxiety. The numerous observations of parental intercourse are represented in the dream by the numerous rifle shells in the door. The dream shows his reaction of hatred to the nightly observations. In this dream he reversed the father's position in order to take revenge on him. The dream demonstrates this clearly: the children are not injured inside the mother by the father's penis, but the father is placed in the position of the children inside the door. The door can be recognized as a symbol of the mother's genital entrance; thus he kills his father with his bayonet; at the same time he achieves illusory intercourse with his mother. His own head injury is linked up with the same fantasy. It may be remembered that his father died of a *"brain stroke,"* and that this fact gave the patient the opportunity to produce unconscious fantasies of revenge for his own head injury as a child, through his father's horse.

Some additional material was furnished by a short outbreak of anxiety which the patient developed the day after the dream, when he had to puncture a child's ear-drum for otitis media. His hand shook so much from excitement that he could hardly hold and guide the lancet. But he accomplished the little operation successfully and felt relief immediately afterwards. In the following analytic hour when he reported this incident he recalled that as a child he had heard that his father was born with a veil, that is, with the amniotic membrane adhering to his head. It was then clear that piercing the membrane of the ear with the lancet represented for him an attack on the father's veil, and that his anxiety related to a fear-wish of injuring the father's head behind the membrane. This injury would have been done in revenge for what he imagined his father had done to the children in the mother's womb behind their amniotic membranes, a revenge which is so well demonstrated in the dream where he thrusts the bayonet through the door and kills his father.

The patient's anxiety hysteria had become manifest when he neglected to examine a child's ear shortly after his father's death. He actually had suspected that the child had otitis media, but repressed his suspicion in order not to be forced to have to puncture the child's ear-drum. The repression was incomplete, however, and did not serve to conceal the anxiety connected with the deeper meaning of the parcentesis. The real reasons for this anxiety were only fully understood at the end of an analysis which of course, was directed not to the theoretical elucidation of this point but to the resolution of the unstable emotional constellations of the patient which made him subject to such episodes of apparently irrational anxiety. These, as has been indicated, proved to be referable to unassimilated childhood situations of the usual sorts.

The Formative Activity of the Analyst

It is neither by mere chance nor as a result of one-sided interest that so many of our papers on psycho-analytic therapy concern themselves with interpretation. Interpretation is and will always remain our paramount technical method in therapeutic procedure, as long as we do not work (Freud, 1904) *'per via di porre'*, that is, by strengthening the repressive forces, but *'per via di levare'*, by undoing repression and thus making the unconscious accessible to the ego so that it can integrate parts of the id and use its newly acquired energy for its manifold purposes. Our ultimate dynamic aim in interpretation is the strengthening of the ego through the addition of instinctual energy which has hitherto belonged to the unconscious. There can be no doubt that interpretation is our main pump in the therapeutic 'draining of the Zuyder Zee' (Freud, 1933; 106).

The fact that the direct interpretation of recognized unconscious material is not usually the means of achieving our therapeutic purpose was a fairly early discovery. Very often the patient is unable to accept the interpretation or even to understand it. Pre-interpretative measures must be taken so that he will be able to understand and accept our interpretations. Such measures consist mainly in the analysis of the ego-resistances or -defences against the expression of unconscious material. Excellent papers by Sigmund and Anna Freud, by Wilhelm Reich, Otto Fenichel, M.N. Searl, Edward Glover, James Strachey and others have been devoted to the preparatory steps of interpretation. In contrast to these, the post-interpretative states and procedures have been neglected in analytic literature. It is in my opinion a necessity that we should focus our attention upon the dynamic situation which exists after a correct and, if necessary, well-prepared interpretation has been given to the patient. For in my experience many analysts stop their therapeutic activity at the point where the interpretation has been supplied to the patient. For such analysts interpretation is the only work.

Read before the American Psychoanalytic Association, Detroit, May 10, 1943.
The Formative Activity of the Analyst, *International Journal of Psychoanalysis*, 1944, 25(3 & 4), 146–150.

Interpretation, and the preparation for it, is their contribution to the therapeutic procedure. The rest of the process has to go on within the patient. He is, so to speak, left alone with the interpretation. In my opinion this attitude on the part of the analyst is a continuation of the 'take it or leave it' policy of the earliest lines of analysis, which is so well expressed in Freud's dream of Irma's Injection (1900). The only difference is that owing to the analysis of the resistance the possibility of the patient's 'taking it' has been enlarged in comparison with Freud's earlier therapeutic measures.

Even if the interpretation of a patient's behaviour, or of his defence mechanisms, is repeated on different occasions, a merely interpretative attitude neglects the further task of the analyst, who must help the analysand to do something with the interpretation, that is, with the newly acquired knowledge about himself.

This merely interpretative attitude on the part of the analyst seems to me an expression of belief in interpretation as a kind of magic formula which works with miraculous efficacy immediately upon its pronouncement by the analyst. But in my opinion the analyst has the further duty of helping the patient in overcoming mental inertia, of showing him how to use the newly acquired insight into himself, into his pathological repetitions, anxieties and defences contructively, so that a re-orientation towards his inner as well as his outer world shall result. The achievement of this re-orientation is our final therapeutic goal, in the light of which our interpretation of the patient's defence mechanisms and unconscious material can be considered only as a preliminary and preparatory procedure. It is true that in many cases the re-orientation for which we are working takes place automatically as soon as the patient develops intellectual and emotional insight into his unconscious as well as into his pathological and inappropriate reactions. But it is far from true that after the patient has accepted our interpretation we can *always* leave it to him to do the remaining therapeutic work of re-organizing his personality. He simply would not do it. The reasons why he does not take advantage of his newly gained insight are many. In general they represent the same forces which we find active against any change in our adaptations, and 'mental inertia' is a term which summarizes them. It is needless to remark that infantile anxieties and unconscious instinctual gratifications may prevent the necessary changes, and that therefore further purely analytic interpretative measures must be taken. But the necessity for changing in itself, the need to give up old ways of restoring the mental equilibrium in favour of new adaptations, creates a type of resistance to which Freud gave the name 'resistances of the id', although we can easily see that the ego too in most instances refuses to undergo changes in its reaction patterns. To me it seems a therapeutic necessity to help the patient in effecting these changes by something more than the preliminary act of interpretation. This additional function of helping the patient, which may even amount to forcing him to establish a re-orientation of his personality and a re-adaptation to his outside world, I should like to describe as the 'formative activity' of the analyst. It no doubt belongs to the 'working through' part of our task.

It is difficult to describe in detail in what this formative activity consists. It is operative within a wide range, from energetic activity to a mere attitude hardly sensible to the patient. Its methods vary with the personalities of patients as well as with their analytic and emotional situations. I am inclined to describe formative activity in a general sense as a continual effort to exert pressure on the patient in order to force him from a state of unhealthy pathological reactions and fixations into better adaptation and a more satisfactory solution of both his inner and his outer problems.

Psycho-analytic treatment has often been compared to orthodontic procedures. Freud once uses the term '*redressement*', probably with reference to the forceful treatment in orthopædic therapy. Both comparisons imply the exertion of pressure from the outside. The means which we use in order to force the patient to change are manifold. In many instances we show him what he did and what he had better have done in certain situations. We use the frustrating effect of interpretation in order to prevent him from repeating his pathological gratifications and reactions. We use his respect for our own opinion in order to make him feel ashamed of his lapses into useless infantile behaviour. If necessary we show him more or less drastically what his repetition of pathological reactions will bring him to, what dangers or frustrations will result from such repetitions. We have to use all these and other means of *personal influence* to mould our patients into a healthier personality formation.

Freud says in his *Introductory Lectures* (1917) that in our therapeutic work, particularly in those phases where infantile conflicts are renewed, we must use 'all our available mental forces in order to press the patient into a new decision'.[1] In my opinion these mental forces consist in per-

---

[1] Translated by the author. The English translation by Joan Riviere does not give the right meaning of Freud's words: 'Das entscheidende Stück der Arbeit wird geleistet, indem man im Verhältnis zum Arzt, in der "Übertragung", Neuauflagen jener alten Konflikte schafft, in denen sich der Kranke benehmen möchte, wie er sich seinerzeit benommen hat, während man ihn durch das Aufgebot aller verfügbaren seelischen Kräfte zu einer anderen Entscheidung nötigt.' (*Gesammelte Schriften* VII. 472.)

[EDITORIAL NOTE: Dr. Sterba's criticism of Mrs. Riviere's translation seems unjustified. Her version of the passage is as follows (*Introductory Lectures*, Revised Edition, 1929, 380): 'The decisive part of the work is carried through by creating—in the relationship to the physician, in "the transference"—new editions of those early conflicts, in which the patient strives to behave as he originally behaved, while one calls upon all the available forces in

suasion and threat, promise of reward, encouragement and praise, as well as all the rest of the mental equipment we employ when we try to make somebody do a thing that he originally does not want to do. However, such means are exactly those which we use in *education* in order to effect the shift from pleasure principle to reality principle. In this respect psychoanalysis is true re-education. As I once pointed out (1932) education can be considered as the extended psychological repetition of birth, that is, of the change from intra-uterine to extra-uterine existence. Analytical therapy is the last act of this psychological repetition of birth, and, like all the preceding psychological acts of birth in the form of education and like the physiological act of birth itself, it must be accomplished by pressure and force.

The dynamic basis of this energetic influence of the analyst on his patient is the transference. Infantile dependence, love, admiration and confidence are the expressions of the positive transference which enable us to direct our patient mentally towards our therapeutic goal. The actual superiority of the analyst's personality to that of his patient is of considerable help in this process. But as in hyposis, so in our formative activity in analysis we work mainly with borrowed energies.

There can be no doubt that formative activity requires certain personal qualifications which should not be missing in a good analyst. Formative activity is a part of our work which can hardly be learned, and for which we can give neither prescription nor technical advice. Such work is truly creative, like the work of good education, and the personal gift of handling other people is requisite in an efficient analyst. Personal influence must be exerted in such a way as to be at the same time flexible and consistent. The comparison with a good fisherman, who knows how to play the fish

his soul to bring him to another decison.' Thus the difference of opinion between the two translations is as to whether the forces that are to be evoked are the patient's or the analyst's own. The actual words seem capable of either interpretation and the question is best settled by an examination of the context as well as of any other passages from Freud that deal with the same point. Two sentences earlier, Freud writes: 'In order to dissolve the symptoms it is necessary to go back to the point at which they originated, to renew the conflict from which they proceeded, and with the help of propelling forces which at that time were not available [mit Hilfe solcher Triebkräfte die seinerzeit nicht verfügbar waren] to guide it towards a new solution.' Similarly, in the *New Introductory Lectures*, 1933, 198 (*Gesammelte Schriften*, XII, 314), where Freud continues the same discussion, he writes: 'Only too often one seems to see that the therapeutic process is merely lacking in the necessary motive force to enable it to bring about the alteration. Some specific tendency, some particular instinctual component, is too strong in comparison with the counter-forces that we can mobilize against it [eine gewisse Triebkomponente ist zu stark im Vergleich mit den Gegenkräften, die wir mobil machen können].' It seems hardly possible to doubt that in all of these passages Freud is concerned with the economic balance of forces within the patient, with the possibility of the analyst evoking one set of forces in the patient to operate against another, rather than with the notion of the analyst bringing forces of his own to bear upon the patient. Further consideration will perhaps convince Dr. Sterba of the correctness of Mrs. Rivere's version.]

after it is caught on the hook (of transference), is a ready one. Formative activity is at once the most difficult and the most satisfactory of our many therapeutic activities. If analytic intuition and insight into the patient's mental content can be compared to the inspiration of the creative artist, the formative activity in our therapy can be likened to the other power essential to the artist's creation: the ability to give his idea *form*, to body it forth into the final artistic product. Intuitive insight into the patient and the ability to use this insight constructively for the transformation of the patient's personality are the equivalent constituents of analytic therapy.

I am well aware of the many limitations we must impose upon our formative activity. We are not supposed to set ourselves for it, neither should we impose upon the patient our own *Weltanschauung* or our opinions on various matters. Even our own personality pattern is not supposed to be a model for our moulding the patient into a new orientation towards life. Much objectivity is needed. The process of temporary identification with the patient and the subsequent ejection of this identification, which resembles the mechanisms described by Ludwig Jekels (1930) in his excellent paper on the psychology of pity, seems to be an important factor in gaining this objectivity. In formative activity more than in any other part of our work the personality of the analyst is a decisive factor.

I know very well that in all I have said I have stepped on ground in the realm of therapy which to some analysts seems as dangerous as a minefield. Such an attitude contradicts their analytic thinking. Their idea of the analyst is a very neutral, colourless and impersonal image, invisible to the patient and without influence upon his decisions, whose only function is to offer the patient material for better judgement. But I may remind those who think in this way that human beings are very little influenced by their intellectual insight, that they need strong emotional support in order to use it for their own benefit, and that the neurotic in particular is a weak person in this respect.

I have mentioned already that I have found very little on this subject in psycho-analytic literature. Our technical papers show a rather rigid attitude in cautiously avoiding discussions of any activity on the part of the analyst that is not merely interpretative. There are some exceptions, however. Franz Alexander (1935), for example, emphasizes the fact that the analyst has the task of assisting the patient's ego in his synthetic endeavours. He states that, 'what we call "working through" has the function of aiding the integrating process', and speaks of the active influence of the analyst upon the assimilating process going on within the patient. 'The standard technique', he says, 'as it is used since Freud's technical recommendations, consisting in interpretations centering around the transference situation, really involves an active participation of the analyst in the integrating process.'

Melitta Schmideberg (1939) recognizes how often steps and activities which are not merely interpretative are applied in therapeutic analysis and how they contribute to the therapeutic result. M. N. Searl and Edward Glover give some indication that they recognize non-interpretative influence on the part of the analyst. Edward Bibring (1937) recognizes that pedagogic measures have their place in analytic therapy.

And last, but certainly not least, Sigmund Freud has much to say about the influence of the analyst on his patients. In this connection Freud uses a term which for us nowadays has a flavour that we do not like to connect with psycho-analytic therapy. This is the term 'suggestion'. For us the term 'suggestion' used in connection with psychotherapy has the connotation of making the patient believe things that are not so, and keeping him from recognizing others which really exist. But this is not Freud's understanding of the term when he speaks of suggestion in connection with psycho-analytic treatment. He, and this he makes quite clear in his *Group Psychology* (1921), uses the term to mean *any personal influence* on the patient.[2] Having this in mind, that in the following quotations, chosen from among many similar ones, Freud uses 'suggestion' to mean *personal influence*, it will be found that in his writings we can discover many clear expressions of what I call the formative activity of the analyst. Again, Freud (1922) speaks of 'the suggestive influence which is inevitably exercised by the physician'. In his twenty-eighth lecture (1917 § 377) he says, comparing hypnosis with psycho-analytic therapy: 'Analytic therapy takes hold deeper down nearer the roots of the disease, among the conflicts from which the symptoms proceed; it employs suggestion to change the outcome of these conflicts. . . The labour of overcoming the resistances is the essential achievement of the analytic treatment; the patient has to accomplish it and the physician makes it possible for him to do this by suggestions which are in the nature of an *education*. It has been truly said therefore, that psychoanalytic treatment is a kind of *re-education*.' Further on in the same lecture (*ibid.*; 381) he says again: 'The change that is decisive for a successful outcome . . .is made possible by changes in the ego ensuing as a consequence of the analyst's suggestions,' that is, under the personal influence of the physician. I quote finally from Freud's *Laienanalyse* (1926): 'This personal influence is our most powerful dynamic weapon; it is the means by which we introduce something new into the situation and bring it into a state of flux. The intellectual content of our

---

[2] [On p. 100 of *Group Psychology* (1921) Freud defines suggestion as 'a conviction which is not based upon perception and reasoning but upon an erotic tie'.—Ed.]

explanations cannot effect this.' In the sentences following this he speaks of the great 'suggestive' influence in psycho-analytic therapy. Many other quotations from Freud's writings could be added, in which he expresses his opinion about the significance of *personal influence* in psycho-analytic therapy which has to be used *over and above* interpretation.

Goethe once declared that man's most important study is man. No other psychologist has contributed so much to that study as Sigmund Freud. But through the analytic method of psychotherapy he did more: he gave us the possibility of remodelling individual personality structures of an unfavourable and neurotic kind. His study and insight into the human mind enable us to form and mould distorted minds and personalities into a better shape. And so we who are psychoanalytic therapists can, by using the vital tool of our formative activity, take into our hands the useless structures and neurotic mazes of distorted personalities, can work, shape and form the valuable energies that have been wasted in them into the living pattern of an efficient human being. And in so doing we go beyond the *study* of man to the active and most important *work* of man, namely the work of building man.

REFERENCES

Alexander, F. (1935). 'The Problem of Psychoanalytic Technique', *Psychoanal. Q.*, 4, 608.
Bibring, E. (1937). 'The Theory of the Therapeutic Results of Psycho-Analysis', *Int. J. Psycho-Anal.*, 18, 188.
Freud, S. (1900). (*Revised Trans.* 1932.) *The Interpretation of Dreams* (Allen & Unwin), 114 ff.
―――(1904). (*Trans.* 1924). 'On Psychotherapy', *Collected Papers*, I., 253.
―――(1917). (*Revised Trans.* 1929) *Introductory Lectures on Psycho-Analysis* (Allen & Unwin).
―――(1921.). (*Trans.* 1922.) *Group Psychology and the Analysis of the Ego*.
―――(1922). (*Trans.* 1942.) 'Two Encyclopædia Articles', *Int. J. Psycho-Anal.*, 23, 104.
―――(1926). *Die Frage der Laienanalyse. Gesammelte Schriften*, XI. 353 f.
―――(1933). (*Trans.* 1933.) *New Introductory Lectures on Psycho-Analysis*.
Jekels, L. (1930). 'Zur Psychologie des Mitleids', *Imago*, 16, 5.
Schmideberg, M. (1939). 'The Rôle of Suggestion in Psychoanalytic Therapy', *Psychoanal. R.*, 26, 219.
Sterba, R. (1932). 'Zur Theorie der Erziehungsmittel', *Z. psychoanal. Pädag.*, 6, 422.

Dreams and Acting Out

From the daily analysis of patients' dreams it is found that the unconscious not only expresses itself in these dreams, but that from a dream we understand much of the dreamer's behavior in the waking state. In analysis, patients' dreams seem to acquire a new significance as a means of communication with the analyst. The connections with a patient's daily activities are, therefore, particularly important and enlightening. In associations to details of the manifest dream we find such connections between actions, thoughts, fantasies, feelings, and the latent dream content. Usually the patient relates a dream, after which he gives associations, and with the analyst's help, comes to an understanding of the significance of the dream, and its psychological connections with reality, the transference, and the analysis.

At different times I have had the opportunity to observe a sequence of events which appears to be the reverse of the usual procedure. I refer to certain incidents of acting out which precede the narration of dreams in the analytic hour so immediately, and which can be understood so clearly after the dream has been told, that one forms the impression that the acting out functions as a preceding dream association.

A patient who lived near my office came to the hour without the spectacles he always wears. He stated he forgot to take them when he left home and that he did not bother to go back for them since he was a little late and could walk the short distance without spectacles. He had never before forgotten his spectacles during two years of analysis. It then occurred to him that he had had a dream the preceding night. He dreamed that he started an argument with another man, and before getting into a fist fight he was taking off his spectacles in order to prevent his eyes from being injured by glass particles if the man should strike back. Acting out in the form of forgetting the glasses and the dream explain each other to a great extent. The other man in the dream is the analyst, and the aggression of the dream is acted out at least to the extent of coming to the appointment without them. This symptomatic behavior is closely associated with the dream, making possible an interpretation of the dream before further associations are produced.

A second example deals with a woman, a patient who had arranged to live where I was spending the summer in order to continue her analysis. The house in which I lived was situated on a hill approximately sixty feet above the road. One day the patient arrived as usual on time, but I saw her running up the path to the house and storming up the few steps to the door. When I opened the door, she did not take off her coat, but rushed into my office, threw her coat on the floor, and flung herself on the couch, completely out of breath. She began immediately to relate a dream from the preceding night, frequently interrupted by attempts to catch her breath. She dreamed that her mother, while talking with her by telephone, had to interrupt her speaking continually because she was short of breath. When questioned about this, the mother stated she was out of breath because she was in labor, in the process of giving birth to a baby. That the patient caused herself to arrive breathless, and without any cause in reality had an important relationship to the content of her dream: her identification with her mother in a state of parturiency. It was very impressive to observe the intensity of the patient's need to express through this action her wish to be identified with her mother in labor. It was the fulfilment of one of the most urgent wishes of her early childhood, and it played the most important rôle in her neurosis.

A man, who had the habit of coming for treatment a few minutes late, once arrived almost half an hour early. In the library where he waited, I found him fast asleep on a couch. When I woke him he was unaccountably angry, to a degree not in keeping with the circumstances. He then related a dream from the preceding night in which he was sleeping in a bed situated in a kind of an alcove. A woman was lying beside him. Suddenly a man came down from the second floor, as if through the ceiling, woke him up, grabbed him and lifted him to the second floor. At this point he awoke.

This dream required extensive analysis. Partially, it repeated an experience of early childhood at the age of three and a half. He was at that time taken by his parents to the Far East where his father had taken a position. The dream referred to a scene which occurred one night while traveling on a train or on a boat. He was in the lower berth with his mother, when his father, who according to the analytic reconstruction of the scene was in the upper berth, came down and lifted him to the upper berth, while he himself got into bed with the mother. The sexual scene that followed was perceived, at least acoustically, by the child. The patient's falling asleep so that I had to waken him, and his anger and indignation about it were clearly hostile feelings against his father which resulted from his incestuous wishes towards his mother, and his rivalry with his father transferred to the analyst. This acting out in connection with the analogous dream content indicated that infantile and analytic situation were fused in the transference.

A last example is the most dramatic I have experienced. A man, who had his analytic appointment at night, rang the doorbell, and when I opened the door I was quite shocked by his appearance. Pale, disheveled, his face contorted with pain, he was holding his right arm with his left hand. With my help he staggered into the room and told me he had had a bad fall in front of my house. On the couch, he was scarcely able to tell what had happened. After a while he became calmer and, though still in pain, related that when he had parked his car in front of my house he had had the thought that he would have to be very careful because the road was icy. By walking cautiously he safely reached the sidewalk which was entirely cleared of snow and ice. He then felt he was on safe ground. Suddenly, he stumbled over a step which he had passed innumerable times without difficulty, and whose existence was completely familiar to him. He had fallen on his right arm and felt an extreme pain in the region of the elbow. As the pain subsided gradually, the patient chose to remain for his hour. He did not believe that he was seriously injured. (An x-ray made the following day showed a fracture of the radius near the elbow.)

He then related a dream from the preceding night, which consisted of two parts. In the first part he observed a little boy who did some damage to the right front fender of a car. In the second part he saw a girl standing in front of a building, a house or a hospital. She seemed to be injured or ill, for two men came and carried her into the building. Again the acting out preceding the narration of the dream explains the dream immediately. It centers around active castration wishes, and retaliation in kind. The patient recognized the little boy who damaged the car to be himself, and the car as his father's. The retaliation involved a part of his body which roughly corresponds to the right front fender of the car. The retaliation itself, omitted in the dream, is acted out by falling and breaking his arm. The dream represents only the result of the symbolic castration: transformation into a girl who is taken into a hospital. That he is the girl is also acted out. He appeared at my door in such a miserable condition that I almost had to carry him into the house. In this example we see that symptomatic action and dream content were interlocked, so that a piece of the dream filled a gap in the action, and vice versa. Both combined offered a complete understanding of the unconscious psychological situation.

In our examples it is clear that the acting out which closely precedes the narration of the dream is unconsciously connected with the dream content. The phenomena described emphasize the importance of the rule that in dream analysis it is necessary not to restrict the focus of attention to the manifest dream content and to the associations produced in direct connection with the dream elements. The diffusion of the analyst's attention over the total picture, what precedes as well as what follows, is necessary in order to recognize the deeper connections and organize them according to the *Gestalt* of the underlying unconscious dynamic currents.

The close connection between the acting out and the dream gives the impression that the acting out functions like an association to the dream which precedes the dream. The dream can often be understood immediately from the content of the acting out. Actually the acting out as well as the dream which it precedes are both the expression of the same unconscious instinctual dynamism which succeeds in breaking through the repressing forces of the ego, particularly when the defenses are loosened up through the analytic work.

On Spiders, Hanging and Oral Sadism

All pregenital instinctual tendencies are ambivalent, that is, they manifest towards the same object and at the same time both friendliness and hostility—the former with the wish to preserve, the latter desiring to destroy. The destructive component represents a danger for the object and this is the greater the earlier the stage of libido development to which the instinctual tendency belongs. The tension of the ambivalence decreases during the course of libido development and almost disappears with sexual maturity. Over a long period of time human beings have known of the ambivalence of the pregenital tendencies and, although this knowledge has not been expressed scientifically, unerring psychological intuition has made man choose two comparisons from the animal world—the spider and the vampire—to represent the oral danger of object love and particularly the danger of being loved. Both of these are symbols to us of the oral destructive danger of being loved and represent the endangered object as a victim of oral aggression. In this way we betray our depth psychological knowledge of the ambivalence of oral instinctual tendencies.

The significance of the spider as a means of representation of dangerous object love was very early recognized by psychoanalysis. Abraham (1) found it used as a symbol of the mother, the bad mother with dangerous attributes, possessed of a destructive male organ. She is the masculine mother, whose embrace injures and kills. Freud remarked, in connection with Abraham's findings that the significance of the spider as a symbol was the reflection of a biological fact, since the male spider is weaker than the female and is frequently devoured by the female after coitus. Abraham discovered further that in dreams the spider's web represents the female

On Spiders, Hanging and Oral Sadism, *American Imago*, 1950, 7, 21–28. From: Spinne, Erhangen und Oralsadisms, *Psychoanalytische Bewegung*, 1932, 4, 268–274.

(1) Die Spinne als Traum Symbol—The Spider as Dream Symbol, Karl Abraham, Selected Papers

pubic hair, while the single thread signifies the male genitals. The sucking dry of the object is to be compared with the destruction of the partner's genitals by castration.

The conclusions of an analysis led me to a hitherto unsuspected connection between spiders, hanging and oral sadism, which reminded me of a story by the German novelist, Hanns Heinz Ewers, in which these three elements are linked together in an amazingly similar manner.

A man who was in analysis with me had, between his sixth and seventh year, attempted a number of times unsuccessfully to commit suicide. Possibly the attempts were unsuccessful because they were not seriously executed. The method of these attempts was unusual, namely, that of hanging. Another attempt at the age of 23 of suicide by the oral incorporation of morphine indicated so clearly the connection between similar intoxicants absorbed by his mother who was seriously ill at the time, that there could be no doubt that the son's attempts at suicide were manifestations of identification with the mother. The analysis revealed that this identification was the expression of his passive-feminine tendency towards the father. It was not difficult to deduce from this that even the childhood attempts at hanging had to be considered as a passive instinctual satisfaction in connection with the father. The tendency towards passive experiences with the father had also been manifested in the form of fantasies produced from his third to his fifteenth year, which centred around the pleasurable idea of being devoured by a giant. Following one of those intuitions which analysts often have to thank for some of the best deductive results in analysis, I remarked to the analysand, as we again spoke of his attempts at hanging, that I had the impression his attempts expressed the desire to be bitten. The analysand's next observations corroborated what I had said. He said that the first time he had tried to hang himself by standing on the toilet the cord had broken, but the noose had remained round his neck; then, astonishingly enough, he went into the bathroom and tried to free himself with a comb, which he placed between his throat and the cord. Not till later did he find a more suitable instrument to free himself. But my conjecture had been verified, for a comb has one thing in common with a devouring jaw, namely the teeth.

The spider too appeared in this analysis as a threatening oral symbol. The patient had the following dream, at a phase in which his passive experience with his father, who had died several years ago, was recognized as the reaction formation to active feelings of hate and aggression towards the father, which were caused by his desire for his mother. This was the dream: From the sky great spidery monsters come down on the earth, causing much death, first of all in central Europe: the patient flees to Italy with his mother. It is clear that behind the spidery monsters which come down from the sky is hidden the threatening father, who has been dead for a number of years and is therefore, according to infantile ideas, in heaven. Spidery monsters can also appear as father symbols, for the analytical interpretation of the spider as the masculine mother is also a proof of father attributes in the spider. The basis of this dream is formed by a novel by Maurice Renard entitled "The Blue Peril", which the patient had read recently. The novel is about invisible monsters which live in the stratosphere and dive down to the surface of the earth which, for them, is equivalent to a kind of "deep sea research". They are invisible to man and once they are on the earth they begin a work of horrible destruction among men. The transference is recognizable in the "deep sea research", which represents the "depth psychological research" of analysis; the monsters consequently represent the analyst who is invisible to the patient. The destruction of the monsters was of an oral nature, in the patients fantasy, and corresponded to the sexual fantasies of being devoured and to his attempts to hang himself.

I would not have ventured to establish a connection between hanging and being bitten if a sensational short story by Hanns Heinz Ewers had not shown in an astonishingly similar manner the connection between spider, biting and hanging. That a story by an author who is regarded by many as a writer of sensationalistic fiction, should be used to support a clinically founded assumption can hardly be an objection, because we can assume that a writer addressing himself to a wide public will make use of common symbol formations in relatively simple disguises. In this connection it may be useful to recall the procedure Freud employed in his paper: "Der Dichter und das Phantasieren" (The Relation of the Poet to Day Dreaming (2) in which he uses for his psychological investigations the unassuming writer of cheap novels and stories which find the most numerous and fervent readers among the greater public.

The content of the story is as follows: In the room of a little Parisian hotel, on three successive Fridays, between 5 and 6 in the evening, three otherwise inconspicuous persons quite unexpectedly committed suicide by hanging. The first was a Swiss commercial traveller, the second an artist, the third a policeman, who had voluntarily set himself the task of solving the mystery of the first two suicides. From each of the three corpses ran a spider, when they were discovered. The guests fled the hotel. A young student wants to try to find out the cause of the suicides and accordingly asks permission to occupy the room where they occurred. The chief of

(2) S. Freud. Collected Papers, IV, p. 173.

police agrees to let him carry on investigations on condition that a telephone is installed in the room, to keep him in continual contact with the police station. The student is glad to get free food and lodging from the hotel owner and thinks he has found a quiet refuge for a good long time. What subsequently happens to him the author indicates by means of an episode recorded in the diary in which the student jots down all his experiences.

It reads as follows: "This morning I watched a little drama. I was walking up and down the corridor while the servant was cleaning my room. Outside the window which looks down on the courtyard hangs a spider's web, with a fat garden spider sitting in it. Madame Dubonnet, the owner of the hotel, refuses to let it be caught; she says spiders bring good luck and she has already had enough bad luck in the house. I saw how another much smaller spider ran cautiously round the web, a male. Warily he crept along the weak cobweb threads towards the centre, but as the female stirred he retreated hastily, ran to the edge of the web and then began to draw closer again. At last the strong female at the centre of the web seemed to accept his wooing and stopped moving. First the male pulled gently and then more sharply at one of the threads, so that the whole web quivered, but his beloved remained still. Then he crept quickly, but with infinite care nearer her. The female received him quietly and abandoned herself passively to his tender embraces. For some minutes they hung motionless in the middle of the big web.

Then I saw the male slowly begin to release himself one leg after the other; it was as though he were trying to move away very quietly so as to leave his partner to continue her dream. Suddenly he let go completely and ran as fast as he could out of the web. But in the same instant the female came violently to life and dashed in pursuit of him. The weak male lowered himself from a cobweb and the female immediately followed suit. Both fell on the window sill, the male throwing every atom of strength into an attempt to escape. Too late, the female already had her grip on him and carried him back to the very middle of the web. And this same place which had served as a bed for their voluptuous pleasure was now the scene of quite another drama. In vain the lover struggled, straining his weak legs in an effort to escape the wild embrace; the female would not release him. In a few moments she had spun him into the web so that he couldn't move a limb. Then she struck with her sharp mandibles and sucked in great draughts of her lover's young blood. I saw how she finally rid herself of the pitable, unrecognizable little lump of legs, skin and cobwebs and disdainfully threw him out of the web.

So that is what love is with these animals—thank goodness I'm not a young male spider.''

Soon after the student had moved into the room he had noticed a woman at the window opposite, with whom he had quickly established visual communication. There is something unusual about this woman: when she is not at the window, looking across at him, she sits spinning at a small old-fashioned spinning wheel. "I once saw a spinning wheel like that at my grandmother's", he thought, "but Clarimonde's (this was the name he had given her) spinning wheel is very small and fine, it is white and looks as it is made of ivory; it must make extraordinarily fine threads." A few other striking details stood out in her personal appearance. "It seems to me as though her little teeth taper off in points like the teeth of beasts of prey". While spinning she wore long black gloves. "It is so strange the way the narrow black fingers take up and draw the threads, as though they intermingled, really almost like a mass of insect legs." Her dress is black, with great purple spots. The relationship between the student and Clarimonde becomes more intimate because he notices that she, as though in sign of a deeper understanding, imitates every movement he makes when they look at each other, which is now more and more often. As a matter of fact a most unusual game develops from this imitation:

"We have invented a strange game, Clarimonde and I; we play it all day long. I greet her from my window and at once she greets me back. Then I drum on the window sill with my fingers; hardly does she see me before she begins to do it too. I wink at her and she does the same thing. Then I stroke the hair back from my temples and her hand is already at her forehead. A real children's game and we both laugh over it. As a matter of fact, she doesn't actually laugh, she kind of abandons herself to a quiet, passive smile, just as I imagine I smile myself.

All this is not really so stupid as it seems. It is not only imitation; I think we would both soon tire of that; there must be some kind of thought transmission between us, because Clarimonde follows my movements in the tiniest fraction of a second; she scarcely has time to see them before she carries them out herself, it often seems to me as though they were simultaneous. The fascinating part of it is to do something unforeseen, different; it is bewildering the way she immediately does the same thing. Sometimes I try to trip her up. I make a number of different movements quickly, one after another; I repeat the same thing again and then again. As a matter of fact, the fourth time I make the same movements but I change the sequence, or else I leave one out, just in the way that children play "All the birds fly away". It is amazing that Clarimonde doesn't make a single mistake, although I change so quickly that she hardly has time to recognize each individual movement.

That's the way I pass my days. But I never, for one moment, have the feeling that I'm killing time. On the contrary, I feel that never in my life have I done anything more important.''

Suddenly the young student makes the extraordinary discovery that it is not Clarimonde who has been imitating his movements, but he who without knowing it has been imitating hers. He writes in his journal: "I have made a discovery: it is not I who am playing with Clarimonde—she is playing with me."

So Clarimonde brings him to complete subservience; he imitates all her movements slavishly, she makes him cut through the telephone wires—which were his means of communicating with the police—and hang himself. He is found, like all his predecessors, hanging from the curtain cords. "But the expression on his face was different from the others; it was distorted into a grimace of hideous terror, the eyes open wide, projecting from their sockets, the lips stretched back, the strong teeth clenched.

And crushed between them, hung a great black spider with extraordinary purple spots on its body.

The analytical connections are so clear that brief indications will be sufficient. The grandmother's spinning wheel suggests Clarimonde, as a mother substitute. The game with the hands is recognizable as masturbation, to which the young man had become enslaved to the point of complete degeneration; this is clearly connected with his incest fantasies. However, the important point for us is the connection between oral aggression and hanging. It was through hanging that the student's death occurred. The observation of the tragic end of the spider couple's love play indicates that this hanging is a substitute for being bitten. "It seems to me that her little teeth are sharp and pointed like a beast of prey", the student said of Clarimonde, and of the female spider: "Then she dug her sharp mandibles into his body". The revenge which the student takes, when dying is of an oral sadistic character, following the Talion principle he does to her what she did to him, he bites her to death. The striking parallel in my clinical observation and in the story, between hanging and being bitten, seems to me to justify communicating the material for, hitherto, analytical literature has observed no connection between being hanged and being bitten, or of the substitution of the one for the other. This connection may well claim the interest of clinical psychology and of criminology.

A Case of Brief Psychotherapy By Sigmund Freud

Brief psychotherapy has recently been promulgated by many analysts as if it were a new therapeutic invention of their own which reaches far beyond the scope of the classical, or, as they prefer to call him, "standard" analyst. (See particularly French and Alexander, *Psychoanalytic Therapy: Principles and Application*.) Freud, they claim, was solely concerned with scientific investigation, his attitude was therefore not therapeutic, and his followers in classical analysis are supposed to adhere rigidly to his "standard" technique.

Therefore, when I found a case of brief psychotherapy conducted by Sigmund Freud in 1906, and described by the patient himself in his autobiography, it provoked my interest, and I considered it important to present the autobiographical description of the case to psychoanalytic readers. The patient is one of the greatest conductors of our time, Bruno Walter, and his neurosis occurred when he was a young but very successful conductor at the Imperial Court Opera in Vienna. His neurotic affliction struck him at a time of particular happiness and security. He describes this experience with Freud in his autobiography, *Theme and Variations* (Bruno Walter, Theme and Variations, New York: Alfred Knopf, 1946, 164ff.) as follows:

"To prevent my being too thoroughly coddled by a friendly fate, the guardian angel to whom my education and chastisement were entrusted had felt it proper to insert into that period of peaceful contemplation an illness that caused me a great deal of anxiety during the year after the birth of our first child. I was attacked by an arm ailment. Medical science called it a professional cramp, but it looked deucedly like incipient paralysis. The rheumatic-neuralgic pain became so violent that I could no longer use my right arm for conducting or piano playing. I went from one prominent doctor to another. Each one confirmed the presence of psychogenic elements in my malady. I submitted to any number of treatments, from mudbaths to magnetism, and finally decided to call upon Professor Sigmund Freud, resigned to submit to months of soul searching. The consultation took a course I had not foreseen. Instead of questioning me about sexual aberrations in infancy, as my layman's ignorance had led me to expect, Freud examined my arm briefly. I told him my story, feeling certain that he would be professionally interested in a possible connection between my actual physical affliction and a wrong I had suffered more than a year before. Instead, he asked me if I had ever been to Sicily. When I replied that I had not, he said that it was very beautiful and interesting, and more Greek than Greece itself. In short, I was to leave that very evening, forget all about my arm and the Opera, and do nothing for a few weeks but use my eyes. I did as I was told. Fortified with all the available literature about Sicily, I took an evening train for Genoa, strolled through the interesting streets of the picturesque town, gazed with awe at the mighty stairways of the ancient palaces, and, after having procured a steamer ticket at the office of the Navigazione Generale, sailed out into the Ligurian Sea and toward Naples on the following morning, not without casting a look of admiration back upon Genoa.

Milan and Venice were the only Italian beauty spots thus far known to me. I had purposely chosen the sea route, because I would have considered it unbearable, if not sinful, to rush in a train through cities like Florence and Rome just to get to Sicily quickly enough and be able to use for the intended purpose what little time my finances permitted me. I arrived in Naples toward noon. When my eyes took in Mount Vesuvius, the town, and its environs, I did not die, but neither did I quite feel of this world. It took all the importunity and cheating tactics of the cabbies, all the smells from the street kitchens, all the noise made by the street vendors, all the naively immoral propositions in the Galleria Umberto, and all the other rather worldly peculiarities of that paradisiac place to get me back to earth again. I was deeply sorry that I had to forego Capri, but I was anxious to get to Sicily, and I took the regular steamer to Palermo the following evening. The boat was small, the seas were high, and I was disgracefully seasick, but I felt richly compensated by the splendid entrance into the port of Palermo and the sight of Monte Pellegrino in the morning air.

Mindful of Freud's instructions, I endeavored not to think of my affliction. In this I was aided by the powerful and exciting effect of my first meeting with Hellenism, which burst upon my eye and soul from every side. I was deeply impressed by the papyrus shrubs, and the temples of

Girgenti. But all these individual sights were outshone by the magnificent landscape with its grandiosely shaped mountains, the sublime solitude surrounding Syracuse, the rivers, the fields, and the nobly shaped bays. This, indeed, seemed an ideal scenery for Goethe's *Walpurgisnacht*. Thoughts of a tempestuous past, of the monuments commemorating it, and of nature made me forget the present and my troubles. In the end, my soul and mind were greatly benefited by the additional knowledge I had gained of Hellenism, but not my arm. Besides, it was cold, and I felt I needed warmth. So I decided to use what little was left of my money and my time on the French Riviera, whose fine sunshine was extolled in newspaper reports.

I had to pass through an uncomfortable hour, which made me wonder if I'd ever be privileged again to bask in the rays of the sun. I had planned to go to Naples by way of the Strait separating Sicily from the mainland. Night found me in a hotel in Messina. I was awakened by a feeling of dizziness, my room seemed to rise and settle down again, and my bed, which had suddenly come alive hurled me to the floor like a bucking bronco getting rid of its irksome rider. This comparison was of course suggested by screen impressions gained at a much later date, but even if I had been acquainted with western habits at that time, I doubt if there would have been room in my mind for anything beyond the thought: an earthquake! When I tried to get up after a few minutes of quiet, a new rising, trembling, and falling of my room and the tumbling of pictures from the walls—what was a paltry steamer trip to Palermo compared with that?—made me think better of it. It seemed wiser patiently to await the end of the terrestrial spasm before entrusting myself again to my bed. How disappointed was I on the following morning when I saw no faces pale with fright, heard no excited tales, but was reminded of my fearsome experience merely by my waiter's polite phrase: *Un piccolo terramoto, Signor.*' Obviously it took shocks of an entirely different caliber to draw the attention of the blasé inhabitants of Messina. I told myself that their indifference was due probably to the frequency of quakes in that vicinity and that I need not be ashamed of having been so violently frightened by my first experience of the kind. It is really terrifying to feel the foundation of our animal existence, the firm ground under our feet, rock and sway. Man's sound instinct probably responds to no elemental events with the abysmal terror caused by an earthquake. When I read, in 1908, that a monstrous seismic catastrophe had brought death and destruction to the beautifully situated flourishing Messina, I was reminded of the *piccolo terramoto* and could imagine the waiter's polite smile freeze into a Medusa-like grimace, while the walls came tumbling down upon him.

A regular ferry service was maintained between Messina and Reggio di Calabria, but after the night's experience, I balked at so prosaic a combination as that of Scylla and Charybdis with a sea-going bus. Heedless of what dangers might be lurking in the passage through the whirlpool, I hired a man and a boat to row it. To my question in Italian whether he and his boat were strong enough for the trip he answered with many a flourish of his arms and a flood of proud assurances uttered in a wholly unintelligible Sicilian idiom. I heard nothing on our trip of the Charybdis roar described in Schiller's *Der Taucher*, but the whirlpool was fierce enough to toss our little boat about violently for quite some time, until my boatman finally succeeded by means of a small red sail, a wealth of imprecations, and calls upon the Madonna and his patron saint in reaching smooth water and, finally, Reggio di Calabria. A night ride by train took me to Paestum, where the sight of the world's most wonderful Greek temple in the light of the full moon impressed itself indelibly upon my mind. From there I went back to Naples. I attended an evening performance of *Rigoletto* at the Teatro San Carlo, and though I was not interested in the performance itself, I admired the magnificent house, enjoyed the noisy enthusiasm of the audience, and was particularly amused by a little incident that, at that time, could hardly have occurred anywhere but in southern Italy. When I got up to leave my seat during the intermission, my neighbors begged me to wait a bit. A few seats away from me a young mother was nursing her infant, and the Neapolitans, so noisy and unrestrained at other times, waited patiently and with sympathetic awe until the baby had drunk its fill. Then, to be sure, they crowded their way out with Neapolitan impetuosity.

Boarding a boat train again, I sailed back to Genoa, where I was met by my wife. Together we proceeded to Monaco. Every day I climbed a rock in order to expose my ailing arm to the sun, but in vain. When I got back to Vienna, I poured out my troubles to Freud. His advice was—to conduct. 'But I can't move my arm.' 'Try it at any rate.' 'And what if I should have to stop?' 'You won't have to stop.' 'Can I take upon myself the responsibility of possibly upsetting a performance?' 'I'll take the responsibility.' And so I did a little conducting with my right arm, then with my left, and occasionally with my head. There were times when I forgot my arm over the music. I noticed at my next session with Freud that he attached particular importance to my forgetting. I tried once more to conduct, but with the same discouraging result. It was at that time that I discovered Feuchtersleben's *Contributions to the Dietetics of the Soul*. I read and studied, trying assiduously to find my way into the lines of thought expressed in the brilliant book, in which a physician, who at the same time was a poet, wisely tried to point out to suffering humanity a way that has since been made practicable. I also tried to familiarize myself with Freud's ideas and to learn from him. I endeavored to adapt my conducting technique to the weakness of my arm without impairing the musical effect. So, by dint of much effort and confidence, by learning and forgetting, I finally succeeded in finding my way back to my profession. Only then did I become aware that in my thoughts I had already abandoned it during the preceding weeks.''

Mr. Bruno Walter was kind enough to grant me an interview when it became known to him through a common friend that I was a pupil and follower of Sigmund Freud, and that I was interested in the therapeutic success which Freud had achieved with the simple supportive method he obviously used in the case of Bruno Walter's professional neurosis. Bruno Walter had little to add in terms of a dynamic explanation of the treatment, but it was clear that he was still deeply impressed by Freud's personality forty-two years later. He stated that it was Freud's sincerity and decisiveness in his advice which made him take the evening train to Genoa, the same day that he had his first interview. He had never met Freud before. He felt confident immediately that he had put himself in the hands of someone who was trustworthy in every respect and who knew about human nature. When he returned form his trip he was discouraged, because no improvement had been made. But he had not lost confidence in the therapist whom he had met only once, and whose advice had not brought the relief he expected, so strong was the transference which Freud was able to establish in him in one interview. And he continued to trust him when Freud encouraged him to conduct. Particularly the fact that Freud was able to take the responsibility that no upsetting of any performance would result from his trying to conduct again made him feel that he could try again and that he had to. In one of the following interviews Freud asked him if in the state of being carried away by the music when he was conducting he did not sometimes forget about his ailment and conduct, using his right arm in an unhindered manner, which Bruno Walter had to confirm. And here Freud set in with further encouragement. He used this fact as a proof to the patient that he was able to overcome his neurotic affliction by conscious effort and encouraged him to continue doing just this. In a short time Bruno Walter had overcome his neurosis. The whole threatment consisted of five to six interviews.

I dare add little to this masterpiece of brief psychotherapy. We do not have sufficient material to venture any hypothesis about the psychodynamics of Bruno Walter's short-termed spell of professional neurosis. But

I think that some points in the therapeutic procedure are fairly clear. Freud must have known intuitively that he was faced with a case in which the disturbance of the dynamic equilibrium which led to the neurotic manifestation was only slight, and that the Ego of the patient was strong enough with some suggestive support to regain control over the muscular functions of which an unconscious inhibition had taken possession. He first distracted the patient's attention from the inhibited activity by sending him on a trip to Sicily, which he knew would satisfy many of the patient's intense cultural needs. When the patient returned, Freud used all the weight of his suggestive authority to press him out of his neurosis. He did this by taking the full responsibility that no failure would occur. But at the same time he was ready to surrender this responsibility into the hands of the patient. He therefore asked him whether he did not forget about his arm when he was intensely absorbed in performing. And as soon as the patient confirmed this, he did all he could to enforce the patient's self-confidence until the latter was successful in freeing himself permanently from his neurosis. The short history of the treatment shows an unusual skill in gauging dynamic relationships and using the influence of the therapist's authority at the right time and in the right way. The success and the katamnesis of forty-two years proves the therapeutic result.

Character and Resistance

To define 'character', we may start with the etymology of the word, derived from the Greek 'charassein', which means 'to make sharp, to cut into furrows, to engrave'. 'Charaktēr' designates in ancient Greek the instrument with which the engraving is done, the chisel, and the sign which results from the engraving. In this sense we speak of Greek, Latin, and Cyrillic 'characters', referring to the letters of different alphabets which were originally engraved in clay. The meaning of character as we use it nowadays developed relatively late in the Greek language. From this it becomes clear that character designates the features of personality which are more or less indelibly engraved upon it, features which of course express themselves in actions and reactions, features that are 'characteristic' of the individual, features by which one ego structure can be differentiated from others. Since actions and reactions as they manifest themselves are the function of the ego, we are accustomed to attribute character to the ego. But character is formed not only by the specific ways of dealing with the multitude of stimuli which rush toward the ego from without and from within, but, in its deepest roots, it is formed also by the specific demands, or better, the specific quantity of demands pressing upwards from instinctual strivings of the id. Character is thus based on the organic substratum of the psychic personality, as was pointed out by Freud: 'The tendency to repression, as well as the ability to sublimate, must be traced back to the organic bases of the character, upon which alone the psychic structure springs up'.[1]

As a third factor the superego, with its specific demands, its rigidity of do's and don't's, is an essential contributor to character formation. We have to take into consideration therefore that all three provinces of the mental structure of the personality contribute to the formation of character.

Read at the midwinter meeting of the American Psychoanalytic Association, New York, December 1948.

[1] Freud: *Leonardo da Vinci, A Psychosexual Study*. New York: Dodd, Mead & Co., 1932, p. 127.

One might define character as the sum total of specific reactions of the individual, determined by the three provinces of the mind according to their inherited and acquired dynamics. Ego, id, and superego are, then, involved wherever character changes are attempted, as in psychoanlytic therapy. I would like to emphasize this threefold origin of character formation, because we often find in psychoanalytic literature that character studies are narrowed down too much to the province of the ego, due to a misapprehended application to studies of the origin of character of the sentence, 'The ego is the carrier of the character'. Especially when we deal with character in connection with resistance we have to liberate the concept in its genetic aspect from its inappropriate limitation to the province of the ego. This limitation was enforced partly through certain phases in the history of psychoanalytic technique. For the purposes of this paper we may term 'resistance' anything that stands in the way of the therapeutic procedure and goal in so far as it originates in the psychodynamics of the neurotic process.

If the two concepts character and resistance show up simultaneously in psychoanalytic literature or discussion, we almost instantly, as if in accordance with a conditioned reflex, react with a limitation of our thinking to a certain type of technical approach. The conditioner, as is well known, was Wilhelm Reich. Wilhelm Reich in his forceful manner usurped the combination of the two concepts by cutting down the vast area of their relationship to his rather narrow term, 'character resistance'. As happens so often in the progress of a science, such a bottleneck is useful for a short period in focusing attention on a narrow strip of the knowable, which is then thoroughly investigated; but it requires afterwards considerable effort to release the free flow of investigation of surrounding areas that were temporarily neglected.

For Reich 'character' and 'resistance' are identical.[2] His concept of character as an armor of defense against intrapsychic and external dangers presented the dynamics of character as so one-sided and limited that he was able to present the resistance in analysis only as an aspect of character in a specific dynamic situation. Character, then, for Reich becomes the expression of ego defense in analysis. As the authoritarian which he is known to be, Reich tried to make a totalitarian system of the study of specific defense reactions of the ego in analysis which was his special interest and his merit.

We owe it mainly to Anna Freud that the combination of character and resistance was broken, and 'character resistance' deflated to what it should

[2] Reich, Wilhelm: *Character Analysis*. New York: Orgone Institute Press, 1945.
Character and Resistance, *Psychoanalytic Quarterly*, 1951, 20, 72–26.

have remained, namely, characteristic ego defense and its dynamic importance as resistance in analysis. But it is Reich's unquestionable merit that he drew attention to how the ego resistances might be approached, and emphasized the necessity of investigating their infantile origin. Anna Freud's The Ego and the Mechanisms of Defense, although it does away with much of Wilhelm Reich's Character Analysis, could hardly have been produced without the latter.

If we make a short survey of resistances as Freud classified them in The Problem of Anxiety, and examine their relationship to character, we become aware that at least four of his five types of resistance, if not all five, are closely tied up with the character formation of the personality. Certainly the 'repression resistance', which Freud mentions as the first of the three ego resistances, is connected with the character of the person. We know that the hysterical character, for example, is inclined to use repression as the main mechanism of defense. 'Transference resistance' in most instances is only another form of repression resistance, formed under the specific psychodynamics of the psychoanalytic situation, and will always be shaped by the characteristic defensive features of the personality. Denial, identification with the aggressor, passive submissiveness in transference against unconscious hostility, and numerous other attitudes in a state of transference resistance are possible only because of the specific character structure of the personality. Even the 'resistance from secondary gain' will depend in its quality and quantity upon the structure of the character. Ego and resistance are so closely connected in psychoanalytic experience that we hardly expect resistances exerted by the ego, the carrier of character, not to be determined by the personality of the individual.

Resistance from the superego can hardly be different, the superego itself being only a step in the development of the ego. Many years ago I pointed out that the concept of superego resistance is somewhat nebulous and unclearly defined. If this resistance stems from the repressing influence of the superego, then it can be subsumed under repression resistance. If, on the other hand, 'superego resistance' refers to the masochistic attitude of the ego toward the superego, as expressed in the negative therapeutic reaction, it should be included among the ego resistances. But in both cases we cannot miss being aware of the close connection between resistances of this type and the total personality.

Let us now turn to the 'resistance of the id,' the last in Freud's classification. In its essence this resistance stems from the 'viscosity' of the libido, the sluggishness of the instinctual drives to develop and reach maturation. Such a deficiency within the id has a definite influence on the character formation, as, in the last analysis, all id tendencies have. Psychological infantilism is a good example of this relationship. Anal stubbornness in giving up an id tendency and its corresponding traits in the ego is another example, so well demonstrated in Freud's History of an Infantile Neurosis. The resistance of the id also is therefore closely connected with character.

We know from clinical experience that certain more or less well-defined character types frequently oppose certain types of resistance to therapeutic progress in analysis. To mention only a few examples, the anal character with its stubborn refusal to give material, its doubtfulness in accepting interpretations, and its sluggishness in giving up libido positions; the passive-feminine character with its superficial acceptance and latent aggressive rejection of explanations offered; the pseudonarcissistic character with conspicuous aggressiveness against the analyst in defense against anxiety. But such classifications have little value in deeper and extensive therapy. They entice particularly the beginner to approach the patient of a certain character type with the expectation of finding 'typical' forms of resistance. Psychoanalytic therapy is extremely individualistic and the single patient approaches patterns and types only very superficially. At the present stage of our science, particularly since we are still far from a unified psychoanalytic characterology, the combination of the concepts of character types and types of resistance should be kept as loose as possible.

Clinical and Therapeutic Aspects of Character Resistance

The term, character resistance, may be found earlier in psychoanalytic literature—though not in Freud's writings—but for those who have participated in the development of psychoanalytic literature since the early twenties, it is tied up with the therapeutic theory and technique of Wilhelm Reich. It is, therefore, not possible to discuss the concept of character resistance without reviewing and re-evaluating the therapeutic ideas of Wilhelm Reich. I refer, of course, to those theories which he evolved while he was still a psychoanalyst; that is, before his sexobiological and 'orgonic' phase. I must confess to a feeling of hesitancy in presenting Reich's ideas because, having lived through the era of his impact on the therapeutic thinking of his time and having struggled out of it, I am not altogether in a position to make a completely objective appraisal of their significance for the present-day psychoanalyst. But judging from the interest in Reich's concepts which persists—especially among students—perhaps my re-examination will be of more than merely historical value.

Reich first presented his therapeutic ideas and developed his theory of resistance and his characterology in two papers: the first, On Technique of Interpretation and Resistance Analysis, (subtitled, On the Lawful Development of Transference Neurosis), published in 1927, and the second, On Character Analysis, which appeared the following year. The whole structure of his therapeutic theory and technique he expanded in his book, Character Analysis, published in 1933 in German, the English translation appearing in 1945.

To make his renovation of analytic therapy impressive and still legitimate within the framework of freudian technique, Reich emphasizes repeatedly that the decisive change in psychoanalytic therapy took place when the

Read before the meeting of the New York Psychoanalytic Society, October 30, 1951.
Clinical and Therapeutic Aspects of Character Resistance, *Psychoanalytic Quarterly*, 22, 1–20.

therapeutic emphasis shifted from the symptom to the resistance. To this we must reply that a state of affairs in which the therapeutic efforts of psychoanalysis were focused only on the symptoms is an artificial construction, based on a confusion of different phases of the development of psychotherapy by Sigmund Freud. Actually preoccupation solely with the symptom belongs to the preanalytic phase of psychodynamic therapy. Psychoanalytic therapy was born when the resistances were taken into consideration, that is, when the symptoms were recognized as a result of a conflict between instinctual drives and ego, and the resistances, therefore, had to be taken into consideration in therapy. What changed gradually was the way in which psychoanalytic technique dealt with the resistances, and in this development Wilhelm Reich participated during a certain phase until further progress, mainly inspired by Anna Freud, nullified and cast into discard the greater part of Reich's therapeutic suggestions, including the concept of 'character resistance' as he had created it. But the interest that this therapeutic technique holds for many even today makes a critical investigation of his concepts necessary. What I shall undertake to demonstrate is that the concept of 'character resistance', as Reich formulated it, has to be discarded as an artifact which owed its existence to the peculiarities of Wilhelm Reich's theory and technique of psychoanalytic therapy.

The main aim of Reich's therapeutic efforts was to make analytic therapy a systematic procedure. Any student of psychoanalysis will agree that the main difficulty which he encounters as a beginner is to know what to consider as important among the wealth of the material offered by the patient, what to choose as the focus of his interest, and on what to make the patient focus and objectivate in order finally to interpret it. It appeared as an enormous help to the neophyte in therapy when Reich established his schematic theory of the structure of the neurosis and the neurotic personality, which was based on his technique of systematic analysis of resistances. I entered the Vienna Psychoanalytic Institute as a student just at the time when Reich took over the technical seminar and thus acquired a forum for the propagation of his technical ideas. Largely because of the impact of his forceful personality, he created the impression that resistances were only dealt with in psychoanalytic therapy since Reich had appeared on the analytic scene. We students were very much impressed; his systematic technical approach seemed to be the answer to our main technical problem and the way out of our therapeutic confusion. I readily admit that the interest he created in therapeutic technique led to considerable clarification and that the discussions in his seminars provided for me the first orientation in the difficult field of psychoanalytic therapy.

I consider Reich's first technical rule still valid with a few qualifications. This rule is to make the first approach to any material to be interpreted from the side of the ego, not from the side of the id; in other words, the defense or resistance has to be dealt with before the unconscious content is told to the patient. This point is particularly emphasized by Reich, one could say overemphasized, concerning all transference situations. It is from the transference situations that Wilhelm Reich develops his theory of personality structure and his characterology. Reich regards all transference situations, particularly in the beginning—in fact all relationship or non-relationship to the analyst—as the expression of resistance. His reasoning is that analytic therapy disturbs the neurotic equilibrium which the patient has difficulty in maintaining anyway. As the disturber of the patient's intrapsychic armistice, as it were, the analyst necessarily becomes an intruder and frightening enemy. The patient, therefore, will react to the analysis either with open rebellion or, if this reaction is felt as too daring or too dangerous, his defense will go 'underground' and he will react with superficial obedience, but underneath he will build up latent 'secret' resistances which are even more 'dangerous' than open negative reactions and to which Reich, therefore, pays particular attention. For Reich initial transference situations are never repetitions of genuine object relationships, which may or may not be used by the need to resist the analytic process. For him transference and resistance are identical. The result of this equation of transference and resistance is that Reich is full of suspicion about every positive transference manifestation at the beginning of treatment. He does not trust it, refuses to accept it at face value and seeks systematically to destroy it. He calls this procedure 'systematic resistance analysis'.

According to Reich the initial transference resistance expresses itself in a specific form which is characteristic of the patient's personality. The distinguishing and important feature of this resistance is not the content, which might be the same with different personalities, but the form in which it is expressed and is felt by the analyst. The defense of a female patient with a male analyst might take the form of masculine aggressiveness, or of superiority and coldness, or of suspicion and mistrust and other similar negative and aggressive features. Reich postulates that the form of the initial resistance against the analytic approach—the 'how' by which it expresses itself—is specific for the personality because this form is taken over and over again by any further resistance that the patient develops during the course of his analysis. Since this form of resistance is characteristic for the personality of the patient, Wilhelm Reich considers it the expression of the patient's character and therefore calls it 'character resistance'. The consistent analysis of this form of resistance Reich presents as his therapeutic innovation, and terms it 'character analysis'. He is particularly concerned with what he calls the 'secret' resistances of the personality, and repeatedly emphasizes how 'dangerous' they are. The danger of secret resistances almost seems to haunt him. He is of the opinion that secret resistances, if neglected, destroy all therapeutic efforts, and he believes that if the analyst interprets beyond them, that is, if he deals with recognizable material from a deeper layer than the one to which the secret resistance belongs, he creates what he calls a 'chaotic situation'. He maintains that analyses conducted in such disorderly fashion are ruined and have to be given up without therapeutic results because the damage done by unsystematic interpretation is irreparable.

One can recognize that Reich's theory of therapy is closely tied up with another systematizing concept of his, that of 'stratification'. For Reich the mental apparatus is structured in the form of layers, and the order of the layers has to be considered in therapy, particularly in the interpretative approach to resistances. In his case histories, in which he shows all his brilliance as a clinician, he demonstrates very clearly what he meant by a systematic approach to a character resistance. If, for example, such a resistance manifests itself as a silent smile which accompanies the patient's productions, Reich considers it useless and even dangerous to interpret any material produced while the analytic situation is under the influence of such a resistance. According to him the only correct technique is to interpret the resistance expressed in this smiling according to the layers of its significance systematically from the most superficial and genetically latest layer to the next one and in proper order down to its deepest significance. In his book he demonstrates the different resistive meanings of the smile of a patient and unmasks it first as an attempt at reconciliation, in the next layer as a compensation for anxiety, and in the third as the expression of a feeling of superiority. He is convinced that had he interpreted the second significance before the first, or the third before the second, or, even worse, the third before the first, the whole analysis would have been hopelessly disturbed and would have resulted in chaotic disorder. Since the analysis of the resistive smiling led to different defensive attitudes established against painful experiences in the patient's infantile past, and since these contain the patient's most characteristic attitudes toward unpleasure, he considers this resistance an expression of the patient's character. He claims that even if this resistance is unfolded and removed by systematic interpretation, it will return with the appearance of every further resistance and will have to be dealt with systematically again, since this typical form of resisting is the most essential constituent of the patient's character. He therefore calls it 'character resistance'.

It might be appropriate to add a few words about the further development of this concept of 'character resistance' into what Reich calls 'character analysis'. When Reich examines systematically the origin of the resistance form of a patient he considers this study a characterological one, since he is of the opinion that it expresses the patient's character, and he makes the study of such a resistance the basis of his characterology. For Reich character is something that establishes a 'typical', specific resistance in analysis which repeats itself always in the same form. From the fact that the attitude of defense characteristic of a person serves as a permanent resistance in analysis, Reich makes the bold conclusion that character itself is a resistance, an apparatus of protection against the outside world and against instinctual drives. Since Reich's characterology is based on technical experience in therapy one could call it 'therapeutic-technical'. His technique, in which he focuses all technical efforts on the resistance expressed in a specific attitude, he terms 'character analysis', since he maintains that this attitude of defense forms the central and most essential part of the character. He claims that his technique is the only correct one because it strives to undermine the neurosis in all directions from a firm stronghold.

The ego's resistive reaction against analysis, representing the 'character' of the patient, Reich tries to trace back to the infantile experiences which were responsible for the formation of the specific way, the 'how' in which the patient resists the analytic effort to uncover unconscious material. Reich tries to establish a metapsychology of the characteristic attitudes of protection. According to Reich character from the topological viewpoint is an apparatus of protection, from the dynamic viewpoint it is composed of frozen resistances against unconscious drives plus instinctual satisfactions obtained through the character attitudes themselves, and economically it serves the avoidance of unpleasure, for example anxiety, as well as the establishment of the neurotic equilibrium mainly due to the satisfaction of repressed infantile drives through the character attitude itself. These metapsychological relationships of defense attitudes Reich illustrates in his book with excellent examples. The case histories are the best part of his book.

Since character and resistance are practically identical for Reich, he arrives at strange concepts about character which he tries to illustrate by a simile. To him character is an armor formed through chronic 'hardening' of the ego. The meaning and purpose of this armor is protection from inner and outer dangers. And from this comparison of character with an armor he makes statements which might be appropriate for the armor of a medieval knight, but hardly for a person's character. For example: character, Reich says, results in a definite limitation of the psychic mobility of the total personality since a person cannot move freely is he is encased in armor. Nevertheless, the armor has to be imagined as somewhat movable with a normal person, for one has to imagine that it has gaps or openings through which the emission and withdrawal of object cathexes can take place. Reich speaks of the 'rigid' armor of the emotionally blocked person, or the 'prickly' armor of the querulent and aggressive type, of 'armoring of the surface' with patients blocked in their emotions or with the compulsive character, of 'armoring of the depth' with the hysterical character.

He further considers the libidinous gratification derived from the specific defense as the linkage between the different defensive attitudes organized in the character resistance, as the putty that fills out the gaps, as the joints between the different parts of the armor, and similar farfetched comparisons. I have presented this thumbnail sketch of Reich's characterology to show that his characterology is the end product of his therapeutic theory, of which the concept of character resistance, the subject of this paper, is the most essential part. I shall now undertake to evaluate Reich's therapeutic theory and technique.

The first postulate against which we have to raise objections is Reich's assumption that particularly the initial transference is exclusively the means and expression of resistance. There is probably no better argument against this notion than the following quotation from Freud:

> The part taken by resistance in the transference-love is unquestionable and very considerable. *But this love was not created by the resistance;*[1] the latter finds it ready to hand, exploits it and aggravates the manifestation of it. Nor is its genuineness impugned by the resistance . . . it is true that the transference-love consists of new editions of old traces and that it repeats infantile reactions. But this is the essential character of every love. There is no love that does not reproduce infantile prototypes. The infantile conditioning factor in it is just what gives it its compulsive character which verges on the pathological. The transference-love has perhaps a degree less of freedom than the love which appears in ordinary life and is called normal; it displays its dependence on the infantile pattern more clearly, is less adaptable and capable of modification, but that is all and that is nothing essential.
>
> By what other signs can the genuineness of a love be recognized? By its power to achieve results, its capacity to ac-

---

[1] Italics added.

complish its aim? In this respect the transference-love seems to give place to none; one has the impression that one could achieve anything by its means.

Let us resume, therefore: one has no right to dispute the 'genuine' nature of the love which makes its appearance in the course of analytic treatment. However lacking in normality it may seem to be, this quality is sufficiently explained when we remember that the condition of being in love in ordinary life outside analysis is also more like abnormal than normal mental phenomena. The transference-love is characterized, nevertheless, by certain features which ensure it a special position. In the first place, it is provoked by the analytic situation; second, it is greatly intensified by the resistance which dominates this situation; and third, it is to a high degree lacking in regard for reality, is less sensible, less concerned about consequences, more blind in its estimation of the person loved, than we are willing to admit of normal love. We should not forget, however, that it is precisely these departures from the norm that make up the essential element in the condition of being in love.[2]

Freud further gives the following advice concerning the handling of the initial transference: 'One must wait until the transference, which is the most delicate matter of all to deal with, comes to be employed as resistance'.[3] Here it is again clear that initial transference and resistance are not identical, but that the transference becomes sooner or later employed by the resistance.

It is one of Reich's basic errors that he denies the genuine character of positive transference, particularly in the beginning of the analysis. Reich's technique of dealing with the transference seemingly is an outgrowth of his own suspicious character and the belligerent attitude that stems from it. This makes him imply 'secret' resistances even where genuine transference-love is established. Under the impact of his technique, which is conditioned by the mistrust in the patient's positive transference reactions and by the disbelief in the genuineness of initial and even later transference-love, the patient must necessarily feel unaccepted and constantly questioned as to the truthfulness of his positive feelings toward the analyst, so that he finally has to develop negative reactions out of his feeling of being frustrated and rejected. If these negative reactions finally manifest them-

[2] Freud: Coll. Papers, II, pp. 387–388.
[3] *Ibid.*, p. 360.

selves in dreams or otherwise Reich is triumphant because it proves to him that the initial transference was not genuinely positive. His whole therapeutic approach is full of aggressiveness and belligerency. It is revealing to observe how regularly he uses comparisons from the battlefield, and the way in which he uses them. Again and again he compares the resistance with a dangerous and tricky enemy who has to be exterminated at all costs. The consistent analysis of the character resistance he calls the 'stronghold' from which the therapist has to 'undermine' the enemies' position. The patient is assumed constantly to deceive the analyst who has to be on guard against 'secret agents' of resistance all the time. At the time he published his book in 1933, his technique had reached a degree of aggression that he himself felt it dangerous for his patients, so that he found it necessary to warn them of the possibility that their egos might break down under the constant hammering at their character resistances. When he claimed at the beginning of his therapeutic crusade that his new technique does away with the directly aggressive approach to the patient's resistance and replaces it by analytic dissolution, we must reply that, on the contrary, the further development of his character therapy is much more sadistic and destructive than the analytic technique as it was developed before him. In his recent book, Listen, Little Man!, he releases all the fury of mockery, abuse, irony and sarcasm toward the suffering neurotic.

When one reads Reich's analytic papers one will recognize that he lacks insight and understanding of one of the basic characteristics in man's emotional life. He ignores the phenomenon of ambivalence. Freud designates as a characteristic of infantile instinctual life ' . . . the fact that the contrasting pair of impulses are developed in almost the same manner, a situation which was happily designated by Bleuler by the term *ambivalence*'.[4] Reich refuses to acknowledge this basic fact of the instinctual life of man; for him ambivalence is not something inherent, an innate characteristic of certain instinctual manifestations, but is acquired in the course of development due to the frustration of instinctual needs. According to Reich our drives originally have only positive and loving aims and attitudes (although strangely enough he denies their genuine reappearance in the transference, at least in the beginning of the analysis); hatred and destructiveness are the result of frustration by reality. This denial of instinctual ambivalence as well as of the ambivalence of feelings or attitudes toward objects is essential in Reich's theory of personality, for it is responsible for his theoretical construction of the personality in the form of layers. If negative signs appear among positive ones in the transference,

---

[4] Freud: *Contributions to the Theory of Sex*. In: *The Basic Writings of Sigmund Freud*. New York: Modern Library, 1938, p. 598.

Reich considers their simultaneous appearance not the expression of an ambivalent attitude but believes that either the negative ones are breaking through the positive surface from a deeper layer or vice versa. The order of the layers depends on the quantitative relationship between the manifestations with opposite signs in the sense that the superficial layer predominates in its manifestation. This layered structure of the personality goes very deep. From five to six layers are sometimes enumerated by Reich. They all are supposed to contribute to the character resistance and, according to Reich, the systematic removal of their contributions to the initial and constant resistance in orderly sequence is supposed to be the only correct analytic procedure in character analysis.

The auxiliary construction of the psyche in the form of layers is not Reich's original idea. Freud used the concept of superficial and deeper layers of the mind repeatedly and emphasized that we have to reach out for spatial relationships in order to gain some plastic concept of the working of the complicated mental apparatus. 'Upper and lower level' are often used in dreams even of persons not psychoanalytically trained to represent the conscious mind and the unconscious.

What we have to object to in Reich's theories is the concept of multiple layers that can and have to be peeled off systematically in therapy with careful avoidance of penetrating a deeper layer before all the others above it are removed. Freud himself made an attempt to demonstrate the relationship of mental contents, or better cathexes of presently actual and regressive formations and tendencies, with a comparison, and when reading it one obtains the impression that he wants to emphasize how incorrect a strict application of the concept of stratification is in connection with mental material. He tries to demonstrate this by a comparison:

> Now let us make the fantastic supposition that Rome were not a human dwelling-place, but a mental entity with just as long and varied a past history: that is, in which nothing once constructed had perished, and all the earlier stages of development had survived alongside the latest. This would mean that in Rome the palaces of the Caesars were still standing on the Palatine and the Septizonium of Septimius Severus was still towering to its old height; that the beautiful statues were still standing in the colonnade of the Castle of St. Angelo, as they were up to its siege by the Goths, and so on. But more still: where the Palazzo Caffarelli stands there would also be, without this being removed, the Temple of Jupiter Capitolinus, not merely in its latest form, moreover, as the Romans of the

Caesars saw it, but also in its earliest shape, when it still wore an Etruscan design and was adorned with terra-cotta antefixae. Where the Colosseum stands now we could at the same time admire Nero's Golden House; on the Piazza of the Pantheon we should find not only the Pantheon of today as bequeathed to us by Hadrian, but on the same site also Agrippa's original edifice; indeed, the same ground would support the church of Santa Maria sopra Minerva and the old temple over which it was built. And the observer would need merely to shift the focus of his eyes, perhaps, or change his position, in order to call up a view of either the one or the other.[5]

From this comparison we gain the impression that Freud definitely was opposed to the concept of simple layers because it misrepresents the spatial coincidence of mental contents as if they were temporal and spatial successions.

Reich's demand for systematic technique based upon the alleged stratification of the character resistance is unjustified since the rigid concept of multiple stratification itself is incorrect. This does not mean that interpretation should not be given in an orderly and organized fashion, in which the sequence—interpretation of the defense first, of the unconscious content second, or id part after ego contribution of the formation to be interpreted—is almost always valid. Reich particularly emphasizes the damaging effect of too early or too deep interpretation which is supposed to upset the whole therapeutic schedule to an irreparable degree. The careful training in psychoanalytic institutes nowadays prevents beginners from making the mistake of making shocking interpretations that could do damage, scare the patient, or severely disturb him. The 'what' and 'how' of interpretation is something that can be taught only to some degree. The rest has to be afforded by the therapist's gift and intuition. Systematization of interpretation impedes the flexibility of the analyst in acting according to the patient's needs and according to the make-up of his own personality.

In my own experience I have found that even the oversight or neglect of an initial 'secret' resistance—the most dangerous mistake in Reich's view—does not have the irreparable consequences that Reich ascribes to such a technical blunder. Some years ago I took in therapeutic analysis a physician who had read about analysis and had friends who were analyzed. In the second or third hour he released a flood of disconnected obscenities, acting, as I thought, according to a misconception of free

---

[5] Freud: *Civilization and Its Discontents*. London: Hogarth Press, 1930, pp. 17–18.

association. Since his profuse profanity made the impression of being exaggerated in its content and quantity, I simply told him, 'Don't force yourself', and explained free association to him. He calmed down and from then on spoke in a much less excited manner. The analysis proceeded in orderly fashion. He was in analysis for two and a half years and improved greatly. Since there was little movement during the last six months in his analysis, we decided to terminate temporarily. He was pleased with the result of his analysis which had produced a decisive change in his personality. From a rather timid individual with relatively limited capacity in his profession, he became a very successful, steady physician who was a strong support for his family, whereas his wife had dominated him before and had been the main provider. There were some slight anxieties which we considered to be the scars left from his neurosis. After a year of all-round success he returned for some more analysis, because he felt something had been left undone. When he was on the couch again, he began with bitter reproaches about my attitude at the beginning of his analysis. When I had responded to his flood of four-letter words with, 'Don't force yourself', he reacted only to the 'don't'. It prevented him from the free expression of his aggression. He never dared to come out openly again with all the dirty words, accusations and reproaches which he had desired to hurl at me and which had been pent up from childhood when his parents applied the 'don't' to his aggressive behavior. In the short period during which I saw him the second time, he released all the resentment that he had accumulated on account of my first 'don't' and which he had not dared to express in his analysis. Only after the first termination, when he was not any more under the direct influence of the analyst, did he accumulate the courage to come back and 'tell me off' and thus complete the analytic work.

According to Reich, the initial mistake which built up a defense against free expression toward the analyst—a typical dangerous 'secret' resistance—should have rendered all further analytic work null and void. The layer of resistance below the surface should have destroyed the effect of all later interpretatins of further material. That this was not so is clearly demonstrated by this brief case report. The analysis was able to progress and achieve satisfactory results despite the secret resistance.

Reich propagates the systematic sequence of interpretation—by which he almost always means interpretation of resistance—because the cardinal resistance, initiating the transference and shaping all subsequent resistance throughout the analysis, is for him identical with the character of the patient. And here our main objection to Reich's concept of 'character resistance' has to be raised. Reich's concept of 'character' is far too limited.

It might be appropriate to say a few words about the definition of character as I understand it. Character, in my opinion, designates the features of personality which are more or less indelibly engraved upon it, which express themselves in our actions and reactions, and by which one personality structure can be differentiated from others. Since actions and reactions as they manifest themselves are the business of the ego, we are accustomed to attribute the character of the personality to the ego. For Reich, character would be only the expression of the resisting ego. But a short deliberation reveals that character is formed not only by the specific way of dealing with the multitude of stimuli which impinge on the ego from outside and from within, but that it is deeply rooted in the quantity of specific pressings upward from the id in the form of instinctual strivings. In this respect character is based on the organic substratum of our psychic personality, as was already pointed out by Freud in his study of Leonardo: 'The tendency to repression, as well as the ability to sublimate, must be traced back to the *organic basis of the character,* upon which alone the psychic structure arises'.[6]

A third contributor to character formation is the superego with its specific, more or less rigid demands. All three provinces of the mental structure of the personality, therefore, contribute to the formation of character. A definition of character, then, would designate it as the sum total of specific reactions of the individual, determined by the interaction of the three provinces of the mind according to their inherited and acquired dynamic contents. Ego, id and superego have to be involved where character studies are attempted.

From all this it is obvious that the concept of character implies more than resistance in analysis. There is no doubt that Reich's concept of character as a dynamic formation which produces specific and constant resistances in analysis is far too narrow and one-sided. A technical-therapeutic characterology is very insufficient to explain the many facets of the personality, and character certainly consists of more than defenses.

Reich's 'character resistance' is outdated and hardly useful nowadays. However, some of Reich's contributions to the theory and technique of psychoanalytic therapy were of considerable value. His ideas and the forceful way in which he presented them led to the clarification of many concepts in therapy. In my opinion the most important result of the commotion he created is Anna Freud's book, The Ego and the Mechanisms of Defense. When I read Anna Freud's book again recently, after having worked my way through Wilhelm Reich's papers on technique, I experienced great

---

[6] Freud: *Leonardo da Vinci: A Study in Psychosexuality*. New York: Random House, 1947, p. 120. (Italics added.)

relief. One feels the pressure of Reich's technique even while reading his papers, and particularly his book on character analysis. Anna Freud's book, when read after Reich's technical papers, produces a feeling of liberation. It is as if, after being hurled in a boat through rapids, one emerged in a calm, wide body of water where the mountains that narrowed the river have receded into the background and a relaxed survey of the open landscape is possible in many directions. Though this comparison may sound somewhat poetic, it helps to illustrate the fundamental difference in the basic attitude of the authors. Anna Freud's concept of character is much broader than Reich's. According to her, character is approximately the whole set of attitudes habitually adapted by an individual ego for the solution of the never-ending series of inner conflicts. Character, then, is the single ego's typical way of dealing with the conflict between the instinctual urges coming from the id, the dangers coming from the outside world, and the threats of the superego which represent the incorporation of a most important part of what was once the outside world, the parental authority. Every ego is characterized by the choice it makes among the instinctual urges which it seeks to satisfy due to its access to motility, by the determination of those instinctual urges which it rejects, and by the methods of defense which it uses against the powers threatening it from outside and from within.

It is significant that in broadening Reich's therapeutic bottleneck Anna Freud emphasizes the concept of defense in contrast to Reich's almost exclusive preoccupation with the concept 'resistance'. It is well known, after the original introduction of the term 'defense' into psychopathology, Sigmund Freud abandoned it for more than forty years because during this time he was investigating mainly one type of defense, repression. In Inhibition, Symptom and Anxiety, he reinstated the concept of defense and put repression back in its place as only one among many typical defenses against inner and outer dangers. The reinstatement of the term 'defense' paved the way, as it were, for Anna Freud's studies of the defense mechanisms. Freud also laid the groundwork for the psychodynamic understanding of the ego. But while Freud's ego analysis was concerned with the ego's dynamic structure, its composition, and the development of its organization, Anna Freud's ego analysis is a study of the ego's activity, or at least of one very important and constantly applied activity, namely that of defense. It is defense analysis. The importance of this step in the development of our science can hardly be overestimated. Only after the study of the ego's activity of defense was added did psychoanalysis become a well-rounded science of man's mind and its working.

It is my impression that the importance of this newest addition to our science has not been sufficiently recognized and that it has not yet penetrated the thinking and therapeutic technique of most analysts. It is easy to understand why this is so. We are still very much impressed, even fascinated, by the id contents which psychoanalysis enables us to discover. The working of the ego is so inconspicuous and silent that we are hardly aware of it. It is only necessary to recall the contrast between the experience of dreaming—which may occur in the most vivid images and with most violent emotions and always manifests itself as a sensual perception—and the forgetting of the dream which occurs so quietly and unnoticed. Without having become aware of any activity within ourselves, we simply recognize the fact that the dream is gone or that we are left with only a few meager memory fragments of an experience that, a few minutes before, had filled us with great intensity of perception and feeling. We notice the result of the ego's defensive activity—in the case of dreams the forgetting through repression—but we are completely unable to perceive this activity itself, and this applies to all unconscious defense activities of the ego. We never can catch them at work; we can only reconstruct them from the result. While one can listen with the 'third ear' to the utterances of the id, it needs a most refined instrument to register the workings of the ego defenses. It has been my observation that it is a most difficult task to teach students to pay attention to these mute and subterranean workings of the ego. Even the experienced analyst must constantly exercise self-discipline in order to remain aware of the ego's defense measures in therapy.

Perhaps it is carrying coals to Newcastle to emphasize here the significance and importance of Anna Freud's contribution to psychoanalysis. But judging from my experience as a teacher, from our scientific meetings and from the current literature I find too little real influence of Anna Freud's studies, although often lip service is paid to them. 'Mechanism of defense' is used glibly to indicate the advanced state of one's analytic thinking, and 'identification with the aggressor' is mentioned in order to display consideration of the ego. I believe it will require a great deal of time and effort on the part of training analysts to make Anna Freud's discoveries of the silent activities of the ego penetrate general analytic thinking and improve psychoanalytic technique so that it will consist of id-plus-ego analysis, applied alternatingly.

I cannot here present all the technical implications and modifications that arise from Anna Freud's studies. I can only contrast them to Reich's therapeutic ideas and his technique. The difference at first sight is not very conspicuous; both emphasize ego consideration. But on closer inspection this difference is very profound; in fact one has to consider it fundamental. Reich looks for resistances, suspects them in every transference manifestation and considers it the only proper technique to bring them relentlessly into the open and to follow them up with interpretations through all layers down to their roots. Reich's ego consideration is only apparent; it concerns itself only with the ego as it resists the analytic process. The ego for Reich is the enemy of analysis, and a deceiving and tricky enemy at that. His approach to the ego, therefore, is a hostile, aggressive one as we have demonstrated. Anna Freud, in contrast to Reich, remains an objective observer of the ego and is only concerned with the understanding of its functioning inside and outside the analytic situation. She objects explicitly to any suspicious inimical and pressing attitude toward the ego's resistance and defense in the analytic situation. She obviously has Wilhelm Reich's technique in mind when she states: 'In my opinion we do our patients a great injustice if we describe these transferred defense-reactions as "camouflage" or say that the patients are "pulling the analyst's leg" or purposely deceiving him in some other way. . . . The patient *is* in fact candid when he gives expression to the impulse or affect in the only way still open to him, namely, in the distorted defensive measure.'[7] Defense mechanisms which the ego learned to use against inner and outer dangers during its lifetime, particularly in childhood, the ego will find useful and will by necessity have to apply in the analytic situation. The therapeutic task is to notice them during the analytic process, to observe them or better to reconstruct their working from the result and to demonstrate to the patient their general application by the personality in the present and past; furthermore, to trace their genesis and their deepest motivation in the form of infantile anxieties; and finally to render their use unnecessary through analytic comparison between the present and past. Only if in this way ego analysis complements the analysis of the id, is psychoanalytic method a study and therapy of the total personality. Only then can we hope to be successful in our therapeutic approach to what Anna Freud calls the 'innumerable transformations, distortions and deformities of the ego which are in part the accompaniment of and in part substitutes of neurosis'.

Anna Freud says especially that she considers the term 'character analysis' not very appropriate for ego analysis and defense analysis. The term 'character resistance' is not used by her at all, and I think it is rightly omitted in her book. Though a specific defense reaction which serves as a resistance in analysis might be characteristic for the patient, we have no justification to identify this defense reaction with the totality of reactions of a personality, which is properly called character. Such an identification is implied if we use the term 'character resistance' for a major defense

---

[7] Freud, Anna: *The Ego and the Mechanisms of Defense*. London: Hogarth Press, 1937, p. 20.

mechanism of a patient in analysis. I therefore feel we are justified in abandoning the term 'character resistance' as inappropriate.

Oral Invasion and Self-Defence

In her paper 'Negativism and Emotional Surrender', presented at the International Congress in Amsterdam in 1951, Anna Freud pointed out that certain children go through a negativistic stage in their early development. These negativistic children refuse the slightest demand or assistance from the part of their surroundings, because they want to be independent. Such negativistic behavior might be repeated in pre-adolescence, in adolescence, and to an extreme degree in psychosis. In the case of such negativism any approach on the part of the surrounding persons is experienced as a claim or a hostile attack.

Anna Freud enumerated the explanations given for this type of behaviour, such as early disappointment in the love object, early seduction, temptations by the object, excessive narcissism. All of these explanations she found insufficient to explain this type of negativism. Anna Freud pointed out as an important reason for the negativistic attitude that for these persons love is a loss and not a gain. Love for them means impoverishment and subjugation. In these persons there exists the misconception and fear that to love anyone means to surrender to the object to an extent which would make them lose their own identity and would transform them into the person whom they love. They would thus be 'invaded' by the love object. Anna Freud illustrated this negativism with very impressive case material. One of her cases in particular demonstrated the fear against which the negativism was established as a defence. It was that of a girl who was negativistic as a child as well as when grown up, and in treatment, with one exception, when she fell in love with a musical conductor, with whom she was absolutely 'hörig' (enthralled) so that during this period she followed him everywhere like an appendix of the love object. Here the 'invasion' by the object which is warded off in the negativistic attitude had actually taken place in a love relationship in form of enthralment (*Hörigkeit*). Anna Freud then stated that in observing these patients during

Oral Invasion and Self-Defense, *International Journal of Psychoanalysis*, 1957, *38*, 204–208.

treatment one obtains a 'dim perception of the mental process' which underlies the negativism of these patients. It is their tendency to fall back on a complete oneness with the object, which oneness, however, would not lead to an enrichment but to an invasion by the love object with a consecutive loss of the integrity of their personalities. Their negativism then has to safeguard the intactness of their own identity.

Anna Freud's paper has not been published, probably because she thought it too preliminary. In the abstract of it (2) she reported only the clinical observations in a very abbreviated form, not her suggestions as to the deepest cause of negativism. She may have wanted to wait until what she calls a 'dim perception' of the process underlying this type of negativism becomes clearer in the course of further clinical observations. But she referred to this paper when she addressed the Detroit Society in the fall of 1952, and again in the paper which she read in 1953 at the International Congress in London (1).

Anna Freud's paper furnished me with the understanding of some of the difficulties which I met during the treatment of two patients. In turn, the analytic material which these patients offer seems to corroborate Anna Freud's 'dim perception' of the process underlying the negativistic resistance which these patients showed in treatment. Both patients are females in the late thirties; both have been in analysis for a considerable time.

The first patient was extremely difficult in respect of technique, and needed most careful handling as far as the transference was concerned. She was a single child. Her father had died in an accident when she was only a few months old; she has no memory of him. The mother was a very dominating character, a lady in high society, of considerable wealth and greatly interested in horses. She was absolutely set in her ideas about social position, educational principles, behaviour, mainly behaviour which signifies 'belonging to society'. She had no doubts as to the right set of values, was very sure of what and what not to do, and was determined to teach all this to her little girl.

The mother nursed the child for almost a year. As a little girl the patient was deeply attached to her mother, partly because she was not able to establish another object relationship. She had a long series of governesses, but these did not provide any lasting objects, since the mother soon became dissatisfied with and dismissed every single one of them. The deep and lasting attachment to her mother shaped the little girl's love life in a particular way with which we will not here concern ourselves.

When the little girl was five years old, the mother married again. The girl made an attempt to attach herself to her stepfather and tried to find in him an ally against the mother's domination. But this attempt at an oedipal relationship soon ended in failure. The stepfather turned out to be a very weak person, completely dominated by his wife. The little girl found out very early that the mother had not much love for her second husband, and recognized her almost contemptuous attitude towards him. The mother knew how to prohibit the girl with a strong hand from forming a satisfactory relationship with the father.

The attachment to her mother had not only the most important influence on the patient's love life, but also on the transference which she presented in the analysis. From the first few sessions on she developed a very deep, impressive, all-pervasive love for the analyst. A few details of her behaviour will demonstrate the extension of this transference-love. She developed an irresistible need for closeness to the analyst which expressed itself in a kind of craving for some at least indirect physical contact with me. She took every opportunity to touch objects that belonged to me, for example, my overcoat when it was hanging in the entrance to my office, or to pick up a worthless piece of paper that I had touched with my hand, etc. Sometimes the urge to touch me was almost uncontrollable. This craving for bodily closeness could without difficulty be recognized as a repetition of her infantile desire to be close to the mother. In the first part of her analysis it was an absolute necessity for her to know where I was going, when I left town. If I did not give her the possible minimum of information she was thrown into utter despair and unbearable anxiety, as if her lifeline had been cut and she was abandoned and exposed to die. She had an almost irresistible urge to follow me on my trips, and in the beginning of her treatment I had to allow her to do this a few times in order to alleviate her unbearable pain and anxiety. One is reminded of the negativistic patient of Anna Freud's who once fell in love with the conductor and followed hm around like an appendage. Hand in hand with this craving for physical closeness with the analyst she showed an intense curiosity about myself, my life, my family. She made all kinds of efforts to find out about me and used all kinds of methods to satisfy this curiosity. In her almost irresistible greed for knowledge about me, which she sometimes actually felt as a sensation in her mouth cavity, she had no hesitation in transgressing the ordinary limitations of the therapeutic situation and even of conventional behaviour. As can easily be understood, the handling of the transference was no easy task with this extremely oral character. The slightest restrictive admonition she experienced as a total rejection which threw her into utter despair with suicidal tendencies. It was necessary to steer skilfully between an at least somewhat permissive attitude and the most cautious restraint. To gauge how much restriction she could stand was no easy task and required much empathy and intuition.

I do not wish, however, to enter into a discussion of the technical aspects of this case. I want only to depict the oral character of the patient through the medium of the technical difficulty which she presented. Her deep and intense love-transference made her outwardly very submissive. But it could easily be seen that behind this submission she was very controlling and dominating and that her love-tendencies were all-engulfing. It was difficult for the therapist to extricate himself time and again from her octopus-like psychic embrace, which was a repetition of her first oral attachment to her mother. However, behind this obvious absorption of the love object, there was established an adamantine resistance to any real receptivity. This resistance was extended over many areas, but was mostly noticeable in connexion with intellectual perception. She herself called her difficulties in intellectual grasping 'compulsive thinking'. They better deserve the name 'defensive thinking'. She showed a peculiar attitude when something was explained to her, some idea, some theoretical concept, even some relatively simple facts. She then listened with extreme eagerness in order to absorb thoroughly what was communicated to her. Her whole body became tense through her fervour in taking in what was explained to her. She repeated the words silently with her lips while talked to, she made movements with her hands as if organizing the material for easier absorption, in short, she appeared as a most ardent receiver of the message conveyed to her. As if in order to understand even better, she asked for more exact information about a detail which she seemed unable to grasp. When this detail was explained to her, she fastened on to a detail of this explanation which she would like to understand better. At times she repeated this procedure even with this secondary explanation so that she demanded a tertiary explanation. In the end one found out that she did not understand the essence of what one wanted to convey to her in the first place. In this way her eagerness to understand turned out to be a defence against the reception of the idea which one wanted to communicate to her.

The material in her analysis showed that the person against whom this resistance was originally established was the mother. The analysis established that an attempt to resist the domination by her mother was definitely made by the patient between two and three years of age. It took the form of constipation as a rebellion against the mother's anal demands. The mother tried to break the spirit of rebellion with the help of enemas and increased demands of obedience. This overpowering mother was outwardly successful. But the resistance went underground and spread into many areas. Almost everything the patient did in later life was in contrast to what her mother had intended for and expected of her. The patient remained unmarried; she chose a humble profession unworthy of the high social position of her family. She avoided the social obligations so important to her mother, she was a failure in horse shows, and she acquired political ideas which her mother abhorred. She stuck to all this with anal stubbornness. But the interpretation and working through of the anal origin of her resistive attitude, mainly in the form of rebellion against the enemas which the governess had to apply at her mother's command, did not sufficiently change it and did not bring about the expected result. The all-pervading nature of the defence, its 'massive' character, suggested that it belonged to an earlier phase of development. I had to realize that particularly for her resistance against intellectual perception an earlier than anal origin had to be postulated. This defence was established against the overwhelming oral penetration by the breast.

In almost innumerable dreams of the patient breast and penis were identified. At the same time the idea of being penetrated by the membrum virile was completely inconceivable to her; the mere thought of it threw her into a panic. One can easily understand how severely this impeded her relationship with men. Her whole sex life was distorted by this fear of being penetrated and 'filled out by the man'. But the defence against penetration did even more damage to her intellectual development. Any explanation given to her had for her the unconscious significance of being penetrated by the idea, of being pierced by the concept, of being forced into oral receptivity and submissiveness to the other person, in the last analysis to the first overwhelming object, the mother, or more specifically, her breast. I formed this opinion in analogy to Anna Freud's description and explanation of general characterological negativism. When I explained to the patient for the first time that her defence against receptivity towards ideas was due to their being identified with a breast that threatened to penetrate and invade her oral cavity and her whole personality, she tried to defend herself in her usual manner by not being able to grasp some details of the explanation. But she reacted to it after the hour in a peculiar way. She always had what is called a 'cast-iron stomach', which could stand even the most indigestible food. But for two days after the explanation her stomach was so severely upset that she had to vomit repeatedly.

During the further course of the analysis it was possible to unearth the earliest manifestation of her resistance against the domination by her powerful mother in the form of an eating disturbance at the end of her second year. With the working through of this early manifestation her 'defensive thinking' markedly decreased.

The second patient from whose analysis I am going to report was a married woman, the mother of two children. Her neurotic difficulties were manifested mainly in the relationship to her children and in her love life, in which she was unable to find complete satisfaction. Another area in which her neurosis led to considerable difficulties was her social contacts. I would like to describe first her social impediment. When she attended a party or had guests at her home she was at first very lively and participated vividly in the conversation; she was what one would call 'in the swing of things'. But after a while she began to feel uncomfortable, and soon had to withdraw from the conversation. She felt inferior, because she considered herself incapable of thinking correctly and effectively, became depressed, and left the party as early as possible. At home she often withdrew from the guests to her room. In the course of the analysis it was not difficult to recognize that her inhibition was a defence against aggressive thoughts and feelings which she was afraid she might express if she continued the conversation. It is of interest, in connexion with our theme, in what way her aggression was mobilized at such occasions. If a controversy arose in the conversation she felt forced inwardly to win her point at all costs. She could not afford to be beaten in an argument. She had to defend her standpoint, because for her admission of the standpoint of her opponent's argument was equal to complete submission, to utter defeat, even to a complete loss of her identity. In order to avoid an obvious fight in polite society she had to withdraw from the conversation entirely. At times even the 'give and take' of the small talk at a party was too much for her because of the implications which the 'take' had for her.

Her aggressive defence, however, became very manifest in the relationship to people who were inferior to her, and to the members of her family. She had to win at all costs in any contact with them. She was constantly on guard against the possibility that someone could 'put something over on her'. Against this possibility she defended herself with the utmost violence. One can imagine what it meant to her children that she had to win all arguments with them and could not suffer disobedience and insubordination. If she was in danger of losing a point in the struggle with a merchant, for example, or the plumber, or the grocery-woman, she became so desperate that her husband had to come to her rescue and win the case for her. Nothing can demonstrate better the reason why she had to defend herself so violently against any form of 'defeat' than a dream that occurred during her analysis after she had lost a minor argument in a social conversation. In her dream 'there was the body of a person run over by a train. The face had been cut off by the wheels so that the body could not be identified. She refused to look at the bloody mess'. I need not point out the castrative meaning of this dream. In connection with our theme its broader significance is of more importance. In the dream-picture somebody—no doubt the dreamer herself—is 'railroaded' into something and in this way loses 'face' and identity. To understand this danger we have to report some material from the patient's childhood.

The patient was breast fed for over a year by a kind but rather firm mother. The patient must have been endowed with insatiable oral needs. She sucked her thumb till she was 12 years old. When she was 5 years old, her mother had another child, a boy. This aroused the intense jealousy of our patient, particularly when she saw the baby nursed by the mother. She pestered her mother incessantly to let her try the breast also. Finally the mother gave in and offered her the breast, whereupon the little girl bit into the nipple so that the mother screamed in pain.

As soon as she gained command of language she developed her resistance against the will and demands of others and started to argue. She was most difficult to handle as a child because of this extreme resistance to any demands, and she remained so throughout her childhood and adolescence. When she came home for the first time from college, she happened to say 'I am sorry' on some occasion. The family was flabbergasted, for it was the first time she had apologized for anything. She had always stubbornly refused to do so. All this gives the impression of anal stubbornness. But the most careful search for connexions of anal material with her stubbornness brought forth very little result. Her intense orality suggested another, earlier basis of her defensive attitude. It had to be assumed that her stubborn refusal to 'submit' in any form was originally established as a defence against oral penetration by the breast or the nipple, a penetration which would result in a dissolution of her personality due to the invasion by the object. In many of her dreams, too, penis and breast were identified. This identification seriously inhibited her sex-life and in consequence of this her whole femininity. There were many instances in her analysis when encouragement in the direction of femininity was answered by a dream in which she was turned into a lifeless mass of protoplasm, or into a dummy with limp limbs that had no personality of its own. The most interesting manifestation of her early defence against submission to the object was a repetitive nightmare which she remembered from earliest childhood and which continued to appear even during her analysis till its oral invasive significance was interpreted to her. She dreamed that 'she is lying in bed when a big, almost gigantic woman approaches her and begins to tickle her, going over her whole body with both hands in rapid motions. The patient becomes completely paralysed as children become when tickled, only more so'. She wakes up in a terror; as a child she sometimes screamed for her father to help her. Although the content of the dream does not refer directly to an oral experience, it is obviously connected with experiences which belong to the earliest period in her life. It presents even in the manifest dream-picture the early handling of the child by the mother, the bathing, the drying, the powdering, the diapering, all passive experiences in which the mother's hands go very actively up and down the child's body. The defence against the wish for re-experiencing this passive pleasure in surrendering to the mother's activity turns it into a nightmare.

As far as it is permitted to take consecutive improvement as proof of the correctness of an interpretation—we know that this proof has only limited validity—I might point out that the demonstration of the oral origin of the characterological defences in both my patients brought about considerable therapeutic results. It decreased their defensive attitude to a marked degree.

As I have mentioned, Anna Freud indicated in her paper that the negativism of her patients could be understood as a defence against the invasion by the object and might be traced back to the earliest union which had for them the significance of an invasion by the love object, i.e. by the mother or her breast. It is 'self'-defence in the truest sense. Something simlar seems to be the case with my two patients. With each of them the character traits which we have described seem to serve as a defence against masochistic surrender on an oral-passive level with the consecutive danger of invasion and loss of self.

We know many pleasureful psychic states—normal as well as abnormal—which are based on the early oral fusion with the only object then existing, breast and mother. They range from the everyday experience of sleep, over the oceanic feeling, to the highest bliss and elation of the unio mystica of the saint in ecstasy.

We have extensive knowledge and understanding of the positive experience of the mother-infant dual-unity. Much less is recognized of the negative aspect of this earliest relationship, although Melanie Klein had long ago pointed it out; perhaps the fact that she did this within the framework of her own concepts, which are not shared by many analysts, made her emphasis on the negative aspect of the earliest oral experiences less acceptable. In this respect, Anna Freud's paper is in my opinion of great importance. Established within the framework of classical analysis, it seems to me to throw light on earliest negative oral attitudes, and considerable doubt on Abraham's concept of a 'preambivalent' oral phase. Ambivalence seems to be our endowment from the very beginning of postnatal existence. The fear of being penetrated by the breast or nipple and filled with mother substance, so that it replaces the self, seems to be an oppositional complement to the third part of Bertram Lewin's oral triad (4), namely the wish to be devoured. It seems, therefore, that what Freud calls 'instinctual ambivalence' (3), the appearance of instinctual desires in pairs of opposites, might be already recognized at the very beginning of extra-uterine instinctual life.

At the conclusion of this paper I might present a hypothesis about early defence reaction of the self. The earlier the defence reaction is established the more totalitarian is it in character. Whereas later defences are sectional in their development and application, the earliest and most primitive defences comprise more or less the whole self. The hysterical defence against oral incorporation is more or less circumscribed and localized in a symptom like gagging or vomiting, based on the phallic phase of libido-development to which the hysterical symptom belongs. The defence against oral surrender and invasion on an oral libido level is not localized; it comprises much wider parts of the personality and spreads out over all kinds of experiences which are only loosely connected with the oral area and activity. We thus see a difference in the result of libido- and of ego development. The primitive self, the ego-id matrix according to Hartmann, starts originally with more or less totalitarian reactions in form of massive defence. Its development goes in the direction of more sectional and independent activity and reactivity, in the direction of departmental functioning which explains the possibility of conflict-free spheres in the mature ego. The development of the libido goes in the opposite direction. It starts with independent, auto-erotic activities at the different erotogenic zones and is gradually brought more and more under the successive primary zones so that a libido-*organization* is established, in which the normal and optimal function of discharge is of more or less totalitarian character. In the mature person then we find massive discharge of libido in orgasm, but well departmentalized and restricted defences, in contrast to the massive defence and the relatively departmental auto-erotic activities of the infant.

REFERENCES

(1) FREUD, ANNA (1953). 'About Losing and Being Lost.' Paper read at the 18th International Congress, London. (For Abstracts see: *Int. J. Psycho-Anal.*, 35, 1954, p. 283.)
(2) ———'A Connexion between the States of Negativism and of Emotional Surrender (Hörigkeit).' *Int. J. Psycho-Anal.*, 33, 265.
(3) FREUD, S. *Three Essays on the Theory of Sexuality*. (London: Imago Publ. Co.)
(4) LEWIN, BERTRAM D. *The Psychoanalysis of Elation*. (New York: W.W. Norton & Co.)
(Received 20 November, 1955.)